"Beneath the surface of every | art waiting to be revealed. This ﹏ us into God's Masterpiece, and in the process helps us restore his Masterpiece in others."

—Mark Batterson,
author of *The Circle Maker*

"I wish all believers loved people who are far from God like John Burke does. Burke captures a unique aspect of a missional life in Christ that we can easily fail to grasp: We can be missional but on the wrong mission. *Unshockable Love* reminds us of our desperate need to join Jesus in the messy work of life-on-life discipleship."

—Ed Stetzer, www.edstetzer.com,
author of *Subversive Kingdom*

"John is a man who not only knows Jesus, but that Jesus *really* saves and redeems broken people and makes them trophies of his grace. This book gets into the heart of the ministry that has characterized John's distinctive contribution to the contemporary church—that Jesus is Lord and Savior."

—Alan Hirsch,
author, activist, dreamer, www.alanhirsch.org

"The phrase 'this is what I was created for' kept running through my mind as I read *Unshockable Love*. My lifelong friend John Burke captures the heart of Jesus to summon the best from each of us. I've watched John live this message for the past several decades. Come and see the bold love of God, who invites everyone—from skeptics to the spiritually stuck to the religiously arrogant—to follow Jesus Christ while surrounded by authentic friendships and energized by a shared mission."

—Ken Cochrum, DMin, global vice president,
Student-Led and Virtually-Led Movements

"Hope is a dangerous thing. This book drips with hope. Burke is a master storyteller and his stories, woven together with the electric stories of Scripture, grab the heart and ignite the mind. Burke helps us believe that God can do more in and through us, with everyday people we meet in everyday situations. Pick up this book, and your hope will rise."

—Doug Schaupp
growth coach, InterVarsity Christian Fellowship,
coauthor, *I Once Was Lost*

"In *Unshockable Love*, John has once again captured a fresh vision of a Jesus who is not only worth following, but orienting and giving our entire lives to. In simply but poignantly looking at Jesus' various interactions with people throughout the Gospels, he is able to underscore the call Jesus gives to us in each conversation, a call that goes beyond clever ministries, strategies, or apologetics. It's the call to be found in a story much larger than ourselves."

—Mike Breen, 3DM global leader

unshockable
love

unshockable love

how Jesus changes the world through imperfect people

John Burke

BakerBooks

a division of Baker Publishing Group
Grand Rapids, Michigan

Published by Baker Books
a division of Baker Publishing Group
P.O. Box 6287, Grand Rapids, MI 49516–6287
www.bakerbooks.com

Originally published under the title *Mud and the Masterpiece*

Printed in the United States of America

Library of Congress Cataloging-in-Publication Data
Burke, John, 1963-
  [Mud and the masterpiece]
  Unshockable love : how Jesus changes the world through imperfect people
  / John Burke.
      pages cm
  "Originally published under the title Mud and the Masterpiece."
  Includes bibliographical references.
  Summary: "Bestselling author and pastor invites readers to love and
  engage with the messy people around them in ways that disarm and move
  them to real relationship with Jesus"— Provided by publisher.
    ISBN 978-0-8010-1650-9 (pbk. : alk. paper) 1. Christian life. 2. Jesus
  Christ—Example. 3. Interpersonal relations—Religious aspects—Chris-
  tianity. I. Title.
  BV4501.3.B873 2014
  248.4—dc23   2014018229

Author is represented by Fedd & Company.

14   15   16   17   18   19   20   7   6   5   4   3   2   1

*I want to dedicate this book to my beautiful bride,
best friend, and ministry partner.*

*Kathy, you have an amazing gift for calling out
God's Masterpiece in everyone you meet,
and I've benefited the most!*

Contents

Introduction

Do You Follow Jesus?

If you ask people on the street for one word to describe Christians today, what would they say? I've asked this question while speaking to Christians and church leaders all over North America, Europe, Scandinavia, and Australia, and I find it very troubling that we all know the answers: "judgmental," "narrow-minded," "arrogant," "hypocritical," "bigoted."

These seem to be the most commonly agreed upon one-word answers. Of course, none of us think we could be rightly accused of these attitudes, and yet maybe it's not just what we're *doing wrong*, but what we're failing to *do right* that brings these negative stereotypes. Maybe it's something we really are not aware of that tends to infect us over time, as it seems to be especially prevalent in post-Christian societies where authentic faith and traditions cross ways.

During Jesus' day, if you asked the average Joe (or Joseph) in Jerusalem to give one word to describe Jesus, I think you'd get a much different set of words. So why doesn't the average person describe the average Christian with words that match Jesus' life and ministry: "loving," "kind," "compassionate," "wise," "merciful," "truthful," "hopeful," "healing," "helping," "caring," "life-giving"?

When you look around you, do you see many people wanting to know about your God because they see a glimpse of a greater love, more abundant life, and new kind of freedom in you and your friends? Is God restoring what's lost and damaged in this world through you? If not, we ought to ask ourselves a very provocative question: "Why aren't we more like the One we follow?"

Right after I wrote these words in JFK airport, I quickly boarded my plane to Scandinavia to speak to church leaders there. I walked back to the flight attendant, Michael, and asked if he could fill up my empty water bottle. He said, "We're not supposed to . . . but here, I'll do it." Michael and I had been talking for about ten minutes when he asked, "So, what do you do?"

"I'm a pastor," I said.

"Oh my gosh, that is the LAST thing I would ever have guessed." Michael kept expressing how shocked he was because I didn't seem like "those people." He told me the horrible experiences he had with Christians and why he became Buddhist. And he asked me, "Why are Christians like that?"

I told him, "Honestly, because not all Christians truly have the heart of Jesus for other people." Now, here's the shocking thing—Michael, who disdained Christians, almost wouldn't let me sleep! He wanted to know more about Jesus and even wanted to attend our Internet campus. Why?

I think because he sensed something. I think he sensed God's heart for him somehow coming through me.

For the last twenty-five years, I've seen the Michaels of the world find faith, follow Jesus, and even begin restoring and leading others to follow Jesus as part of his church—his bride. After seeing this happen in thousands of lives, I'm convinced that our problem is not that we need more evangelistic tools, methods, apologetic arguments, or missional strategies—in fact, none of these will be worth anything if we don't first see ourselves and others through the eyes of Jesus. I truly believe people intuitively sense how we *feel about* them (even in a ten-minute conversation), and that makes the biggest difference of all.

This book flows out of an intensive study looking at every encounter Jesus had with people—all people. What caused so many people who seemed far from God to flock to Jesus? Why did he have such a magnetic pull on people? I observed and analyzed his words, his attitude, what was recorded about his body language, and how people must have experienced him. I realized that people could see something in the eyes of Jesus that conveyed an attitude we must adopt.

I looked at the actions of Jesus and what he had his followers do to walk in his footsteps. I looked at his kind words, his hard words, and the timing of all of them. I studied the four Gospel accounts of Jesus' life and teachings in chronological order (through what is called a Harmony of the Gospels*), and I discovered revealing insights into the timing of Jesus' words and actions. And accidentally, I noticed something else.

I noticed the encounters of the Pharisees with the same people.

I found it shocking to realize that Jesus' one-word descriptions of the Pharisees were very similar to the average person's description of Christians today. In fact, I noticed the way the Pharisees seemed to think about, treat, and talk about people outside their "church parameters." It matched what I've sometimes noticed among Christian groups I've been a part of and have even led. I realized I, too, have sometimes looked less like Jesus and more like a Pharisee.

This led to an important realization that can help all of us if we're willing: Falling into the trap of the Pharisees is not something anyone ever does intentionally. It happens slowly, gradually, in little incremental ways that rob us year by year of becoming the kind of people Jesus intended us to be—people who actually follow Jesus in attitude and action, bringing life, love, and a truth that sets people

*If you are interested in reading the Harmony of the Gospels I used, see Robert Thomas and Stanley Gundry, *A Harmony of the Gospels* (San Francisco: Harper & Row, 1978).

free. And I'm convinced we all must fight pharisaical creep. For us to become the kinds of people God intended, we have to let God restore us into more of the Masterpiece he intended us to be. We must see ourselves through the eyes of Jesus so we can cooperate with him in restoring others.

Part 1 of *Unshockable Love* will help you experience Jesus in a new light. We will explore his attitudes toward people, all people, imperfect people, and those who thought they weren't so bad. Through exploring stories of imperfect people, your heart will change as you experience God's merciful, masterful restoration of the most sin-stained works of art, both today and in Jesus' day. You will begin to see yourself and others the way Jesus did, and that will change everything.

In the stories I tell, I've chosen to change everyone's name unless they specifically asked me to use their real name. I've indicated real names with a diamond (♦). I've included many stories because they demonstrate God's merciful attitude toward imperfect people today, and how Jesus is still actively restoring those whom the Pharisees wrote off as hopeless. I believe if we are willing, God can restore us into truly life-giving people whom others really want to be around, because they see in us what people saw in Jesus.

Once we get an attitude adjustment, we will be ready to participate with God in the greatest restoration project of all time—the reclamation and restoration of God's Masterpiece, his image artistically incorporated in every human being we meet. Jesus left his followers with an example to follow and a plan for bringing restoration to the world around us, life by life. In part 2, we will learn from Jesus' instructions to his followers, and we will explore a way to follow his Spirit together, so that we begin to see the same life-giving, loving impact that Jesus brought to a damaged world.

In order to align our attitudes with that of Jesus, we must position ourselves to see in new ways. At the end of each chapter, there will be the opportunity to take time to reflect in prayer on attitudes that may subtly infect you. Then I'll encourage you to take a risk and try some things that will challenge pharisaical tendencies and allow God to bring your heart in line with his heart. As that happens, be sure to check out next step resources at www.unshockablelove.com.

Through motivating stories of ordinary, restored followers of Jesus all around the world, you will catch a vision for a life of adventure with God and others that will be contagious. I pray that through this book, you will see that there's hope for all of us because God is a Master Artist who wants to restore his crowning creation. Let the restoration project begin.

PART 1

SEEING THROUGH THE EYES OF JESUS

1

A Glutton, Drunk, and Friend of Sinners

The Return of the Prodigal Son, Rembrandt (1668–69)

Photo: Album / Art Resource, NY

ill you pray for us? We need help." I stood in disbelief, trying not to show it, as Derek and Zoe approached me after a service. First, I could hardly believe they were at church—Zoe had only come once or twice—but even more amazing was her willingness to seek prayer and help. If you knew what I knew that day, you'd be amazed too!

Zoe was a young mother of two. She longed to give her kids a better life than she had. I looked into her eyes, full of emotion, and I wondered what I should say. After all, she knew that I knew she was living with Derek, and this was the first time I'd met her. But there's more to the story.

I knew Zoe's story through Derek. I had met Derek a year before. I was on my way to visit my mother when a voice behind me called, "Young man—wait!" I turned around to see an elderly woman racing her wheelchair down the hall toward me. "Aren't you the pastor of that church full of young people?"

"Yes, I am. I'm John, what's your name?"

"I'm Susan, and my grandson Derek is in the hospital. Will you visit him? It's really important because he just got out of prison, and he needs to go to your church."

Requests like these are always awkward. Probably the last thing her grandson would want is some unknown pastor-dude showing up at his grandmother's request. I tried to explain that to Susan, but she was insistent, so I finally said that I would have someone go visit him even if I couldn't.

The next week was my son's thirteenth birthday, and I had planned a daylong Man Quest, where he would complete a series of assignments that would teach him what it meant to be a man like Jesus. The quest for courage came first (at the skate park!), followed by the quest for compassion. I had planned for us to serve at our food pantry, but it was closed. So in a panic, I prayed for some way to teach my son about compassion, and instantly, Derek came to mind.

It turned out Derek was incredibly grateful for our visit to the hospital that day, and he shared with us how drugs had landed him in prison. He had just given his life to Christ and was given early hospital release the same month. We encouraged him that day, and he started coming to our church. Soon his brother and his father were also coming. And several months later Derek met Zoe. They got sexually involved and moved in together. Until that morning, I hadn't seen Derek in months. But I knew of the mess he had gotten into.

Derek's father informed me that Derek had fallen in love with Zoe's kids in the past four months living with them. And yet his relationship with Zoe was so tumultuous, at times it was borderline violent. And I knew from Derek's friend Ted that Zoe was not a single mom. Actually, she was still married—to a guy who traveled a lot and didn't mind an "open marriage." I knew this situation was volatile, but what should I do?

All these things flashed through my head like lightning as the words "Will you pray for us?" still hung heavy in the air that Sunday morning. I knew from experience that this was a moment pregnant with the potential to bring forth spiritual life, or the potential for miscarriage. What I said, but even more important, what I held in my mind's eye and in my heart for these two people was critical.

"Will you pray for us?" Is that what I *should* do? Is that *all* I should do? What would you do? What would you be thinking? What would be in your heart?

I've come to realize how critical the answers to these questions are for those who truly want to be like Jesus to the people around them.

The Mud or the Masterpiece

If you talk to people who seem far from God, many tend to admire Jesus, but often can't stand his followers. Jesus still has an intriguing and mysteriously attractive pull on people, but many

Christians create a repelling force. That's troubling, especially when you consider how the Dereks and Zoes of Jesus' day felt a magnetic attraction toward Jesus, but were repelled by the condemning religious leaders. In fact, Luke tells us "all the tax collectors and the sinners were coming near [Jesus] to listen to Him" (Luke 15:1 NASB). To discredit him, the Pharisees called Jesus a glutton, drunk, and friend of sinners (Luke 7:34), mainly because Jesus had an enormous, life-giving impact on so many like Derek and Zoe.

Maybe the reason people today are drawn to Jesus but not to his followers is because many Christians are NOT like Jesus—we don't really *see* what Jesus sees in other people. We don't really *feel* the way Jesus felt toward people straying far from God, living messy lives. Christians can subtly become pharisaical without even realizing it!

Ultimately, the impact we have on the people around us will tell us if we're more like Jesus or more like the Pharisees. "You will know them by their fruit," Jesus said (see Luke 6:44). "Everyone who is fully trained will be like their teacher" (Luke 6:40). The backbone of this book comes from an in-depth study through the Gospels analyzing every encounter Jesus had: How did he treat people? What was he feeling or thinking? What was his attitude? What did he say? What did he do? What did Jesus convey that contrasted so sharply with the Pharisees? As we learn from Jesus' encounters, I want you to wrestle with this question throughout this book: "Am I more like Jesus or more like a Pharisee to the people around me?" The answer may not be as black and white as you think.

When my wife and I lived in St. Petersburg, Russia, I got to see one of my favorite paintings housed in the Hermitage Museum. It's Rembrandt's masterpiece *The Return of the Prodigal Son* (see page 19). It depicts that moving scene in Jesus' parable when, "filled with compassion" (Luke 15:20), the father ran toward his wayward son. The son had squandered his inheritance with loose living, but came begging for mercy. The father embraced him, saying, "My son was dead but now is alive, was lost but now he's found" (see Luke 15:24). Jesus paints this beautiful, priceless picture in answer to the religious people's complaint that he "welcomes sinners" (Luke 15:2). The painting is worth a fortune.

Now, just imagine if one day you visit St. Petersburg, and there in a back-alley dumpster you discover Rembrandt's masterpiece, but it's hardly recognizable. It's covered in mud and dirt, it's stained, and the canvas has been torn. You wouldn't recognize it at all, except you notice the famous hand of the father on the ragged son's back.

How would you treat the painting? Like trash? It's covered in mud, stained and torn—is it worthless? Do you treat it like it's worthless? Or would you treat it like a million-dollar masterpiece that needs to be handled with care and restored? I'm guessing all of us could see past the mud and even the damage to recognize the immense value inherent in this one-of-a-kind work of art—simply because it was created by Rembrandt's own hand. We wouldn't try to clean it up ourselves; we would bring it to a master, who could delicately restore it to its original condition.

So why do we struggle to treat people like the immensely valuable, one-of-a-kind Masterpiece God created with his own hand? As I study the life and interactions of Jesus with very sin-stained, muddied people, it becomes evident that Jesus could see something worth dying for in all the people he encountered. Jesus could see past the mud to the Masterpiece God wanted to restore.

What do you see most when you encounter the Dereks and Zoes of the world? What do you see when you look in the mirror? Do you see the *mud*? Or do you see the *Masterpiece* God wants to restore? What you focus on determines who you become and the impact you have on people around you! That's the heart of this book.

The Pharisees primarily focused on the mud of sin that covered the lives of the irreligious. They prided themselves in mud-avoidance. They fixated on mud. They tried to clean the mud off others with their own dirt—it didn't work then, and it doesn't work now!

23

Jesus was different. Jesus demonstrated a spiritual vision that he wants to impart to us—to see the Masterpiece he sees in us, and to renovate us to become people whose hearts reflect what God sees, under even the most sin-stained life. Jesus saw God's Masterpiece, waiting to be revealed by his grace, and as a result, many people actually became what he envisioned them to be.

The Artwork of Grace

That's what God's grace is all about! God's grace cleanses and restores all willing people! We may trust in God's grace, but do we live in it? Do we exude grace to others? And how do we show grace like Jesus did to sin-stained Masterpieces?

Paul explains what God's grace did through Jesus:

> Because of his great love for us, God, who is rich in mercy, made us alive with Christ even when *we were dead* in transgressions—it is by grace you have been saved. And God raised us up with Christ and seated us with him in the heavenly realms in Christ Jesus, in order that in the coming ages he might show the incomparable riches of his grace, expressed in his kindness to us in Christ Jesus.
>
> Ephesians 2:4–7, italics mine

Notice what this says—we were all dead spiritually. Damaged, sin-stained paintings tossed in the dumpster. None of us brought ourselves back to life spiritually, nor can we clean ourselves up and restore ourselves into what God intended without God's help. But by his grace—his undeserved favor, good will, loving-kindness offered freely—we can be restored!

And notice the words describing God's heart—he has *great love* for you, me, Derek, and Zoe; he has *abundant grace* to give, demonstrated through his *kindness*, and he is *rich in mercy*. As we will see, love, kindness, and mercy flowed liberally from Jesus' life, but the Pharisees' well was dry when it came to mercy. Paul continues:

God saved you by his grace when you believed. And you can't take credit for this; it is a gift from God. Salvation is not a reward for the good things we have done, so none of us can boast about it. For we are God's *masterpiece*. He has created us anew in Christ Jesus, so we can do the good things he planned for us long ago.

Ephesians 2:8–10 NLT, italics mine

The word translated "masterpiece" or "workmanship" is the Greek word *poiema*—from which we get the word *poem*. It's a Work of Art—the work of a Master Artist. Do you realize *you* are God's Masterpiece, his Work of Art? Next time someone says "Wow—you're a piece of work," just say, "That's right, I am!—Artwork, buddy!"

"By grace you have been saved" (Ephesians 2:8). A person living in Jesus' time would hear the Greek word *sodzo*, translated "saved," and think of being carried to safety, made whole, or restored—restored to the original condition. God saves us—he restores us to right-relationship with himself, he makes us secure by adopting us as his own children, and he begins a lifelong process to restore the original Work of Art he imagined before we were born! In fact, God sees it already completed. He already sees us raised with Christ and seated with him (see Ephesians 2:6).

Grace tells you that all God needs is your faith—giving yourself in trust back to your Creator, giving him permission to renovate and restore and bring to life his Masterpiece in you! *That's true for all human beings* (John 12:32). God pictures you as someone more awesome and wonderful than your imagination has ever dreamed. Do you see yourself like God does—as a living Work of Art he's wanting to restore to its full value? Do you see others that way? What you see matters!

Skydiving With Jesus

When I first met Bruce, I never would have imagined God would change so many men's lives through his. Bruce was a mess! But his mud was the acceptable kind in the world of business. As a young twenty-something with a greed-starved drive to make millions, he got involved in a brokerage firm where ethics and moral integrity were optional. He played right along with the game until both his bosses almost landed in jail.

When he moved to Austin, Texas, he started his own business and invested all his profits, making a small fortune. The only money he'd spend was feeding his wild side—thrill seeking, sky-diving, streaking down the aisle of a commercial flight at 30,000 feet (obviously pre-9/11!), trips to Cancun or Vegas, where he'd drink all night and wake up in the bed of some woman he didn't know.

And then Jesus showed up!

Bruce had just begun to follow Jesus when we met. We started a small group in his house that became Gateway Church. Bruce was always the spark, the life of the party. I could see God's gifts—that risk-taking zest for life, adventure, laughter, fun—those were all gifts from God, hidden gems of faith getting misdirected. God started restoring Bruce, but Bruce kept degrading himself.

Later that year, I had to lovingly confront Bruce because God was uncovering a Masterpiece in him, but Bruce kept hiding it under more and more sin. I saw a pattern in him of dating and using weak-willed, anorexic-looking women.

"Bruce! Why do you keep dating women who are not healthy, then using them sexually? Is that really who you want to become?" I asked one night on his driveway.

"I had never thought about it before," he answered. Bruce later reflected how that conversation and another one got him focused on the Masterpiece instead of the mud. "I didn't see it until that night, but as I reflected on it, I realized it was another symptom of the deeper disease—trying to play God of my life. My only criteria was thin, sexy, and broken women because I could control them. It was the same insecurity driving everything—my hoarding of money, my effort to be in power over women, my inability to truly connect and love and give to others."

Bruce and Joe started meeting as Spiritual Running Partners.* At first, every week they confessed their failures—but nothing seemed to change. Accountability wasn't working. "I'm a terrible person," Bruce heard Joe say in shame one day. He felt the same way. But as they committed to reading Scripture and memorizing passages about who they are in Christ, something dawned on Bruce. "You're not a terrible person—you're all these promises in Christ. We need to help each other believe them and let God chip away this other stuff that's foreign to who God made us to be."

That made all the difference! I've gotten a front-row seat to watch God's amazing restoration of my friend from greedy to generous, from stupid-risky to full of risk-taking faith, from unethical and immoral to one who loves people and cares about how his actions impact them. And it didn't take long for that gift of faith to kick in, and Bruce started taking other muddied men on faith adventures—calling out the Masterpiece in them. I've watched God use Bruce to transform hundreds of men's lives. And God wants your life not only to reflect his Work of Art in you, but for you to be a paintbrush in the hand of God to restore others.

Attitude Adjustment

Your life, as we will see, was meant to be a tool of restoration in the hands of the Master Artist. But we must become more like Jesus than the Pharisees—and that starts with the right attitude of heart. Jesus must have pictured what he created people to be, and that vision affected how he felt about them. I'm sure those he encountered picked up on his attitude toward them, and that's probably why so many muddied people flocked to him—in his eyes they saw a glimmer of hope for who they were meant to be.

*Spiritual Running Partners consist of two to four people meeting regularly to help each other run this marathon of faith, following a format of confessing sin, encouraging spiritual fruit, and helping each other put intentional practices in place to grow.

I'm convinced that people intuitively pick up on our attitude toward them. What's in our hearts toward people will be felt by them. Do we have good will toward all people? Are we for people, or really against some of them? Do we truly believe they have immense value and worth to God? Or are we secretly disgusted, bothered, shocked, judgmental, wanting to "fix them" quickly? I've come to believe that many Christians repel those who don't follow Christ because we don't share God's heart for them. Why?

Some of us may have come to faith in Christ under a gospel of mud management rather than a gospel of restoration grace. Maybe we think God saves us, and then *we* clean ourselves up out of gratitude, while trying hard to avoid mud. First, that doesn't work (read Galatians). Second, it misses the point—Masterpiece restoration is a work only the Master Artist can do!

Some of us are highly critical—trained to see what's wrong. Mud-spotting, flaw-finding, failure-anticipating might even be our profession. My father was an engineer, and I, too, have an engineering degree and worked as an engineer, and I have a critical eye for what's wrong. I've discovered this works really well with problems, but not with people! I've discovered personally, I must allow Jesus to restore in me "eyes to see" what he sees. As I begin to see value in people like Jesus did, and even point out how I see God drawing individuals to himself, many seek him and find him.

Chip and Dan Heath, in their book *Switch*, give many examples demonstrating how pointing out progress motivates forward movement.[1] For instance, Dave Ramsey helps people climb out of deeply entrenched debt. But his approach is counterintuitive. Most financial advisors would instruct a person to pay off the highest interest rate debt with the greatest balance first (because it's costing you the most interest—which makes sense). But Dave found that approach usually doesn't work. People get so demotivated by how much needs to change, they stay stuck. Instead, he suggests the Debt Snowball. List all debts from smallest balance to largest, then make only minimum payments on every debt except the smallest (regardless of interest rates). Throw every dollar available toward that smallest debt until it's paid, then move on to the second smallest debt, then the third smallest and so on. What Dave found is that with each debt conquered, greater progress can be seen, and motivation grows. He's helped people with close to $100,000 of debt, stuck for years, finally slay the debt dragon. There's something motivating about someone pointing out progress versus pointing out how far you have to go!

I've seen the same pattern in Jesus' encounters, and I've seen it motivate thousands of people to come to faith in our day. Jesus would point out progress: "You are not far from the kingdom of God" (Mark 12:34), "I have not found such great faith" (observing a Roman centurion, Luke 7:9). A gospel of mud management focuses only on the mud. A gospel of restoration grace sees God's progress and hope because he's already paid all of our debts! They just have to receive it.

Which gospel we hold affects how we actually *feel* about ourselves and other muddied people. If we picture God's goal for life as mud management, we will quickly judge and push away muddied people, or try to scrape off the mud ourselves, or just avoid them so we won't get muddied. But that was not Jesus' approach. That was the way of the Pharisee.

Zealous for What?

It does little good to call ourselves followers of Jesus if our lives and our influence don't reflect Jesus' life. Jesus said, "Very truly I tell you, whoever believes in me will do the works I have been doing, and they will do even greater things than these, because I am going to the Father" (John 14:12). God fully intends your life, as performance art lived in concert with his Spirit, to have the same influence on the world around you as Jesus did.

"We are God's workmanship, created in Christ Jesus to do good works, which God prepared in advance for us to do" (literally, "to walk in," or "live in," Ephesians 2:10 NIV 1984). What you do in life following God's lead becomes a living Work of Art—poetry in motion. God prepared you in advance for a unique purpose only he knows—a masterful picture of a life well lived, that truly brings purpose, fulfillment, and eternal beauty to you *and* to the people around you—just like Jesus did! All he needs is faith—you growing to trust his leadership more and more. That's what I hope to help you do, so that you have his impact.

But it's not just up to you. God intends Christ-followers to work together as his body on earth. Through your church or Christian Network working as one body, Jesus will re-present himself restoring the world around us. I've seen him do it through hundreds of ordinary people like you'll read about in the stories of this book—ordinary people having an extraordinary impact because they're seeing what Jesus sees and following his Spirit in their encounters with people.

Today in Christian circles, I'm hearing more and more about being missional Christ-followers, meaning the church should never be a place where people sit and listen and do nothing good in the world. The church is people, being Jesus' body, on Jesus' mission with him. That's what this book is about. But I believe Christians can be missional on the wrong mission, and not realize it! That's even more what this book is about!

How do we make sure we are truly on mission with Jesus rather than falling prey to the mission of the Pharisees? We might reject the notion that we would ever be pharisaical, but I find it's not so black and white. We can subtly find our hearts becoming pharisaical toward the very people Jesus came to restore.

Missional on the Wrong Mission

The Pharisees were not all bad. When we see them through such polarizing glasses, we set ourselves up to be blind to the same tendencies that deceived many well-intentioned religious people in Jesus' day. The Pharisees were actually reformers—that's why

Jesus' harsh confrontation of them shocked so many. The Pharisees saw the moral decay increasing all around them due to Roman influence, and they were concerned for God's laws given through Moses (Matthew 9:11). Many Christians today have similar concerns and great zeal for moral reform, but how do people really change according to Jesus?

The Pharisees loved the Scriptures—they diligently studied! (John 5:39). They prided themselves on staying true to Moses and the prophets, but they missed the heart of it all! (Matthew 23:1–3). The hard truth we need to see here is that it is possible to diligently study the Bible, yet miss Jesus' mission entirely.

And the Pharisees were evangelistic! They valued making converts to the one true God. Yet Jesus said, "Woe to you, teachers of the law and Pharisees, you hypocrites! You travel over land and sea to win a single convert, and when you have succeeded, you make them twice as much a child of hell as you are" (Matthew 23:15). They were missional on the *wrong mission*!

Is it possible that many Christians today who desire moral reform, love the Word of God, and pride themselves on teaching truth could be missional on the wrong mission—failing to demonstrate the heart of God to a broken world?

Absolutely!

Hey, if Jesus called Peter "the rock," and yet Peter was deceived at least twice, if James and John missed Jesus' heart several times, if Paul was zealous for God yet persecuted the church . . . who do I think I am if I proudly say, "Not me!" Phariseeism can sneak up on all of us!

So what was it that caused the Pharisees to be zealous for the wrong mission?

They had no mercy or compassion for broken, muddied people! They did many things right, but they didn't see themselves or others accurately. They had an "us/them" mentality. They believed God belonged to the "good people" (us) and wanted nothing to do with the "bad people" (them). So they separated themselves. That's where Jesus and the Pharisees collided.

The Heart of Jesus

Marc owned two bars on Sixth Street—where everyone from Austin goes to party. Most of his life, wherever Marc went the party followed, so he decided to make a living of it. Triple Play (Marc's sports bar) and The Loft both made great money—enough to fund his rockstar-style drug habit. For years the alcohol, drugs, sex, and crowds of people living the *vida loca* with Marc helped him outpace the emptiness and deep insecurities he had run from his whole life. But now at the young age of twenty-eight, they finally caught up with him.

One night after closing time, Marc sat at the bar with his head in his hands, thinking, *There's got to be something better!* Marc recalls, "My drinking and drugging had become unmanageable, but I wouldn't admit it. I relied on it to maintain the only identity I knew—'life of the party Marc.' My girlfriend couldn't take my out-of-control behavior and left me. I was despondent. I knew something had to change."

Marc had encountered several people in his bar who mentioned Gateway Church. They had been invited by others and started to explore life with Jesus, and the picture of life they were starting to see was worth talking about. Longing for a better life, Marc started coming to Gateway.

Bruce, the guy I mentioned earlier, heard that Marc spoke fluent Spanish and asked him to go to Mexico on a trip he was organizing. A group of men were going to build a house for a family in need. When Marc met Bruce, he wasn't planning on going—he didn't feel worthy.

"Bruce's first words to me were, 'You're Marc, the one who's gonna translate for us in Mexico?—that's so awesome!'" Marc recalls. "Bruce was so excited and passionate about it, I didn't have the heart to tell him no, so I went. Responding to that invitation changed everything."

Matthew sat in his tax office, gainfully employed in his crooked business when Jesus came and said, "Follow me" (Matthew 9:9).

Jesus had been hanging out in Matthew's region of Galilee for about a year, and no doubt Matthew had heard about Jesus and probably followed him around. But Matthew had not yet left his despised trade—known among the religious to attract immoral, unethical, "sinful" people—tax collectors were the "bad guys." In today's terms, it would be like Jesus walking into the bar saying, "Marc, follow me."

Matthew must have seen in Jesus' eyes a vision of something better he could become. He was so excited, he threw a big party for Jesus at his *big* house (an indication of his wealth gained from his unethical business). Though he only had a glimpse of the Masterpiece Jesus saw in him, it was attractive enough to want all his friends to have the same.

Even though Matthew had been hanging around Jesus, he was also still hanging out with his friends who partied, drank too much, had immoral tendencies, and were dishonest, because that's who came to the party. Mark even points out "there were many of them, and they were following [Jesus]" (Mark 2:15 NASB). That's what convinced the religious people something was wrong with Jesus.

> When the Pharisees saw this, they asked his disciples, "Why does your teacher eat with tax collectors and sinners?" On hearing this, Jesus said, "It is not the healthy who need a doctor, but the sick. But go and learn what this means: 'I desire mercy, not sacrifice.' For I have not come to call the righteous, but sinners."
>
> Matthew 9:11–13

Don't miss Jesus' biting sarcasm! Who were these "healthy, righteous" people Jesus was talking to?

The Pharisees who would eventually have him killed!

They weren't *healthy*; they were *hiding*! They weren't righteous; they were playing religious "us/them" games to feel good about themselves—but their hearts were far from God (Mark 7:6). Jesus points this out—they used religion to mask what was missing inside: *mercy*!

Jesus tells them to go learn what this means. He quotes Hosea 6, where God calls Israel's love a mist—it appears and then is gone— they've been unfaithful to God: "For I desire mercy, not sacrifice; and acknowledgment of God rather than burnt offerings" (v. 6). God is getting at the heart of what he wants for his people—not just religious sacrifices ("I don't do that like *they* do"), or offerings ("look at me; I serve, I tithe, I attend, I'm good!"). God wants something else. He wants hearts like his, full of a mercy that flows like a river of love from the One who offers mercy to me, and you, and Marc too.

As we will see throughout the Gospels, Jesus doesn't have an "us/ them" picture of people—those who are "healthy" and then those "other people" who need God's mercy and help to find restoration. Jesus just sees "people"—all of us broken, muddied, sin-stained, marred Masterpieces that only the Master Artist can restore. Jesus came for all people who are honest about their desperate need for God's restoration work. Is that you? If so, fantastic! Pray that God uses this study of Jesus' life and encounters to align your heart with his and fulfill his restoration mission in you and through you.

Life by Life

As we will see, Matthew and friends followed Jesus for one year, and then Jesus sent Matthew out to do the very things Jesus did for him. Two and a half years later, Jesus commissioned Matthew and friends to *lead his church*, restoring the world wherever they went. And I'm convinced Jesus wants to do the same thing through you and your friends! In fact, if we look around three to five years from now, and none of our "tax collector, sinful" neighbors are following Christ and even leading his restoration mission forward, we need to reconsider if we are missional on Jesus' mission. I've watched hundreds of ordinary people, in churches and Christian Networks around the world, restoring God's artwork, life by life. You can too.

Marc recalls, "On the way to Mexico, all these men were telling their stories of where they'd been in life—many had been right where I had been—but the difference I saw was that they weren't doing life alone anymore. They were in it together, and they were helping each other become what God intended—I wanted that! I opened my heart to Christ, got baptized, and got involved in a recovery group and a men's small group—which helped me overcome drugs and grow tremendously."

Though making great money with his bars, Marc felt God leading him out of the bar business—a huge step of faith, but he found huge blessings on the other side. One of our church Networks now meets in his old bar! (We'll talk about how you can start a Network in part 2.) Marc's girlfriend saw such positive change, she started hanging around Marc's new friends and found faith, and today they're happily married.

Several years later, Bruce challenged Marc to start his own men's group, and Marc invited Corey to join it. Corey had moved from Miami to work in Austin as a physical therapist, but got involved in the same life Marc had come from. Corey saw in Marc the vision of the man he could become. Corey started following Jesus in that group of men, allowing Jesus to do his restoration work in him. Within a couple of years, Corey was making radical decisions to be an instrument of mercy and restoration in the hands of the Master Artist.

Serving refugee families with others at Gateway, Corey decided to move into the low-income part of town to be a minister of mercy and hope among refugees. Marc equipped Corey to lead, and today Corey spiritually leads a group of men. Corey got his group involved demonstrating mercy and love to the elderly. They started visiting the retirement community where I met Derek's grandmother.

And there Corey met Derek!

Corey and Derek have become friends. I have no idea how the story will unfold, but I see Corey showing love and mercy to Derek and Zoe, calling out the Masterpiece under the mud—just as Marc did for him, and Bruce and others did for Marc, and I did for Bruce, and Randy Worrell did for me. And someone must have done for you too!

That's why I could look Zoe and Derek in the eyes that Sunday morning and say, "I'm so glad you're here. I'd love to pray for you. God has great plans for both of you if you're willing to follow him." That's how God the Artist restores his Masterpiece, life by life! And he will do the same in you and make a huge impact through you—if you're willing. Are you willing to let God's restoration process begin with you?

QUESTIONS AND ACTIONS

1. Reflect on this: Do you tend to focus most on the mud or the Masterpiece when you see yourself? How about when you see others muddied by sin and brokenness? Why is this?

2. Try this: Ask God to lead you to people this week who look muddied to you. Engage them in conversation. Your only goal is to ask questions, listen, and learn about them as people, uniquely created by the Master Artist.

2

Unshockable

Supper in the House of the Pharisee, Pieter Rubens (1618)
Photo: Scala / Art Resource, NY

L et's just go for fun! We'll see how much we can push their buttons," Amy✦ (diamonds indicate a person's real name) teased her girlfriend, who didn't like the idea of hanging around a bunch of Christians. "Come on," Amy insisted. "I hear their motto is 'Come as you are.' I just want to prove that they're 'come as you are' . . . unless you're gay."

Amy had been in a nine-year lesbian relationship that had broken up, leaving her wondering why her deepest longings could never be satisfied. She and Rachel had just started seeing each other when they decided to attend one Sunday morning.

"I came on a mission to shock people," Amy admits. "Rachel and I would hold hands in front of people, but instead of the disgusted looks of contempt we expected, people met eyes with us and treated us like real people. So we started coming to church weekly. We kept moving closer to the front each week, trying to get a reaction so that we'd be rejected sooner rather than later. When we couldn't shock people, we stopped trying and started learning.

"Not long after that, Rachel and I stopped seeing each other, but I kept coming to church because I was searching for something," Amy admits. "I definitely wasn't looking to change. It wasn't my lesbian lifestyle that I was bringing to God, but I wondered if God had answers to my deeper longings. Problem was, I didn't trust God at all!

"The more I listened and learned about the teachings of Jesus, the more I started to actually believe that God really did love me. I heard more and more about being his Masterpiece, and in time, I actually started to believe it. The more I believed God actually could see something of value in me, the more I trusted him."

Over time, Amy slowly opened her heart and struggles to Christ. "It took several years, but as I moved closer and closer to Christ, he gently took me on a very surprising journey. First, I found out my father had nine affairs while I was growing up—a secret that rocked my world. Jesus began to show me how the roots of my

38

sexual issues tie together with my dad's—I was just like him, using people to find comfort, life, and love outside of God."

Amy continued to grow in her knowledge of the Scriptures, falling more and more in love with the Lord. The following year, God had another surprise for her: "I went to the seminar called 'To Be Told,' hosted at Gateway. I wanted to see how God could put closure to my brokenness, but what he showed me *shocked me*," Amy recalls.

"As Dan Allender was telling a story of a bully, I suddenly had a flashback of getting off the school bus. I lived down the street from Jimmy, a boy who had bullied me all year. But this particular day, Jimmy acted nice to me as I got off the bus," Amy recalls. "He apologized for being so mean, and he invited me to come to his house."

That day in the seminar, all else faded to black as this vivid nightmare crept back to life. Amy saw herself walking through Jimmy's front door, noticing all the shades pulled down. Startled, she spied two teenage boys eyeing her with a ravenous look as the door slammed shut. Her screams never escaped the evil darkness that enveloped that house. They pinned her down and raped her.

She was only nine!

Amy swam in a pool of tears as she experienced this divine epiphany. She realized the Lord had been drawing her near to strengthen her for this revelation—to show her the source of so much sexual struggle hidden for years beneath layers of protective mud.

"After that, I realized God knows more about me than I know about myself," Amy recalls, "and he wants to bring healing to these wounds, so I fully gave him my heart and body—everything. As I continued to seek intimacy with him, the lesbian struggles fell away. I'm not saying that's how God works with everyone, but it's how he's healing me. The more I focus on God's intimate love for me and try to see his Masterpiece emerge, the less I want anything to get in the way of his work in me."

Seven years later, Amy leads our ministry to help people find healing and wholeness from all kinds of sexual and relational struggles. She's helping others become God's restored Masterpiece.

Jesus Is Never Shocked

Do you realize that Jesus is not shocked by the shocking things people do? Jesus knew Zacchaeus had robbed people blind and profited off much unethical behavior, yet Jesus was not shocked. He did not offer Zach correction, but relationship. "Come down, Zacchaeus. I'm staying at your house tonight" (see Luke 19:5). That shocked everyone! Yet relationship changed Zacchaeus.

Jesus knew that the Samaritan woman at the well had been married and divorced five times. He knew about her current "hookup" and how sexually entangled she was with the guy she was living with (John 4). Jesus was not repulsed. (Samaritans of Jesus' day were treated by the religious community like gay people often get treated by some of today's Christian community.) None of this kept Jesus away or kept him from offering her living water. Jesus wants Christ-followers who will be less like the Pharisees and more like him—unshockable.

Luke tells of a time Simon the Pharisee invited Jesus to dinner. Jesus and his disciples went and "reclined at the table" (Luke 7:36) along with Simon's religious friends. His friends were skeptical about Jesus' true identity—mainly because he showed more love for "sinners" than love for the Law of Moses (Jesus had just made it clear this wasn't true; he came to fulfill the *intent* of the Law of Moses). They invited Jesus there to judge him, not learn from him.

Middle Eastern dining style consisted of a one-foot-high table with pillows on the floor for seating, usually with feet stretched out to the side or behind them. As the meal proceeded, an immoral woman crashed the party. She sheepishly made her way over to stand behind Jesus. Luke makes sure we know she had "lived a sinful life" (v. 37). She did not just have a few slipups, but rather had made a life out of her sexual deviancies, and everyone knew it! Her mud was public knowledge. Her whole life, she had felt judged and condemned by the religious establishment, so to go into the house of her tormentors took enormous courage.

Yet there she stood . . . because Jesus was there! Somehow word on the street had traveled to her through the crowd she hung out with—there's hope in Jesus for the muddiest human. Hearing he had come near, an unstoppable force welling up from within had drawn her to his feet. As she stood in his presence, hope burst through the dam of all that pain that had driven her mudslinging behavior—she started to cry. Her tears accidentally landed on Jesus' dirty feet (that his host had not shown the common courtesy to wash).

The tension in the room mounted; everyone's shoulders tightened as she fell to her knees behind Jesus, bent down, and wiped his wet, dirty feet with her hair. She took out a bottle of oil mixed with perfume, took the oil in her hands, and gently stroked his feet with the oil—kissing them as she anointed him with the perfume.

Jesus just sat there, never flinching, eyes fixed on the Pharisees, watching them react in shock and disbelief—flames of contempt shooting out of their merciless eyes.

Simon could stand it no more. This outrageous scene had proven his point. He muttered to himself and his "more respectable" guests, "If this man were a prophet, he would know who is touching him and what kind of woman she is—that she is a sinner" (Luke 7:39).

In other words, if Jesus were truly a prophet, he would know about her scandalous sexual sin, and he would be shocked. But Jesus did know and was not shocked!

Now you have to realize, this *was* a controversial situation. Imagine a known prostitute coming up to your pastor, kissing his feet and rubbing oil on them after the Sunday service. It would be his last Sunday at most churches if he didn't put an end to it fast! What *was* Jesus thinking? Why didn't this shock Jesus like it would all of us?

Jesus looks at the heart. It's about the heart. Jesus confronted the unloving hearts of his host and friends while this woman demonstrated a heart overflowing with love. Jesus said, "Simon, I have something to tell you" (v. 40).

"Two people owed money to a certain moneylender. One owed him five hundred denarii [a whole lot of money], and the other

41

fifty [one tenth as much]. Neither of them had the money to pay him back, so he forgave the debts of both. Now which of them will love him more?"

Simon replied, "I suppose the one who had the bigger debt forgiven."

"You have judged correctly," Jesus said. [The only thing Simon had judged correctly that day!]

Then he turned toward the woman and said to Simon, "Do you see this woman? I came into your house. You did not give me any water for my feet, but she wet my feet with her tears and wiped them with her hair. You did not give me a kiss, but this woman, from the time I entered, has not stopped kissing my feet. You did not put oil on my head, but she has poured perfume on my feet. Therefore, I tell you, her many sins have been forgiven—as her great love has shown. But whoever has been forgiven little loves little."

Luke 7:41–47

It's all about love! Don't miss this very critical point Jesus makes to us all—if you truly recognize how much it cost God to forgive you, it will flood your heart with love for God and others who need more of the same. It's all about love! Not a love that ignores the mud and the damage that destroys God's Masterpiece, but a love that recognizes how much loving mercy God has given a messed-up person like me! That great love brings grace and truth together to give hope to a broken world in need of forgiveness and restoration.

Jesus never ignores her sin (he speaks of "her many sins"), nor does he ignore the seemingly less expensive sins of the Pharisees (judgmental, ungrateful hearts that show no love or mercy, yet cost Jesus the same price to forgive—his life!). What Jesus does is point out that both this woman and the "good" religious people around the table owed a debt they couldn't pay! Both could be forgiven that debt, but neither could pay.

In Jesus' day, if you couldn't pay your debt, you went to debtor's prison or became a slave (Matthew 18:30). The predicament was the same for those who couldn't pay *a lot* as those who couldn't pay *a little*. Maybe the reason we get so shocked is that we don't really feel grateful or in need of God's grace in an *equal way*. In other words, we don't see ourselves accurately. Therefore, we don't experience the magnitude of God's love and grace extended to us, so we don't have much love or mercy in our hearts for those who need the same!

Is that you? Does your attitude resemble that of the Pharisees or that of Jesus? Are there certain kinds of people that you treat as irredeemable—too far gone? Do you secretly judge yourself as being a better person than "those" people; therefore you owe God less debt? Do you realize you could not cover your debt, and neither can they, and Jesus' point was really this—there's no difference between any of us, except some realize the cost of forgiveness, others don't; some are more grateful, others less grateful; some love more as a result, others love less.

Full of Shame

Jesus did not recoil in shock and disbelief at people's relative "badness," because he identified the person with the Masterpiece rather than the mud. The reason I believe Jesus wants his followers to be unshockable has nothing to do with hating sin or not hating sin. It has to do with seeing sin for what it is—it's foreign matter. Sin is not our true identity—that's the whole problem. We need to help people identify with God's image in them.

Paul explained it this way: "It is no longer I myself who do [wrong], but it is sin living in me [i.e., sin is not me]" (Romans 7:17). When people identify themselves with the mud (which is *not* them), they act like mud! When people identify themselves with the Masterpiece God created them to be, they're more willing to allow the Master to do his restoration work.

Shame tells us, "You equal your bad behaviors. You are the sum total of the things you've done that you're not proud of. You are

43

ugly and dirty and unworthy of love. You will never amount to anything of value—you're mud." The problem with shame is that it keeps us acting like mud, so we just keep wallowing in it, and dragging others through the mud with us. Jesus removes the shame of all willing people and identifies them as his treasured, beloved, adopted children who *will be* restored fully (Ephesians 2:3–5). Helping people see "what kind" of people God created them to be can catalyze God's restoration work in them!

A St. Lucian Kind of Person

The St. Lucia Parrot, one of the most strikingly beautiful birds in the world, was destined for extinction. By 1977, only one hundred of these exquisite birds remained on earth, all on the tiny Caribbean island of St. Lucia. The striking turquoise, lime green, and red beauty of the St. Lucia Parrot had been taken for granted, hunted, trapped, eaten, and their natural habitat decimated for decades. One biologist forecasted that the parrot "could not escape oblivion by the year 2000."

That's when Paul Butler, a twenty-one-year-old with no authority or money, took on the challenge to convince St. Lucia that they were the *kind of people* who protected their own. He did everything in his power to help the people see that "this parrot is ours. Nobody has this but us. We need to cherish it and look after it." He hosted puppet shows, distributed T-shirts, cajoled bands into recording songs about the parrot, and asked ministers to preach about stewardship of the parrot. All focused on convincing St. Lucia that "we are the kind of people who care about our parrot." And it worked! Rather than becoming extinct, the population of St. Lucia Parrots has grown over 600 percent since Butler started his Identity Campaign.[1]

Our view of "what kind" of people we are changes our behavior. The Pharisees identified the immoral woman by her mud. "If [Jesus] were a prophet, he would know . . . *what kind* of woman she is" (Luke 7:39, italics mine). What kind of a woman *is* she? They could only see the mud, so they treated her like dirt. Jesus saw *what kind* of woman she was *created to be*!

It's an identity issue. Do you see the image of God in every person? Can you imagine God's original intention for one life? That must have been what Jesus could see! He somehow helped people identify "what kind" of people God created them to be. The Pharisees did not have the spiritual vision to see *what kind* of woman she was created to be, so they inadvertently did the work of the destroyer, who keeps people enslaved to their sin by keeping them identified with sin. What kind of people are we? That's a critical question. How do we see ourselves and others?

Condemnation Is a Given

All people grow up under the condemning voice of shame. We all feel it because apart from God's grace, it's the truth. People know deep down the words Paul penned, "I have the desire to do what is good, but I cannot carry it out. For I do not do the good I want to do, but the evil I do not want to do—this I keep on doing. . . . What a wretched man I am! Who will rescue me?" (Romans 7:18–19, 24). Paul identified how shame drives us to feel wretched and condemned. What hope is there for me if this is the truth? People naturally feel this hopeless sense of judgment, so they run from God.

Apart from God's grace, apart from knowing that God holds out hope that can restore the most damaged Masterpiece, people live feeling condemned. Identifying people with mud just pushes them farther away from the Master who can restore them.

Steve, an agnostic skeptic, had a very bad opinion of organized religion and really didn't want to think about God or the claims of Jesus. His wife talked him into coming to our church, and as he started to understand God's vision for his life, he emailed me his insight:

Up 'til now I have not wanted to think this much about God, because it would mean that I have to come to grips with all the wrong I have done in this world—all the people I may have hurt, all the bad things I have done, even the thoughts in my head. I don't want to face that—I don't want to know that—I don't like that person. Why then am I so dead-set on staying that person? I want to be better. I don't want to hurt people. I want to be rid of these desires to do bad things. I am not ready to deal with all of my past, but perhaps in time I can come to peace with what I have become. Anyhow, I think I am now ready to move forward and follow the path of God to be a better version of me.

Relationship Is the Solution

Can you hear the shame and condemnation that keeps driving people away from God's restorative grace? Unless we, like Jesus, offer some really "good news" about God to offset this bad news that everyone secretly understands, people just keep running from him.

So we must be like Jesus. We must start where Jesus started, with muddied, wretched-feeling people. Jesus didn't start with the mud, but the hope of this "good news" about a God of grace who offers damaged people a relationship to become the people they were intended to be (we all need that).

Think about it: Jesus didn't confront Zacchaeus about his thieving practices, he offered relationship, and that changed Zach! Jesus didn't make sure the woman at the well understood that sex outside of marriage is wrong (though he taught it was at other times), he offered her living water that made the muddy water distasteful. Jesus didn't remind the woman caught in adultery that she broke the Ten Commandments—he didn't have to—he set her free from condemnation so that she could "go and sin no more" (John 8:11 NLT). He offered a chance to live a new life! Relationship was Jesus'

46

solution to sin. Can we offer restorative relationship to very mud-died people? That's what it takes to be like Jesus!

Sunni♦ glanced in the rearview mirror. Something about the innocent, big brown eyes smiling back at her from the car seat struck a deep chord in her soul. *She deserves better than I got,* Sunni thought. The bright, beautiful day contrasted vividly with her dark teenage memories of losing her mom to an overdose. Sunni had mostly stopped stripping for a living since her daughter was born, but kicking the alcohol and drugs did not come as easy.

My beautiful little girl deserves more than an addicted mom in unhealthy relationships. How do I get out of this? Sunni thought back over the men she'd been with, always hoping for a knight-in-shining-armor rescue. *I stay with men who are liars, manipulators, alcoholics, and cheaters because I'm so desperate to be loved by someone,* Sunni thought, *yet I always feel empty, like something's missing.*

"Mommy, when can we go to church again?" Autum's♦ four-year-old voice cut through Sunni's introspection. Having good memories of attending her aunt's church as a kid, Sunni had tried church a year earlier. She always left feeling small, dirty, unworthy of God's love, and like there was no way she could ever redeem herself in God's eyes. And she knew if these people found out her past, they'd surely reject her.

"I don't know, honey," Sunni told Autum. Yet that very day, driving along listening to her favorite rock station, Sunni heard a radio ad that made her laugh. "It surprised me that it was a church," Sunni recalls, "but what stuck in my mind were the last words: 'Come as you are—no perfect people allowed.'"

Sundeos is a church we helped start in Oregon. Sean,♦ the pas-tor, recalls meeting Sunni that Sunday. Sunni came once and felt like people were genuine and real, but past memories still haunted her: *Maybe they're faking it,* she concluded. The people seemed fake and judgmental at the last church; she just expected the same here—especially if they knew her past. Two weeks later, Sunday morning found her so hungover her body shook from dehydration.

"'Come as you are' kept filling my mind," Sunni recalls, "so I decided to put them to the test and see if they would push me out"—better sooner than later, she figured. Sean saw her come in, introduced himself as the pastor, and asked how she was doing.

"I have a massive hangover," Sunni blurted out, intending to jolt a judgmental reaction.

"Oh, then you need some coffee," Sean responded. "Can I get some for you?"

Sunni was shocked. She tried again and again with other people, working hard to get a reaction to her "massive hangover." Instead, she felt like the people there were less concerned about her hangover than they were about her—it blew her away.

"I continued to come to Sundeos and began building amazing relationships with people there, and as trust built, I began to say less words for shock value (which was a defense mechanism I used to keep people from getting close enough to hurt me), and I began to allow myself to be ever-so-slightly vulnerable. Sean, Collette, Chandy, and a few other people brought me into their lives like I was family. No matter what I said or did, the response was, 'I love you for exactly who you are, and exactly where you're at, and so does Jesus.' Nine months later, I almost overdosed like my mom had, but I cried out for help—this time to God and my new Christian friends."

Sunni entered recovery to get clean of drugs and alcohol, and Sean baptized her for faith in Jesus. Today Sunni celebrates nearly four years of sobriety. "God led me to an amazing Christian man I've been married to for a year now, I'm back in college, and I know Autum will have a better life than I did, because God's leading us all."

Jesus offered mercy to people who needed mercy. He brought good news about God's heart for people who felt condemned, judged, thinking God saw no hope for them. He offered people relationship that restored. As followers of Jesus, do we first bring something "good" relationally to people in need of good news, or do we bring a gospel of mud management that says, "Until they see the mud, they won't see their need for God? Until I help them see the 'bad news' about how wrong their sin is, they won't see their need for forgiveness"? Jesus didn't do this, but the Pharisees did.

This doesn't mean Jesus ignored or denied the seriousness of our sins against God or our wrongs against each other. Jesus didn't deny the truth about sin (as we will see in coming chapters). Instead, he put the spotlight of grace on the Masterpiece, so people could see why the mud needed removing.

What would happen if you went into your workplace, your neighborhood, your home and really started treating people just like Jesus did? What if you were unshocked by mud . . . motivated by mercy . . . and committed to restoring value? We must learn to hold a new framework in our minds. God may need to chip away some of your rough spots to get you looking more like Jesus than a Pharisee. Will you let him? We must learn to replace shock with a mercy that restores value rather than devalues people. But how? Here's a powerful truth you probably never thought much about: How you choose to see people matters more than what you say or do.

QUESTIONS AND ACTIONS

1. Reflect on this: Circle each "kind of person" you might feel uneasy or uncomfortable striking up a conversation with. Feel free to write in new categories that come to mind. Ask God to show you why you feel this way and why these categories could limit his work through you:

   a drug addict   a lesbian   a liberal   a conservative a Muslim   a Hindu   a Buddhist   a vocal Christian a gay couple   a convicted felon   a Wiccan   a stripper a convicted molester   a vocal atheist   someone of a different culture or ethnicity   a "successful" person   a "beautiful" person   a person in a wheelchair   a troubled person

   Other _____   _____   _____

2. Try this: Look for people to interact with this week who make you uncomfortable or seem very different from you. Again, just ask questions about what they like to do or what was the most fun they've had recently. If they say something shocking or maybe hurtful, pray, "God, show me the priceless value you created in this person."

3

Restoring Value

Hawkeyes
Photo: Travistank.com

T his is just not right!" Tracy thought. "How am I supposed to worship God with *that* right in front of me?" Tracy sat completely distracted by the woman with short, spiky blue hair occupying the seat in front of her. She quickly processed the information—no makeup, short hair, blue jean jacket, pierced, and tattooed—and delivered the verdict. Tracy nudged her husband, pointed to the woman, and slid him a note, "She's gay, let's move."

Tracy and her husband came to Gateway at the request of her daughter. Tracy had been in church her whole life, even worked on the staff of a church for decades. She knew right from wrong, and this was wrong!

"My husband seemed a little less interested in analyzing her than I did," Tracy recalls, looking back. "I think I stared back and forth at her during the entire church service. I was angry. Yes, I was! I felt as though she had no right to even be in church, much less sit in front of me. I was there to worship Jesus, and she was a total distraction. I peered inconspicuously at her 'friends,' wondering what perverted things they probably did. I was totally disgusted, absolutely disgusted! As I tried to pay attention to the message, my eyes were drawn back to her over and over again—still sizing her up, watching her gestures, analyzing, judging. I felt creepy sitting behind her, in church of all places. I wondered, *Why, oh why, couldn't I have just sat where we normally sit?* As the service was concluding I thought, *Good! I can leave.*"

But as they stood to sing the closing song, something grabbed Tracy's attention and threw her over backwards. The tough-looking woman was wearing a skirt! A very feminine, white lace skirt. For some reason, it confounded Tracy so much that she couldn't stop watching, even following this young woman all the way across the courtyard. People she knew to be strong Christians greeted and even hugged this woman. Then it happened! Tracy watched in shock as this woman turned and gave a big hug . . . to her daughter. The rest of the day, Tracy felt troubled, conflicted. That night, her daughter came over, and they had a long conversation about "that woman." Tracy found out the rest of the story about Lisa.

Lisa grew up with a mom addicted to hard drugs. Her father left them only to be replaced quickly with a stepdad who sexually abused Lisa before she was old enough to know the word *sex*. After enduring years of abuse, wanting to protect her younger sister from getting abused, Lisa went to court to testify against her stepdad. She was too young to be believed, and her whole family turned against her. She was forced to move in with her biological father at age twelve, not only having the close friendship of her sister ripped away, but her biological father quickly began to sexually molest her as well.

Lisa turned to drugs in middle school to calm the hurricane of anger and disgust she felt toward men. She didn't trust men, or her dangerous femininity. The only guy she felt safe to date in high school was very feminine himself. But when he got her pregnant, he too turned into a violent monster. He beat her so badly, she miscarried her baby at age sixteen. Feeling horribly alone by age twenty-two, Lisa tried to reconcile with her mom, who then introduced her to crystal meth.

"I couldn't stop the waterfall of tears," Tracy remembers, "as my daughter shared the amazing, healing work Jesus had been doing in Lisa's life since she got baptized one year earlier. I found out Lisa had overcome a drug addiction, worked the twelve steps, and even forgiven her family. She was in a small group, and an older couple now mentored her like loving parents. And the skirt?—well, Lisa felt like Jesus had made it safe enough to start to love her feminine identity again.

"I was brokenhearted as I saw myself more clearly than ever before. *I was a Pharisee!* Yes, I had a rote response to sin, a rulebook of do's and don'ts, and I was a Pharisee. I felt sad, ashamed, and prideful. One year later, I see that day as a divinely orchestrated appointment. Jesus used Lisa to help me see my own sin, and I too am overcoming by his power. I have forgiven myself and am enjoying this new and fresh perspective on life."

Framing the Right Picture

What you hold in your heart toward a person, the mental framework in which you picture them, is what people react to interpersonally. Understanding this can transform you into a more life-giving person. You may have heard about a study showing that words make up only about 10 percent of effective communication. The rest of what gets communicated is nonverbal: tone, body language, facial expressions. I would like to suggest something even more subliminal gets communicated too—heart.[1]

Four decades of research in psychotherapy has now demonstrated that the most influential factor that changes a person during therapy is the relationship. How the therapist *feels about the client* makes the biggest difference! In over one hundred studies, clients indicated it was not the therapeutic ideas or techniques that helped most, but the feelings of warmth ("you listened and cared"), empathy ("you understood me"), and genuine relationship ("you respected and liked me") that made the greatest impact on a person's behavioral change and life outlook.[2]

We can actually perceive what's in the heart of another person—how they feel about us—and that makes a huge difference! This is a powerful truth when encountering others. If people feign interest in you, but they are not really genuine—maybe they just want to look good by acting interested—you can tell!

If your boss uses the latest management techniques on you—sitting on the edge of the chair to practice active listening, inquiring about family members to show interest—none of that matters. You will respond to the way that boss *actually feels* about you when doing these things—somehow, you intuitively know.

In a marriage, you can go to a skilled counselor and learn great conflict resolution and communication skills. You each might do the right things in the right ways technically. But none of that will matter if one of you holds contempt in your heart toward the other—you'll know and that's what will get the reaction![3]

The same holds true for every Christ-follower encountering others. People perceive how you *feel about them*, intuitively, and that's what they respond to. Training in what to say, arguments that prove you're right, tracts or pamphlets, and good books can either help or hinder depending on one thing: what's in your heart toward that person. That's what matters most! That's what influences people the most, even if they can't consciously articulate why.

Which means, if we are going to be influential people—life-giving people, people who are more like Jesus—we must pay attention to the *mental frameworks* we put people in. The picture we hold of them in our hearts, the way we feel about them more than the words we say, techniques we use, or truth we proclaim—these have the greatest impact.

If you are truly *for people*, if you hold *good will* toward them in your heart, if you *highly value* them, people can hear all kinds of difficult things because they'll know you are on their side. But if what you hold in your heart toward another person is devaluing, judging, condescending, manipulative, or self-centered, people sniff that out like dogs in the dog park.

But how, you may ask, can we hold good thoughts in our hearts, when people are so bad? Great question!

I Desire Mercy

Jesus offered mercy to people who deserved judgment. In Luke chapter four, Jesus stood up in his hometown synagogue and read from the prophet Isaiah foretelling the Messiah's mission (which should be our mission!). Jesus said, "This is being fulfilled in me" (see v. 21).

"The Spirit of the Lord is on me, because he has anointed me to proclaim good news to the poor. He has sent me to proclaim freedom for the prisoners and recovery of sight for the blind, to set the oppressed free, to proclaim the year of the Lord's favor." Then he rolled up the scroll.

Luke 4:18–20

He said, "I've come to let struggling people, brokenhearted people, people captive to addictions, people stuck in dark spiritual places know that now is the time of God's favor—*God is for you, not against you!*" Do people perceive that you are for them, not against them?

But Jesus cut Isaiah's prophetic words off in mid-sentence. He read, "to proclaim the year of the Lord's favor," then he rolled up the scroll. Yet Isaiah said, "to proclaim the year of the LORD's favor and the day of vengeance of our God" (61:2). Why did Jesus leave that part out? Why cut out the part about vengeance and judgment?*

Because that's coming—a day is coming when God will set all things straight and justice will be done. But first, he offers mercy to everyone who realizes they need it. He offers restoration to all who will receive God's help. Jesus said, "I did not come to judge the world, but to save the world" (John 12:47). If Jesus did not come to judge and condemn, but instead restore and set free, if that's the age we're in, do we represent his message well? Do we picture others in the frame of mercy, or the frame of judgment? People expect judgment, and it keeps them running from the only One who can help them. Listen to this email I got from Jenny:

> For years, I was so scared to even think of walking into a church. There were many times I would come to tears just thinking of the judgment I would get if I tried. For the past two years, I have suffered from great depression. I have had four miscarriages and one abortion (two miscarriages were my husband's babies, the others were from "my past"). I gave myself so freely and aborted a baby; I figured these miscarriages were my punishment.

---

* The day of vengeance and the day of God's judgment are synonymous. Jesus said, "I have come into the world as a light, so that no one who believes in me should stay in darkness. If anyone hears my words but does not keep them, I do not judge that person. For I did not come to judge the world, but to save the world. There is a judge for the one who rejects me and does not accept my words; the very words I have spoken will condemn them at the last day" (John 12:46–48).

Mercy matters to God. When he reveals himself to Moses, God says, "I will proclaim my name, the LORD, in your presence. I will have mercy on whom I will have mercy" (Exodus 33:19). "He passed in front of Moses, proclaiming, 'The LORD, the LORD, the compassionate and gracious God'" (Exodus 34:6). Mercy and compassion define the character of God.* Jesus says, "Blessed are the merciful, for they will be shown mercy" (Matthew 5:7).

Mercy and kindness demonstrated by women at our church convinced Jenny to attend a group called Forgiven and Set Free. It brought healing to the scars of abortion and led to a turning from her past. Jenny explained, "I got baptized several months ago and started doing the *Soul Revolution* experiment learning to listen to God's promptings. My life is changing with every step I take. My husband and I are growing strong again in our marriage, and it is because of God."

It's God's kindness that leads people to repentance (Romans 2:4). Jesus gets angry with people who have been shown kindness and mercy, but refuse to extend it to others (Matthew 18:33). We may tend to think we can't fall into this trap, but Jesus' encounters reveal a slippery slope religious people often slide down.

Unmerciful Religion

The second time Jesus told the Pharisees to go learn what God meant when he said, "I desire mercy, not sacrifice" (Matthew 12:7), Jesus and his disciples had picked grain and eaten it on the Sabbath. The Pharisees accused Jesus of breaking the Law of Moses by working on the Sabbath. Jesus insisted he and his disciples were innocent (the Pharisees didn't understand the heart of God's law). What tie did Jesus find between the Pharisees' use of the Law of Moses and a lack of mercy?

---

*The next verse also refers to God's justice, saying, "He does not leave the guilty unpunished" (Exodus 34:7). But justice is God's job description, not ours. Jesus bore the punishment for all who receive it. We are told to show mercy; we are not told to punish the world for their sins.

Though Jesus did not actually break the law, he justified his actions with two examples that technically *did* break the Law of Moses. David ran for his life from King Saul, lied to the priest so as not to betray his presence, then took the consecrated bread only the priests could legally eat. Jesus refers to this incident and makes the point clear: "[They] ate the consecrated bread—which was *not lawful* for them to do" (Matthew 12:4, italics mine). Yet the Scriptures do not condemn David and his men. Why?

Jesus confronts their very approach to the Scriptures that cannot value mercy (in David's life-threatening situation) over judgment (technically breaking the law). They didn't understand what Jesus' half-brother James came to realize: "Mercy triumphs over judgment" (James 2:13).

Jesus did not negate the Law of Moses; he fulfilled it in a way the Pharisees never could (Matthew 5:17–20). He poked a finger in the chest of the Pharisees for missing the whole point by valuing the technicalities of law more than the people the law was there to serve. In Mark's account of this encounter, Jesus said to them, "The Sabbath was made to serve us; we weren't made to serve the Sabbath" (Mark 2:27 THE MESSAGE).

The Pharisees' motive was not love for people, but love for themselves. They loved the law because they used the law to feel valuable. See, the problem is the same. Pharisees don't see themselves as God's Masterpiece mercifully being restored. They see themselves as muddied people who cleaned themselves up (or didn't need restoring). How do you view yourself? Does this view lead you to value "being right" or "knowing truth," even more than showing compassion or mercy to a broken world Jesus wants to restore?

After coming to faith, I became an avid Bible student and eventually went to seminary. But because most of my sense of worth or value still came from "being smart" or "being good" at whatever I was doing, my knowledge and use of Scripture was about me. I used it to prove myself smart or right. When I started teaching, I subtly slid into phariseeism. My love for truth was more about proving myself right than helping others find restoration.

Mark records another Sabbath controversy where Jesus got genuinely angry because the religious leaders cared more about proving they were right about Sabbath law than they cared about a man with a withered hand Jesus wanted to heal (Mark 3:1–6). Honestly, I see evangelical Christians all the time who appear to value "speaking truth" and "being right" significantly more than they value lifting a finger to help broken, hurting, wandering people. I think that's a good clue we've lost the truth about the heart of Jesus!

I got an email from a pastor who had the guts to honestly look in the mirror and turn from phariseeism. Listen to what he says:

> I was raised in a very conservative and traditional Christian church framework. I went to college and seminary within that same framework. What I took away from that training was the concept that we are in a battle for the truth, and when we encounter our culture we must engage in that battle and seek to win the argument.
>
> Reading *No Perfect People Allowed*, I really identified with your story about sharing the gospel with an individual whose response was, "Yeah, I understand what you're saying, I just don't want to be like you." When I read that, I sat down and cried. God convicted me that I was more interested in being right, working for the passage of legislation to protect my vision of culture, and making sure everyone knew what I stood for, than I was interested in the brokenness of the culture right in front of me. I had inadvertently become a barrier to people finding grace. That is hard to admit, but it is the reality.

Realizing this truth, he worked hard to get his church to see and care about the culture around them, but they were unwilling. One person even told him, "I know these changes are needed, but you can make those changes when I'm dead and gone."

Courageously, at the age of forty-seven, he and his wife left their security and started The Harbor Community Church in St. Louis, and many people beaten and battered by life's storms have found faith in Jesus as a result!

Not Judgment

Pharisees love to judge people! Jesus instructed us, "Do not judge, and you will not be judged. Do not condemn, and you will not be condemned" (Luke 6:37). As you read their encounters with Jesus, again and again the Pharisees judge others and have no mercy or compassion for those who can't live up to their standards. Jesus rebuked them, "You load people down with burdens they can hardly carry, and you yourselves will not lift one finger to help them" (Luke 11:46). Rather than compassionately helping people, do we burden them with judgment when they don't live up to *our* standards?

That's the key to phariseeism—you must judge not on God's standards, but on your own standards. That's what bothered Jesus the most: Pharisees are hypocrites! They don't judge themselves by God's standards, but they quickly judge everybody else by their own standards. People can sense it in their condemning eyes.

Are we more like Jesus or the Pharisees? It's not so obvious. I find that pharisaical judgmentalism grows weeds in my garden of good deeds, and I'm blind to it. For a whole week, I tried to be more conscious of what I hold in my mind's eye about people. Here's what I discovered:

Judging is *fun*!

Judging others makes you feel good, and I'm not sure I've gone a single day without this sin. In any given week, I might condemn my son numerous times for a messy room; judge my daughter for being moody—which especially bothers me when I'm being moody (but I have a *good* reason!). I judge my wife for over-involvement in service (because it raises the bar for me); even my dog gets the hammer of condemnation for his bad breath (though we feed him junk but don't brush his teeth). Some of you may be thinking,

"Wait, are you saying that correcting my kids for a messy room is judging?" NO! But there's correction that values with mercy and there's correction that devalues with judgment.

I watch the news and condemn those "idiotic people" who do such things. Most reality TV shows are full of people I can judge as sinful, ignorant, stupid, arrogant, or childish. I get in my car and drive and find a host of inept drivers who should have flunked their driving test—and I throw in a little condemnation on our Department of Public Safety for good measure!

At the store, I complain to myself about the brainless lack of organization that makes it impossible to find what *I'm* looking for, all the while being tortured with Muzak—who picks that music anyway? I stand in the shortest line, which I judge is way too long because—*"LOOK PEOPLE—it says '10 items or less,' and I count more than that in three of your baskets—what's wrong with you people?"* And why can't that teenage checker—what *IS* she wearing—focus and work so we can get out of here?[4]

Judging is our favorite pastime, if we're honest—but we're not! We're great at judging the world around us by standards we would *highly resent* being held to! Judging makes us feel good because it puts us in a better light than others—we put ourselves in the place of God, the standard bearer! Jesus confronted this God complex in those who judged by their own standards, but didn't judge themselves by God's standards of mercy, justice, and faithfulness (Matthew 23:23).

The Pharisees felt superior and had *no mercy* for people who didn't live up to *their standards. What Jesus detested most in the pharisaical heart was a lack of mercy. Jesus said to them, "If you had known what these words mean, 'I desire mercy, not sacrifice,' you would not have condemned the innocent" (Matthew 12:7). More than all our self-justifying sacrifices ("I do this, I don't do that—look at what a good person I am—at least I'm not as bad as Steve"), God wants hearts that receive his mercy, and then offer it to others. Only when we stand under the umbrella of God's mercy can we address the mud and stain in our own lives, not feel judged or condemned for it, and let God remove it. That changes us, and others. So how can we be people who, like Jesus, restore value?

Restoring Value or Devaluing

Hawkeyes has lived on the streets for years. Abused and discarded by his father at a young age, street survival is the only life he knows. He and his wife, Lady Hawk, live in a tent in the forest but work the streets to survive.

Travis Tank decided to go out to the streets and shoot a photo essay called "No Homeless in Heaven." His mission was simple: to listen to the stories of those on the streets and ask them how God helps them. As a professional photographer, he would combine their stories with their pictures to create a photo essay. In the process, he hoped to pass on the message that God loves them, and they have · value to him. When Travis photographed him, Hawkeyes casually mentioned he had never owned a picture.

Several weeks later, Travis tracked him down with a beautiful, framed eight-by-ten photo of Hawkeyes and Lady Hawk kissing. He also brought several other glossy photos, including a stunning shot of Hawkeyes that made him look like a model of strength—standing tall with his Texas flag, long dirty-blond hair framing his tan, weathered face—it was striking! (His picture introduces this chapter.)

When Travis gave him the photos, this rough, brazen, street-worn man burst into tears! Something about those photos, or maybe the value they conveyed, moved him deeply. He stood to his feet and embraced Travis. As a result, Hawkeyes and Lady Hawk decided they wanted to know more about a God who would value them like Travis did, and that's how I met Hawkeyes. At the time of this writing, he and his wife sit on the left at our 12:30 service, Texas flag standing tall. He sometimes shouts out when he has a strong opinion. We've seen many people find faith and hope and a path off the streets and out of addictions—but it usually starts with restored value.

As I studied the life of Jesus and his encounters, I made some shocking discoveries. People alienated by the religious establishment wanted to be around Jesus and "there were many who followed him" (Mark 2:15). Their lives changed, and I've become convinced it was primarily because of the way he felt about them. What he held in his heart toward them is what they perceived. Jesus' mercy saw through the mud to something of great value and worth, and in his eyes they saw hope for who they knew they were meant to be. Jesus restored value!

The religious Pharisees, on the other hand, devalued people based on a perceived weight of sin. Of course, it wasn't an equal scale. Their own sins of judgmental pride or greed didn't hold much weight, but unethical tax collecting, drunkenness, sexual sins, not holding right religious practices—these weighed a ton. In Pharisee minds, weighty sin subtracts value from a person. How about in your mind?

 So here's an important question in evaluating if I'm more like Jesus or more like a Pharisee in my encounters with people: Do I restore value or mentally devalue people? Do I hold in my mind's eye the picture of a person's true worth (from God's perspective), or do I mentally subtract value based on my judgment about their relative muddiness?

What's It Worth?

Several years ago, we had to sell my mom's house. I grew up in this house. I learned to walk, talk, ride a bike, build a tree fort, drive a car—all in that house (I didn't drive the car into the house . . . actually, that was another house, and another story). I helped my dad landscape the yard, and we built a pond and waterfall in the back. My mom had lived in that house for thirty years. All our memories were in that house. But we needed to sell it.

So we listed it for what we thought it was worth. And it sat and sat and sat on the market. The realtor said, "You need to lower the price. It's only worth what someone's willing to pay for it." We valued that house based on the time and creative energy put into it, plus the sentimental value no one else could see.

Another year passed. Finally, we lowered the price, and the house sold. The realtor was right: The true value of anything is established by the highest price a person will pay for it.

So what's the true value of the muddiest human being? What is the highest price someone will pay? "God paid a ransom to save you from the empty life you inherited from your ancestors. And the ransom he paid was not mere gold or silver. It was the precious blood of Christ" (1 Peter 1:18–19 NLT).

Jesus said, "When I am lifted up from the earth, [I] will draw *all people* to myself" (John 12:32, italics mine). God set the value of *each person* by what he was willing to pay. He values you, me, Hawkeyes, gays, drug addicts, sexual predators, crooked corporate CEOs, nice happy people, every person with an eternal value—all he could pay! Why? Because he sees what we are truly worth to the Artist, who put in creative energy and holds in his mind an eternal memory of his image in each unique Masterpiece.

So what would possess us to devalue people? How can we claim to follow Christ if we don't restore value to people he valued with his own lifeblood? Maybe the problem is that we just don't see what Jesus sees.

What Do You See?

Pro baseball player Matt White had an aunt who struggled to make ends meet for years, living on fifty acres of property in Massachusetts. When her health started to decline, she was forced to sell her property to pay for health care. As an act of kindness, Matt bought the land from his aunt for the appraised value of $50,000. While exploring the land to see about building a house, he discovered outcroppings of stone ledges.

Matt contracted a geologist, who surveyed the land and informed Matt this stone had commercial value for patios and landscapes and could actually be sold for $100 a ton . . . and he had about 24 million tons on the land. The appraised value on the surface was $50,000; beneath the surface the land was worth over $2 billion![5]

As Jesus looked out at the masses of people, he saw something of great value beneath the surface. "When he saw the crowds, he had compassion on them, because they were harassed and helpless, like sheep without a shepherd" (Matthew 9:36). To be like Jesus to others, we must see what Jesus sees beneath the surface that's of infinite worth to God. What must we picture in our mental framework as we encounter messy people?

Endless Treasures Available

Jesus must have seen beneath the spiritual poverty, imagining God's endless treasures made available to each person by faith. Paul understood this: "[God] gave me the privilege of telling the Gentiles about the *endless treasures available* to them in Christ" (Ephesians 3:8 NLT, italics mine). Paul could look at a pagan, idol-worshiping, sexually misdirected Ephesian and see that beneath the surface, endless treasures lay available in Christ. He could picture them living out what he goes on to pray for: people boldly and confidently living in God's presence, empowered by God's unlimited resources to live with inner strength, roots sunk deep into God's nourishing love, experiencing the love of Christ that makes a person whole and full of life! That's what Paul prayed for people because that's what he could see available (Ephesians 3:12–19).

Is that what you see beneath the surface? If you did, it would move you with compassion and mercy to want that person to know the love, joy, peace, kindness, self-control, fullness of life . . . endless treasures available to them. You would do everything you could to communicate to people, all kinds of people, how valuable they are to God that he would make endless treasures available to them for eternity—despite the mud!

The Restorers Are Few

When Jesus looked beneath the surface, it moved him with compassion because he saw people distressed, downcast, wandering, alone, and disconnected from the God who alone sees their true value. Then Jesus says something shocking to his followers: "The harvest is great, but the workers are few" (Matthew 9:37 NLT). So he commands them to pray for more workers! Then he sends them out to be restorers (9:37–10:1).

The problem is not primarily that people don't feel broken by sin (many are distressed and downcast). The problem is not that God doesn't care (he has compassion). The problem is not with people's openness or willingness to respond (the harvest is plentiful). The problem is with us!

The problem is that God's restoration plan for each of us involves guiding us to care for others—and that requires our willingness. Those willing and available to partner with God in his restoration work are few! Are you available to God to do his restoration work? Or is your life just too busy with more important things? The workers are few—that's the problem!

Think about it this way: Have you ever felt a stirring or prompting in your mind to stop and help someone in need, but you were too busy and ignored it? Have you ever had a thought urging you to go comfort someone or challenge them spiritually, but you decided it might be intrusive? Have you ever felt led to say something encouraging, but it felt awkward? God nudges everyone, but most everyone says no! The workers are just plain unavailable.

A few years ago, two Princeton University psychologists did an experiment inspired by the parable of the Good Samaritan (Luke 10:25–37). Jesus told a story about a traveler who was mugged and left for dead on the side of the road between Jerusalem and Jericho. A priest and a Levite (religious leaders in Jesus' culture) walked by on the other side of the street. The only one to stop and help was a Samaritan (an outcast in that society). Jesus twists the expected around and makes the Samaritan the hero who showed mercy and therefore fulfilled the law because he loved his neighbor. Then he told the religious lawyer who had tested Jesus and provoked the story, "Go and do likewise" (v. 37).

John Darley and Daniel Batson decided to replicate the story of the Good Samaritan with Princeton seminary students. A few variables were introduced. The seminarians were interviewed and asked why they wanted to go into ministry. There were a variety of reasons, but the vast majority said they went into ministry to help people. Then they were asked to prepare a short talk—half of them on the story of the Good Samaritan and the other half on other topics.

Finally, they were told to go to a building across campus to present their talks. Along the way, the researchers had strategically positioned an actor in an alley to play the part of the man who was mugged in Jesus' story. He was slumped over and groaning loud enough for passersby to hear.

The researchers hypothesized that those who said they went into ministry to help people and those who had just prepared the talk on the Good Samaritan would be the most likely to stop and help. But that wasn't the case. There was one more variable introduced by the researchers.

Just before the seminarians left to give their talk, the researcher looked at his watch and said one of three things. To some he said, "You're late. They were expecting you a few minutes ago. You'd better hurry" (high hurry). To others, the researcher said, "They're ready for you, so please go right over" (intermediate hurry). To yet another group he said, "You're early. They aren't expecting you for a few minutes, but why don't you start heading over there?" (low hurry).

The results? Only 10 percent of the seminary students in the high hurry group stopped to help (90 percent didn't help a guy slumped over groaning *because they were in a hurry*), while 63 percent of those in the low hurry group stopped to help. In several cases, a seminary student going to give his talk on the parable of the Good Samaritan literally stepped over the victim as he hurried on his way!

Darley and Batson concluded that it didn't matter whether some-one wanted to help people or whether someone was preparing to teach the parable of the Good Samaritan. *The only thing that mat-tered was whether or not they were in a hurry.* They concluded, "The words 'You're late' had the effect of making someone who was ordinarily compassionate into someone who was indifferent to suffering or the needs of others."[6]

Simply Available

If we want to be more like Jesus than the Pharisees, we must make ourselves available to God's Spirit to see and value those in need more than we value our own agendas. What if we simply made ourselves available to respond with mercy and compassion when God prompts? What might he do to begin restoring others through us if the workers were just available?

While speaking on this very topic, I had one of the craziest, busiest weeks in a long time. I got a text from a friend I play soc-cer with asking if I wanted to do lunch, and I said, "Maybe next week" without thinking about it. The following week I realized that God had tested me. I'd been praying that my friend would seek God, and here he was contacting me—but I wasn't available! Instead of beating myself up, I leaned into God's grace and asked God to give me another chance to be available.

I read a couple chapters of the Bible every night. That week, I read something I know I had read before, but it struck me in a fresh way, and I underlined it. The next day, I was flying to L.A. to speak at an inner-city ministry, and I was sitting next to a very friendly woman from Thailand. I did not want to talk because I only had that flight to prepare for the talk I was about to give.

She kept chatting on and on about her son in Austin, how she's worried about him. I got this quiet nudging that God wanted me to engage in conversation. I prayed, *"Lord, if that's what you want, make it clear, 'cause I have to get this talk ready, but I want to be available."* So I kept working on my talk, when she asked, "Is that from the Bible?"

Clear enough!

I set aside my agenda and said, "Yes, have you read it?" She explained how she grew up Buddhist but was introduced to Christ and got baptized. Shortly after, she lost her first baby, and she felt so hurt and let down by God, she just stopped seeking him.

I shared with her my own story of disappointment with God when my father died, and how I understood that feeling. I explained that this world does not go according to God's will—it's broken. And then it hit me. Isaiah 65!

I told her, "Last night I read something in the Bible that struck me funny, and I underlined it—but I think I underlined it for you." I pulled out my Bible and let her read silently what I had underlined: "I will rejoice . . . and take delight in my people; the sound of weeping and of crying will be heard in [my city] no more. Never again will there be in it an infant who lives but a few days" (Isaiah 65:19–20).

She looked at me, and her tear-filled eyes said it all. I told her, "Don't give up on Jesus—he hasn't given up on you. He wants you to know how much he cares for you." She told me how her son had gotten into trouble, and she told him, "Pray to god, any god, some god—maybe god will help you." She agreed that Jesus wanted her to pray to him again, and the whole flight she kept saying, "This is such a strange coincidence."

No, this is the God who wants to show his mercy and love to a hurting, broken world, through us. Will you be available to co-labor with him? If so, then we need to learn how to call out the Masterpiece in others. That's what we will explore next.

QUESTIONS AND ACTIONS

1. Reflect on this: When do you find yourself subtly looking down on others, valuing yourself as "better than," maybe giving off a

condescending air that says, "You need God's help more than I do"? Ask God to show you what reality looks like from his vantage point. How might you restore value to people this week?

2. Try this: Often we're just too busy to make ourselves available for God's restoration work. Tomorrow and the next day, wake up saying, "Lord, show me your assignment for me today. I'm available." With each person you encounter, ask, "Lord, what do you want me to see? How can I encourage or restore value to this person?" See it and say it.

4

Calling Out the Masterpiece

Statue of David, Michelangelo (1501–04)
Photo: Ying Feng Johansson, Dreamstime.com

One of the most recognizable works of art in history is the statue of David, sculpted by Michelangelo in 1504. Every year over one million tourists come to gawk at this impressive seventeen-foot-high block of white marble, carefully crafted into David with a sling over his shoulder, preparing to do battle with Goliath. It has become a symbol of strength and human beauty.

Michelangelo thought of sculpting as the highest form of art because it mimicked divine creation. He worked under the premise that the image of David was already in the block of stone, and his task was simply to reveal the masterpiece underneath the rough, jagged edges. Michelangelo explained,

> In every block of marble I see a statue as plain as though it stood before me, shaped and perfect in attitude and action. I have only to hew away the rough walls that imprison the lovely apparition to reveal it to the other eyes as mine see it.

That's exactly what I'm hoping you will see. God, the Master Artist, created you, me, and every person in his image. That image has been hidden under layers of false identities, encased in walls of insecurity and fear, marred and muddied and damaged by the sins of others and the sins we have done. What we often see in ourselves and in others around us is just an unimpressive block of marble with rough, jagged edges protruding.

God sees a Masterpiece waiting to be revealed in Christ. He sees his Spirit chipping away anxiety to reveal peace, chiseling off impatience and rage to reveal a calm kindness, stripping off empty pride and hollow self-promotion to reveal a powerful other-centered love, hacking away the chains of addiction to free and release self-control, polishing off the ugliness of self-centered ways to reveal the luster of self-giving mercy and love.

Jesus not only pictured this Masterpiece in every encounter, he called out the Masterpiece. He pointed out the true identity of people that God wanted to reveal by chipping away everything that wasn't the image he imagined. We must learn to do the same.

Change Starts With Identity

The moral law doesn't change people. Cigarette smokers know that smoking kills, but that knowledge does not change many smokers' behavior. Drinking and driving can kill, yet that knowledge doesn't seem to eliminate drunk driving. Knowledge of right and wrong doesn't create lasting change in people. So what does change people's behavior?

Identity! How they see themselves.

And this comes through faith by God's Spirit. "After starting your Christian lives in the Spirit, why are you now trying to become perfect by your own human effort? . . . For the Scriptures say, 'It is through faith that a righteous person has life.' This way of faith is very different from the way of law" (Galatians 3:3, 11–12 NLT).

New Testament scholar Klyne Snodgrass notes, "The whole of Jesus' teaching is geared to confront and rearrange a person's thinking about identity. . . . The assumption of Jesus' teaching is that the identity he described is the identity people should have, what God intended from the beginning, and that if people see that identity, they will want to choose and *can* choose that identity and by God's grace grow into it."[1]

James March, political science professor at Stanford University, says when people make choices they rely on one of two models of decision making: the *consequences model*, which weighs the costs and benefits to maximize immediate satisfaction; or the *identity model*, which asks *What kind of person am I? What would someone like me do in this situation?*

The consequences model can influence short-term decision making, but because identities are central to the way people make lasting decisions, any change effort that is not rooted in someone's identity is likely doomed to failure.[2]

March also notes that people's identities change and grow and greatly influence their decisions. Remember in chapter two what convinced St. Lucians to save their parrot? They started to see themselves as *the kind of people who protect their own*. There were no cost-benefit reasons to protect the St. Lucian Parrot, but identity change provided the motivation. This same identity-formation strategy has worked in conservation efforts in fifty different countries! Many examples exist pointing to change in identity as the key to lasting behavioral change.

Brasilata manufactures cans in Brazil. It's a slow growth, hard to change, not very exciting business. But Brasilata decided to change identities. They began calling their front-line employees "inventors," and had every new employee sign an "innovation contract," challenging them to be on the lookout for potential improvements. Twenty years later, the average employee at Brasilata came up with 145 ideas per year, fueling incredible cost savings and growth. Simply because managers "called out" a new identity in these line-worker employees: "Inventor."[3]

If we are going to become life-giving people like Jesus, people who help others find faith, grow, and change, the question we need to ask is, How can we make change a matter of identity rather than a matter of consequences? How can we help people identify with what God intended when he created them? In this chapter and the next, let's consider some pictures you can hold in your mind to help you call out God's Masterpiece in every person you encounter.

A Unique Work of Art

We are physical, temporal creatures here on earth, but our temporary bodies will be transformed in eternity, and our physical bodies will last! Jesus said, "About the resurrection of the dead—have you not read what God said to you, 'I am the God of Abraham, the

God of Isaac, and the God of Jacob'? He is not the God of the dead but of the living" (Matthew 22:31–32). God sees an immortal identity, a unique Work of Art he created to last eternally. C. S. Lewis reflects on how myopic our vision of other mortals can be in light of what Scripture says:

> It is a serious thing to live in a society of possible gods and goddesses, to remember that the dullest and most uninteresting person you talk to may one day be a creature which, if you saw it now, you would be strongly tempted to worship, or else a horror and a corruption such as you now meet, if at all, only in a nightmare. All day long we are, in some degree, helping each other to one or other of these destinations. It is in the light of these overwhelming possibilities . . . that we should conduct all our dealings with one another, all friendships, all loves, all play, all politics. There are no "ordinary" people. You have never talked to a mere mortal.[4]

God sees what we one day could be . . . should be! Something awe-inspiring now, just from an artistic perspective, but even more so considering the possibility that "Our bodies are buried in brokenness, but they will be raised in glory." "We will share his glory" and "shine like the stars in the heavens" if we trust in Christ (see 1 Corinthians 15:43; Romans 8:17; Daniel 12:3).

Just think for a second about God's artistry displayed in every human body. Whole libraries of books have been written on human biology, anatomy, and physiology. You could study for the rest of your life and still not understand all of the creative mysteries of the human body.

What does this reflect about the mind of the Artist and the value of his art? Consider the tiniest human cell, almost with a mind and life of its own, mysteriously capable of reproducing and differentiating itself into all parts of our bodies. Every little microscopic cell contains a *library's worth* of information. One hundred trillion of these cells make up a giant symphony orchestra playing the composer's unique melody in every human body.

Think about the intricate, interdependent systems that keep our bodies running. The life force rhythmically keeps the beat for every second of our existence, beautifully orchestrating the pounding of our hearts with the breathy melody of our lungs to bring oxygen and nutrients to feed every cell.

The lymphatic system wages a daily war against germs and disease that could harm us. The 200 billion neurons of the nervous system coordinate messages to and from every part of our body, so complex and yet so elegantly simple that we take for granted this concert of communication. Do you see the glory of the Artist in the glory of what he's created?

And then there is the mind. More mystery surrounds the mind and the brain than knowledge at this point, but reflect on the mind's reasoning power that can imagine and construct the seven wonders of the world, giant skyscrapers, airplanes, and spacecraft that can take us to the moon, and we're left in awe of the Artist, realizing we don't even understand our own mental capabilities fully.

Now think about one tiny finger on a newborn baby—the imprint signature of the Creator, verifying that this little one is another unique Masterpiece. There is not another identical Work of Art like this precious child. If the Maker weaves this much artistic wonder into our bodies, imagine how much more artistry he has invested in the human soul!

Consider how tragic it is when we disconnect from the Artist and lose sight of the Masterpiece he created us uniquely to be. We don't want to be ourselves; we want to be somebody else. Think of all the people who are discontent with their uniqueness! Think of all the nose jobs, face lifts, breast implants, tummy tucks, steroid-enhanced, Botox-injected bodies. These are just symptoms that we've lost our true identity.

I was talking to a guy the other day who was hard to look at. Heroine use had hollowed out his eyes and rotted away his teeth. He was telling me how he just doesn't know who he is. He keeps trying to find himself in a relationship or in what others think of him, but it just keeps leaving him feeling discontent and empty.

Over the course of his life, this identity crisis has gotten him in all kinds of trouble with drugs, the law, and unhealthy practices that have destroyed his body. I explained to him that God's restoration plan is to first restore our identity, rooted in our Creator, so that we feel secure in our uniqueness, comfortable in our own unique skin. Then we can stop trying to be like everyone else and learn to fully be ourselves.

The problem is not our uniqueness; the problem is a fallen, sin-stained humanity that doesn't see or value the work of the Master underneath it all. But we can be part of God's restoration work! God wants his followers to call out the valuable uniqueness God created, so people will identify with their Creator.

Broken Bodies

A man whose body was "covered with leprosy" begged Jesus, "If you are willing, you can make me clean." To touch a leprous person was a violation of the Law of Moses and would make Jesus unclean. Jesus had healed many from a distance, so why does it say, "Jesus reached out his hand and touched the man. 'I am willing,' he said. 'Be clean!'" (Luke 5:12–13). Jesus restored not only the leper's physical body, but also his identity as a person who deserves touch.

Can we be like Jesus, who reiterated to people that they were a unique, known, valuable creation of God?

Look at the birds of the air; they do not sow or reap or store away in barns, and yet your heavenly Father feeds them. Are you not *much more valuable* than they? Can any one of you by worrying add a single hour to your life? And why do you worry about clothes? See how the flowers of the field grow. They do not labor or spin. Yet I tell you that not even Solomon in all his splendor was dressed like one of these. If that is how God clothes the grass of the field, which is here today and tomorrow is thrown into the fire, will he not much more clothe you—you of little faith?

Matthew 6:26–30 (italics mine)

Jesus reminded his disciples, "Not one [sparrow] will fall to the ground outside your Father's care. And even the very hairs of your head are all numbered. So don't be afraid; you are worth more than many sparrows" (Matthew 10:29–31). Since "God does not show favoritism but accepts from every nation the one who fears him and does what is right" (Acts 10:34–35), he must see the same valuable, unique creation in each person.

When Jesus encountered a man blind from birth, his disciples asked if it was caused by his sin or the sin of his parents (John 9:2). Jesus cleared up this mistaken notion (we'll talk more about it in chapter 7), and he let his disciples know that when God's kingdom finally comes, all broken bodies will be restored fully. But God allowed this for a reason. God's glory can come through brokenness as his followers learn to restore others.

Team Scottie

Scottie* was born with spina bifida. The doctors told Sarah,* his mother, to unplug life support. The baby wouldn't survive a year. Sarah refused, and Scottie survived the first year, then the second . . . then the tenth . . . and twentieth! But life wasn't easy for Sarah. She had seven sons (two who died tragically). In his twenties, Scottie had his legs amputated and was wheelchair-bound. The father abandoned the family, leaving them destitute and forcing Sarah to move into low-income housing. Without a wheelchair ramp, for fifteen years Scottie found himself confined to their apartment while Sarah worked.

The new manager of Scottie's apartment noticed Scottie. She had just started following Christ and was learning how God's Spirit prompts us to value those the world discards. Nudged, she took the risk to invite Sarah and Scottie to church one Sunday. Sarah declined because they didn't have the right clothes. The manager assured her our church was "come as you are." They did, and Sarah and Scottie kept coming.

One Sunday, Bill Aguayo* passed by Scottie and reacted in disgust. Thinking, *Oh, he's just a nub of a man, misshaped head bent to the side, no legs,* he steered clear to avoid the awkward feelings that erupted. Bill recalls, "All day, God wouldn't leave me alone. I kept thinking about the value God placed on this deformed man who repulsed me, and I knew God wanted me to go meet him."

Bill tracked Scottie down, seeking to help him. "But Scottie helped me," Bill admits. "God used Scottie's broken, 'worthless' body to restore my broken view of a person's worth to God." Bill got Scottie involved serving with him on the grounds team, and a strong friendship developed. Scottie had never been part of a team. He'd never had a job or felt like he had something to contribute. Bill made him a valued, integral part of our church body. First thing every Sunday morning, I would see Bill blowing leaves with Scottie motoring around in his wheelchair picking up trash to beautify our courtyard for those coming to the service.

When Bill learned that Scottie had never been to the movies, seen a game, or played a sport because he couldn't get out of his house, Bill rallied the body and Scottie was included. Men with gifts of craftsmanship helped Bill build a ramp at Scottie's apartment complex. Sarah joined the hospitality team and began to feel like a valued part of every Sunday. Soon both Sarah and Scottie started following Christ, and I'll never forget watching Bill lift Scottie into the pool to baptize him—two men washed clean and being restored!

Kate Raidt* kept seeing Sarah and Scottie and sensing God wanted her to meet them, but she kept resisting. "One Sunday, I felt like God practically pushed me out of my chair to go meet them," Kate recalls. Kate visited their house, realized the intensity of their situation, and knew God wanted her to mobilize more of the body. Kate and Bill connected and thus began Team Scottie.

Since then, twenty people with different gifts and resources and abilities have helped Sarah plug into a support group, they helped Scottie get an interview with Easter Seals for his first job, an attorney did some legal work for free, and others gave him computer lessons. Team Scottie threw Scottie his first birthday party ever—on his forty-second birthday!

Three years after his baptism, Scottie's earthly body finally gave out. But not before bringing incredible glory to God. When I did the funeral, all the members of Team Scottie stood to talk about how God led them to serve Scottie, but what God did through Scottie changed them.

Can you be like Jesus, seeing the Masterpiece through the most leprous, untouchable people, and point out their value to God? Part of his restoration work in you is to help you call out that Masterpiece in others. Not only does God use us to restore others, he will use others to restore what's broken in us too! This gets back to what it means to be created in the image of God—to love others, use our creative imagination to see what God sees in them, and call out their true identities.

Imago Dei

The fact that God created us in his image made the incarnation possible. We're so like God that Jesus became fully human forever.[5] Since God's image resides in every human, we can learn to see and call out that image shining through the cracks in the mud of sin and brokenness. Theologians have debated for centuries what exactly constitutes God's image, or the *Imago Dei* residing in humanity, but for our purposes, several characteristics that differentiate us from the animals can be called forth in others: Our ability to create, manage, and love. When you see traces of his image, point them out. Help people identify with their Maker and seek him with all their hearts, because God promises when they seek, they'll find him (Deuteronomy 4:29).

Creating in His Image

"God created mankind in his own image, in the image of God he created them; male and female he created them" (Genesis 1:27).

God's image shines through our ability to create! As God created us, so we create in ways the animals cannot. Think of the bottomless well of human creativity.

Think of the millions of unique songs we've created—from David composing hundreds of psalms sung in 1000 BC, to the hymns Jesus and the disciples sang in AD 32, from Beethoven and Bach all the way to rock, country, rap, and pop. Can you see his valuable image in the creativity and imaginations of others?

You have imagination and an ability to *see something that is not, and then dream it into being*. Every one of us has that creative ability because of the image of God hidden under the mud. It may come out in painting, music, dance, crafts, or in microprocessor design or interior decorating. Some of us, as we allow the Artist to do his restoration project, will find freedom to dream, imagine, and create again. The image got muddied and damaged, but God wants to restore it. Can you call out his image in people far from God by valuing their creativity, dreams, and imaginations? Letting them know that these gifts come from God will point them to the Creator.

James* grew up like many boys today—fatherless. He had five brothers and sisters, and his mother, a single mom, didn't have much time to spare. To compound the pain, he knew his father lived around the corner, but he was never allowed to see him. James's dad was still married, but not to his mom. James felt like an unwanted, painful reminder of the affair. For years, James ran from God and ran to alcohol, drugs, and sexual conquest to numb the pain of so much relational disappointment. But James could not run from his gift.

God gifted James with a creative, poetic imagination. Poetry had always served as a salve when his heart hurt; it was a friend he returned to often for comfort. Whenever his creative juices flowed, he felt alive, free, in touch with something bigger, better, transcendent. But James kept his gift buried for years under fear of rejection. Then a friend coaxed him into entering a slam poetry contest. He found validation and encouragement to enter more and more poetry nights at local bars. Soon he had a group of friends validating his gift. In his twenties, James decided to go for it—he moved to New York City to make a living in the emerging spoken-word movement.

One year later, battered and bruised by the sheer struggle to survive and devastated by a hurtful falling-out with his mentor, James moved to Austin to start a new life.

"Justin kept inviting me to check out this church," James recalls. "He said it was incredibly artistic. I guess his persistence finally persuaded me. I was a doubter spiritually, but the art I experienced intrigued me, so I kept going."

Matt* met James after one of our services, found out he was a slam poet, and began encouraging him. At that point, James had almost given up on poetry. After the horrible conflict with his mentor and the subsequent falling out with his poet friends, the door to poetry slammed shut, so James stopped using his gift.

Matt introduced James to Tony.* "Matt and Tony became real friends to me," James said, looking back on his journey to faith. "Tony was rough around the edges—like me. He was a musician who had made his living in bars and nightclubs in the past, yet now his faith was solid. Matt and Tony took an interest in me, not just as an artist, but as a person. Matt kept telling me I had a gift, and it was from God. I began to open my mind to the possibility that God really did exist, and had gifted me for a purpose.

"I still had a lot of anger and resentment from my New York nightmare, and now I associated all that pain with poetry. Tony reiterated that I wrote well, but he also helped me see it's not about me. When our creative gifts become laser-focused on serving us, they can end up burning us rather than producing life. Matt and Tony's friendship and encouragement made me want to trust their guidance. I got in a small group to learn about God.

"I began to focus my gift in a new way. Matt and Tony taught me it's not just about what I want to say, but also about what needs to be said. I began to offer my poetry to this God I was starting to believe in—to serve him and others. As I used my poetry more and more, I found a new validation—a realization that God could use my gift for a much more fulfilling purpose—to bring light to others. I started to pray as I would write, *God, speak through me to bring your light to the hearts of others.* I found a new freedom I had never known before—not only a life-giving freedom that's made my poetry more prolific, but freedom in every area of life as I follow Christ."*

Ruling in His Image

Another aspect of God's image we can point out in others is our ability to govern or manage. "In the image of God he created them . . . [and he said], 'Fill the earth and *govern it*'" (Genesis 1:27–28 NLT, italics mine). Our ability to rule, or govern over projects or people, or manage with justice and righteousness reflects God's image in us. Again it gets muddied and marred when we live disconnected from God. Often we use and abuse our God-given stewardship over his earth and his creatures when we work and manage others. But when his image shines through, people notice.

Betsy* didn't know Christ and didn't want to; she wanted to prove her worth to the world as a high-powered business consultant. But she had an employee who made "beautiful spreadsheets." In Betsy's words, "She would always go above and beyond what was expected to make the most incredible spreadsheets to present the data I requested. I knew it took way longer than was needed, so one time I told her, 'I need this by tomorrow, and don't bother making it pretty; that will cost the client too much money in billable hours—just get me the data.' Her reply caught me off guard. She said, 'Oh, I won't charge the client. And I'm always careful about how many billable hours I charge. But I need to do it right because I do all my spreadsheets and my work as a way to honor God.'"

Betsy was confounded by this. She never forgot what her coworker told her, and she observed her behavior even more closely. The next morning, there was another beautiful spreadsheet!

*To see and hear James's poetry, check out www.poetjames.com.

"Something about her doing her work with excellence to please God just got under my skin, and wouldn't let go. That actually opened me up to exploring more about this God who produced that kind of responsibility and respect to do her best." Today, Betsy's on our staff leading our church to serve others with excellence, because of "beautiful spreadsheets" that revealed God's image!

God wants to restore our ability to be good stewards of all we govern over, and use the responsibilities and authority that he's given us in line with his will. God's image can shine through in the way we treat employees, the way we treat our children, or the way we take care of things entrusted to us. How we manage reflects the image of God or the distortion of that image.

When you see people resistant to God, yet they care for the earth as God intended, or lead and manage others with integrity, or use their power or influence to seek justice and do good, do you see and point out the image of God shining beneath the mud? As you learn to call out what comes from God even in the most ungodly, you will better serve the Creator in restoring his Masterpiece in yourself and others.

Marcus grew up following his father to the temple to make sacrifices to the Roman gods. "Jupiter must be honored," his father would say. "Sacrifice to Diana if you hope to have offspring." As a soldier, Marcus worshiped Mars, the god of war who must be appeased to ensure success on the battlefield. Honoring the gods mattered to Marcus because he knew deep within that he needed help to be what he was intended to be.

When Marcus got promoted to centurion, he was less than thrilled at the location—that Jewish outpost of rebellion and uprising—Capernaum in the territory of Galilee. Nevertheless, Marcus did his job well to honor the gods. He was a good man who cared about respecting authority and cared for those under his authority. He took his job seriously.

Knowing that keeping the peace (*Pax Romana*) would please those in authority over him, Marcus showed kindness to the Jewish rulers by building them a new synagogue in Capernaum. Not long after, a stirring of the peace caught Marcus's attention. A man named Jesus had created quite an uproar, supposedly doing miraculous healings right in the synagogue Marcus built. Some of the Jewish leaders called Jesus a sorcerer, but others called him a Son of the God Yahweh.

Over the course of the next year, Marcus kept hearing more and more miraculous stories from his Roman soldiers. "Could this be a son of the gods?" his men kept asking. Marcus didn't know but kept a close eye to ensure no trouble erupted on his watch.

Then tragedy struck! Diocletian came down with a terminal illness. Diocletian was just a Greek slave, but Marcus cared for those under his authority, and had even come to love young Diocletian like a son. No doctors' visits, no prayers to the Roman gods had healed him. He would soon die. Desperate, Marcus thought of Jesus. "If he is a son of the gods and these stories are true, he could heal my servant. Perhaps one of the elders of the synagogue I built can persuade him to come." Jesus responded to the elder's request, but on his way, Roman soldiers stopped Jesus with a message from Marcus:

> "Lord, don't trouble yourself, for I do not deserve to have you come under my roof. That is why I did not even consider myself worthy to come to you. But say the word, and my servant will be healed. For I myself am a man under authority, with soldiers under me. I tell this one, 'Go,' and he goes; and that one, 'Come,' and he comes. I say to my servant, 'Do this,' and he does it."
> When Jesus heard this, he was amazed at him, and turning to the crowd following him, he said, "I tell you, I have not found such great faith even in Israel." Then the men who had been sent returned to the house and found the servant well.
>
> Luke 7:6–10

What did Jesus see in this pagan Roman centurion? Great faith! But we don't even know if Marcus had faith in "Jesus as Messiah," or in "Jesus as Son of God" or even in "One true God." It would be

. Well, Jss sd w do.

85

a stretch to make that assumption given where Marcus grew up. But perhaps Jesus saw the image of God shining through the cracks in the mud. A man who used his authority and power to do good for the Jews, a man who cared for those under his authority, even his slave whom he "valued highly" (Luke 7:2). And he demonstrated faith in what he did know about Jesus—and Jesus praised him for it!

This must have shocked the Jews who thought, *God only values us,* because in Matthew's account, Jesus points out that many will enter the kingdom of God from east and west, yet those who thought they were in will be thrown out (Matthew 8:11–12).[6]

I had an executive of a pharmaceutical company come talk to me about an ethical dilemma he was having. He told me honestly, "I don't know what I think about God yet, but I've got a problem, and I need some advice. I know the mainstay drugs we sell are addictive, and I keep getting pressure to push them because they make up the largest percentage of our revenue, but I feel this is wrong. If I speak up, it's gonna cost me my job, but I can't work there anymore in good conscience."

I told him, "I think this conviction you have is from God. God is at work in you already, and you are responding with a willingness to do the right thing. He will honor that." (Why wouldn't he, since "the requirements of the law are written on their hearts" by God—Romans 2:15–16?) I could see the light bulb coming on inside this executive as he felt empowered to do right, but he also identified with God that day in a way that put him on a path to find faith in Christ.

Think of all the ways to call out God's image in those who don't know Christ by complimenting those who govern well as they manage others, or acknowledging those who do their work with excellence, or encouraging those who take seriously the justice and integrity God created them to display, or telling those who care about the earth that their desire is God honoring. This simple *calling out* of the Masterpiece can begin the process of a person identifying with the God of Jesus. We've seen many come to faith when Christ-followers simply point out his image shining through the cracks in the mud.

Loving in His Image

A Christian woman interested in helping her neighbors find faith said something very revealing to me. She said, "As I've gotten to know my neighbors, they want nothing to do with God, but honestly they're really good people. They love their kids and they're really great parents—I feel like I don't have anything to offer them with Christian faith that they don't already have. I'm at a loss for how to show them where they need God."

I told her, "Why don't you just encourage them on what great, loving parents they are and tell them God must smile seeing how kind and loving they are to their kids, because 'love comes from God.' They've probably never pictured God pleased with them, but they are displaying his image by loving their kids well. Maybe this will open them to hearing more about God if they realize he's the source of all they love."

She said, "I've never thought about it like that—I actually never considered that God would be involved with them at all, since they don't believe in him." As we will explore more in coming chapters, this false idea that God doesn't show up or get involved until we introduce people to Christ actually creates unnecessary barriers to faith. Instead, we should be shining a bright light on the most important aspect of God's image deposited in every human—our ability to love!

Love is the most important aspect of the image of God in us. God created us for himself—not just as an Artist, but as a Lover, as a Father, as a Mother, as a Friend (he uses every human analogy to describe what he desires)! I have led many couples to faith in Christ by pointing out to them that the love they have is from God. Many had muddied up the image of his love by getting sexually involved before marriage, living together, or controlling and dominating one another rather than submitting to God and each other in love.

Yet all this presents an excellent opportunity to connect them to a new vision—a new identity rooted in their loving Maker who wants to help them better love each other.

In every loving act, and in every experience of love, people reveal the image of the Artist. Yes, we muddy up the expression of his love in innumerable ways, but it still comes from him: "Let us love one another, for love comes from God" (1 John 4:7). Yes, humans are totally depraved in every aspect of our being, but that doesn't mean God's good image is gone. It's still there, sometimes shining through the cracks in the mud, waiting to be revealed in Christ!

God may need to chip away some of your rough spots to enable you to see and call out his image in others—I pray you'll let him. Imagine if Christians became known as "the most encouraging, creative, loving, life-inspiring people I've ever met." What if people far from God said about you, "I want to be around him because he calls out the best in me"? Why don't we see ourselves with that identity? After all, Christian just means "little Christ." Jesus called out the Masterpiece, and he did so with both grace and truth. That is what we will explore next.

QUESTIONS AND ACTIONS

1. Reflect on this: How secure is your identity? Do you pay more attention to what God says about you or what others think? What are some specific ways you can call out God's Masterpiece in others around you?

2. Try this: Try to see God's image in others and call it out—say something affirming or encouraging. Make a game out of it. See if you can keep it up all week, affirming at least one person each day.

5

Speaking Truth in Love

Pietà, Michelangelo (1498–99)
Photo: Bryan Busovicki, Dreamstime.com

L aszlo Toth dashed past the guards, running furiously with sledgehammer in hand directly toward Michelangelo's famous *Pietà*. The crowd in St. Peter's Basilica in Rome, patiently awaiting the Pope's arrival for mass, let out a collective gasp as they watched the madman charge the famous statue depicting the crucified Jesus, cradled in Mary's arms.

Vaulting a marble balustrade while screaming, "I am Jesus Christ," Toth assaulted the white marble statue with his sledgehammer. With fifteen blows, he knocked off Mary's arm, removed part of her nose, and chipped her eyelid before the guards tackled the cultural terrorist.

Art historians around the world wept over the seemingly irreparable damage done. Toth was found to be insane and sentenced to an Italian asylum. Whatever his motives for damaging Michelangelo's masterpiece, against all odds, his work of destruction did not endure. Under the careful guidance of art restorationist Deoclecio Redig de Campos, a team of professionals used marble dust and special glue to delicately reattach pieces of the arm, carefully re-craft the nose, and patch the nicked eyelid. Several months later, the masterpiece was fully restored to its original splendor.[1]

No Masterpiece of God is beyond hope of restoration. But what tools does the Master Artist use to restore his original image in us? God uses a team approach through his body, the church (as we will see in subsequent chapters), and the two main tools he wants to teach us to use are grace and truth—but not by themselves or we can do more damage!

Jesus "came from the Father, full of grace and truth. . . . For the law was given through Moses; grace and truth came through Jesus Christ" (John 1:14, 17). The law brings truth without grace—it condemns us (Romans 3:19–20). If we are only damaged, dirtied works of art with no hope of restoration, then we are fit only for the dumpster; but if there exists a Master Artist with the skills to restore and renovate (and by grace, he's willing)—then there's hope!

When you were a kid, did you ever play with magnets? Remember how the positive charged ends of two magnets repel each other? If you have two really strong magnets, it takes a lot of strength to push the two magnets together and hold them there. Grace and truth can feel like the positive polarities of two magnets. For some reason, Christians find it very difficult to hold them together in tension. They tend to repel each other. As a result, people grab hold of one or the other, either all grace with no truth, or all truth with no grace. Jesus held grace and truth together in tension by a stronger force . . .

Love!

Grace, Truth, and Love

If we want to be like Jesus to the world around us, we must learn to keep grace and truth together in tension. That only happens when love is the force that motivates our interactions with people. We must learn to hold grace and truth together in tension because God uses these tools in tandem to restore human beings.

All grace with no truth is unloving. Some Christians desiring to offer grace completely ignore the gravity of our wrongs against God, others, and even ourselves. We minimize the serious consequences of sin under the guise of grace. But this is not a loving thing to do.

If I love my daughter and son, I will give them certain "laws" because I want to protect them from harm. "Thou shall not play chase on the busy street," would be a law I give to keep them from danger. "You must study math even if you don't like it," might be a law I give because I know it will provide a better future for them. When they are young and immature, they don't understand all the reasons why, but I give laws because I love them.

God's will has been revealed for a purpose—to *protect* us and others from harm, or to *provide* something better in the future. When people go against God's will, it does damage to the Masterpiece—in us or in others. So God's love motivated God's law given through Moses. Jesus did not negate the Law of Moses—he fulfilled the intent of it (Matthew 5:17). The intent of the law is to help us know what love does and does not do! When we are *not* acting like loving people, the law shows us that our actions are unloving according to God's definition of love.

But the law can't make us better people! Law (which is true but not the whole truth) without grace just makes people feel condemned. Grace offers a way to become truly loving people. Grace reminds us that God's presence and power will be with us by faith through the restoration process of life, even when we fail to live up to the law. We must seek to be people who live "full of grace and truth" drawn together by love. These are the tools God uses to restore his Masterpiece in us and others. Let's look at some of Jesus' examples of calling out the Masterpiece using the tools of grace and truth united in love.

God Has Great Plans for You

Jesus could see God's great plans for muddied people, and he would often point them out. Mark 10:17–21 tells us of an encounter when a man ran up to Jesus, fell on his knees in a dramatic display of piety, and said, "Good teacher, what must I do to inherit eternal life?" In almost every encounter Jesus had, I find he led with grace (the message of God's favor and goodness available to all who are willing). Here, Jesus subtly led with truth, but look how he combined it with grace by asking questions!

"Why do you call me good?" Jesus asked him. "No one is good—except God alone." We later find out this guy worshiped his wealth—he derived his value from money. Jesus knew the truth about him; he had not really made God first in his life, and he was trying to prove himself good by his deeds. That's why Jesus asked, "Do you realize that no one is good—and in calling me 'good' do you recognize *who* I am?"

Jesus continued, "You know the commandments. . . ." But before Jesus could finish, the brash, young high achiever cut him off with, "All these I have kept since I was a boy."

What came next is just classic: "Jesus looked at him and loved him." Stop and ponder this powerfully insightful commentary. Mark must have observed love bleeding out of the heart of Jesus, reflected somehow on his countenance. Everyone could sense Jesus loved this guy just by the way he looked at the man! But why did Jesus feel love for him? The guy was totally deceived—he was trying to prove his worth, thinking he was good and had kept all the commandments, yet he hadn't even kept the *first* of the Ten Commandments: Love God first and "have no other gods before me" (Exodus 20:3). That's the truth that Jesus knew all along. In fact, Jesus purposely left out the first four commandments (all about loving God above all else) and the last one (about coveting) to make a point with the man. Still the guy didn't clue in at all!

Yet Jesus didn't take out the hammer of truth and say, "You're deceived—you selfish, greedy, arrogant sinner. Money is your god. Repent and you'll be saved." Jesus could have done this, and it would have been completely true (in chapter 9 we will see times when Jesus did bring the hammer of truth to hard-hearted people), but in this case "Jesus looked at him and loved him."

Love motivated Jesus to bring grace together with truth. He could see the great plan God had for this man's life, and so, motivated by love, Jesus called him toward that great plan: "One thing you lack . . . go, sell everything you have and give to the poor, and you will have treasure in heaven. Then come, follow me."

Jesus offered him something even better! Jesus wasn't taking anything away; he said, "You still lack (you just don't know it yet)." He offered him riches and purpose that would last. He called him to something greater that God created him to do. Can we call people toward the great plans we imagine God has for them?

In this case, the man walked away sad. Jesus didn't chase after him. Sometimes we will call out the Masterpiece of God's greater purpose with grace and truth, speaking what we imagine God might do if only that person will fully follow, and they might walk away. But in time, they may see God's greater plan and return!

Leading With Truth in Love

I was hanging out enjoying the beautiful Austin Hill Country views at an outdoor wedding reception one Saturday when I spotted Chad talking to Maria near the bar. Maria had recently given her life to Christ and had invited Chad to Gateway. I knew Chad had been hanging out at church for about six months, and I knew he considered himself an agnostic. Chad busied himself with extreme sports whenever he wasn't working. It was the height of the high-tech revolution in Austin, and he was extremely intelligent, doing very well at a young age in a startup tech firm.

I asked Kenny, one of our staff standing next to me, "Where's Chad spiritually? Is he seeking or stuck?"

"I think he's pretty closed," Kenny replied. "My impression is that Gateway is more about seeking women than seeking God for Chad. I think we missed our chance with him anyway," my friend casually mentioned. "He got a promotion that's moving him to New York soon."

When Kenny said that, something struck me in the gut. I had this strong sense of compassion for Chad. Here was a young guy who was tearing up the world in business, living to the extreme of where his adrenaline rush could take him, thinking he had success in the bag. And in the world's eyes, he did. But as I stood there watching him, I was reminded of the rich young ruler whom Jesus loved, and I had this nudging that I needed to speak the truth in love to Chad before my opportunity evaporated.

Expecting the response Jesus got from the rich young ruler, I approached Chad. "Hey, Chad, congratulations! I hear you have a new job offer in New York—sounds like a huge promotion."

"Thanks! I'll miss the outdoors of Austin, but the pay and opportunity are too much to resist." Chad filled me in on the details of this new high-tech venture and the stock options he would amass as a signing bonus. Less than a decade ago, he was a pimple-faced latchkey kid entertaining himself in the emerging world of cyberspace. Now he was a rich young ruler.

"Chad, you've been hanging out at Gateway for a while now. Where are you at with God? Are you any closer to belief?" I decided on the direct approach.

Chad nonchalantly shrugged out his answer. "I respect what you all are doing, but it's just not for me."

This was not my first spiritual conversation with Chad, so I decided to bet all my chips on calling out the greater purpose I imagined God gifted Chad to accomplish. "Chad, you're an incredibly intelligent person. I know you love to learn and it's paying off for you. But think about this: You succeed wildly, make tons of money, and prove to the world how smart you are. Then you die and find out there really is a God who loved you and had a bigger purpose for your life than just living for Chad. Imagine how you'll feel if you missed using all these amazing gifts God gave you because you were too busy doing what Chad thought was best for Chad—that wouldn't be too smart would it?"

To my surprise, he agreed. So I challenged him to take the next two months before he moved and truly seek—heart, mind, and soul. To allow himself to be open like never before, asking God to reveal himself. I suggested several books I would give him, and told him after reading them, we could meet to discuss his issues and questions.

Chad's move was postponed, but over the following four months Chad worked through his issues by reading, talking with others, and meeting with me. He opened his heart to Christ, joined a small group, and experienced significant spiritual growth. The following December he wrote me a Christmas card from the East Coast: "Thanks for spending so much time with me so I can know Jesus! He's changing my life for the better. Merry Christmas."

I See Godly Character in You

Jesus led with grace in almost every encounter recorded, but always combined with truth. Truth is just *reality*, from God's vantage point. Truth does not merely point out the reality about sin, it also points out the reality about God's image shining through God-given character traits. Often, Jesus would speak encouraging words about godly character traits he saw emerging in a person. We too must learn to see those godly character traits and call them out in others, even under the mud.

When Jesus first encountered Peter, his name was still Simon. He looked at Simon and saw who he would become—a man with zealous faith. "I see something in you, Simon. I see a Rock of faith— I'll call you 'Peter'" (which in Greek means "The Rock"). (See John 1:42.) But there was still a lot of mud that needed polishing off before Simon would fulfill Jesus' vision, "On this rock I will build my church" (Matthew 16:18).

Yet surely Jesus knew the dark side of Simon's zeal and his people-pleasing ways. Jesus knew Peter would do some foolish things: wanting to strike people down, cutting off someone's ear in zealous violence, cowardly denying Jesus three times. Even after Peter had led the church for years, Paul rebuked Peter for people-pleasing sin (Galatians 2:11–13). Yet Jesus called out this positive character trait of zealous faith.

Jesus called out godly character traits in Nathanael when he met him for the first time: "Nathanael, you are a man without guile—a genuine person with real integrity" (see John 1:47). Jesus looked for those character traits he could encourage, and he called them out in people—giving them a chance to respond to God's restoration work, sometimes in crazy ways.

Consider the way Jesus trusted Judas—who never believed! Maybe Jesus saw in Judas a gift with finances. Just like some people seem wired to be good stewards, maybe that was a God-given character trait of Judas. Jesus appointed Judas the treasurer of his ministry (John 13:29). Talk about believing in someone against all odds!

When people far from God demonstrate godly character traits that the Lord would surely want to polish up and use in this world for good, can we take risks to speak the truth, encourage that trait, even take risks to let them use those gifts to serve with us though they may be a Judas?

A Pharisee wouldn't, but Jesus did.

Supernatural Forgiveness

Jessica* came up to me one Sunday with her boyfriend, asking for prayer. She had moved to Austin several years prior from a small town in upstate New York. I picked up from things she said that she probably wasn't a Christ-follower. She told me she had recently started coming to our church with her boyfriend. Several months earlier, her mother in New York had been murdered. They still had not caught the murderer, and they had no motive or reason for this random homicide in her mother's own home. Jessica needed prayer.

"Jessica, I'm so sorry. I can't even imagine what you must be going through," I said, trying to picture how I would be reeling from such news. We talked a little while longer about how she was handling it, and I wanted to make sure she gave herself freedom to grieve. Still sensing she was not a Christ-follower, I wanted her to know this hideous violence grieved God too. Then Jessica said something that floored me.

"I've decided to forgive my mom's killer."

"You have! How?" I was taken completely off guard.

"I just started thinking about how tormented and disturbed he must have been to do such an evil thing, and I know that holding resentment will only hurt me more."

Here it was—a chance to call out God's obvious work in her life, despite the fact that she didn't believe in Christ. I said to her, "Jessica—that's from God. Do you realize that? People don't naturally forgive such horrendous injustice. God is really doing something in your heart to be able to forgive like that."

She said, "I think you're right, because I don't know why I feel a peace about this. I'm still terribly sad, and want him to be caught so that he won't hurt others, but it is strange."

I encouraged Jessica to keep seeking God because he was clearly with her in this. Encouraging that godly trait of forgiveness got her on a path where she got involved in a small group, and later that year, she got baptized for faith in Christ. She realized she needed to take a break from her boyfriend for them to both grow spiritually, and the Lord began to show her some of the sexual sin from her past continuing to muddy up her life. Nine months later, the Lord led them back together with a commitment to honor God with their sexuality, and they are now in premarital counseling. She made huge changes because she began to identify herself as his Masterpiece.

Three years later, Jessica is part of a ministry in prisons where she tells her story and helps prisoners find freedom through repentance for crimes they've committed. God took that character trait of supernatural forgiveness and now uses it to restore others through Jessica!

You're Worth Being With

Sometimes Jesus looked past the mud to simply say, "You're valuable—you're worth being with despite the mud. You don't have to prove yourself to me." Think about Zacchaeus—a notorious little gangster with a Napoleon complex, trying to overcome his small stature by amassing large amounts of wealth and power at any cost.

Luke tells us in Luke 19 that Zach was the chief tax collector—the leader of the mob—the head of all the crooked traitors who would sell their souls to work for the despised Roman oppressors, while robbing their fellow Jews to gain wealth and power. The whole city of Jericho hated him.

Yet Jesus saw something shining through all that mud! He saw God using even Zach's brokenness to draw him close. Jesus spotted

Zach up in a tree, trying to get a look at this rumored "Messiah," and said, "Zacchaeus, come down immediately. I must stay at your house today" (Luke 19:5). What most don't notice is that Jesus "was passing through" (v. 1) when he spotted Zacchaeus. Jesus rearranged his plans to be with Zacchaeus! He went out of his way to spend time with Zach and simply convey "You're valuable—you don't have to prove yourself."

Luke notes that the whole city started to grumble when Jesus decided to spend the night at Zacchaeus's house because they couldn't see the Masterpiece for the mud! Jesus valued him simply by being with him. And that changed Zacchaeus! We don't know what all Jesus said, but Zacchaeus decided to give half his wealth to the poor and pay back those he had stolen from fourfold! Nothing but a new identity could motivate such change. All because Jesus saw something of great value that needed to be restored and rearranged his plans to simply *be with* him. Zach's restoration prompted Jesus to restate his mission: "For the Son of Man came to seek and to save the lost" (Luke 19:10).

The Value of Turkish Violas

Dervish was heartbroken. He had followed the love of his life around the world, from Turkey to Austin. But now she had broken his heart, and his two years in Austin felt wasted. Why did he give up touring Europe with a world-renowned orchestra for a woman? He felt like throwing his expensive Turkish viola across the room, but it was too valuable to waste on a flash of fury.

Love had lured him to Austin. He just didn't realize whose love. Distraught, not knowing what to do with himself, Dervish went to Dominican Joe, his favorite coffee shop in Austin. Sitting outside next to a group of people laughing and talking, Dervish noticed Phillip, who seemed to be leading this group in some kind of discussion. Eavesdropping, he overheard talk about life and meaning.

Dervish felt drawn to them. He asked what they were discussing. Phillip encouraged Dervish to join their quote study. Little did Dervish know, but he had just been led to a Gateway Network composed of musicians, filmmakers, and artists (we'll explore Networks in part 2). Their quote study, based on wisdom from the book of James and other recognizable quotes from authors or artists, was a way the group engaged people in spiritual conversation after they played a set of music in local venues. That night Phillip invited Dervish to a birthday bash at his house.

Later that week at Phillip's party, Dervish met Ramy (our Egyptian pastor to artists). Dervish had never experienced such an authentic combination of laughter and honesty about real-life struggles. Sitting around the fire pit that night with Ramy and others, Dervish opened up about his own broken heart. From this group of strangers, he felt genuine care and concern. There was a love that wasn't verbalized, but it was palpable to Dervish.

"Dude, you need to come hang out with us more!" Ramy said before they parted ways. "You know, sometimes you follow the wrong things to the right place! Come to my house next week. This group meets regularly to help each other grow as artists, musicians, and spiritually. You'll fit in perfectly! You'll love it."

Just feeling loved and valued by fellow artists felt comforting to Dervish. He kept coming to Network events, and even though he was Muslim, he got the clear message "You're valuable—just come be with us and grow with us!" As Dervish learned more and more about these "Jesus people" and what they believed, he became more open. They listened to his religious views with respect, focusing on God rather than religion, and he felt loved and valued and wanted regardless.

Dervish joined one of Ramy's small groups that was reading and studying the Bible. He also decided to read the whole Qur'an, something he had not done. Ramy invited Dervish to play viola with the band, sometimes at gigs, sometimes for worship at church. The love and value his heart experienced kept him openly seeking to understand the God of the Bible.

Two years later, I felt prompted one night to ask a question. "Dervish, you've been hanging out with us a few years; where are you with Jesus?" What he said showed amazing insight.

"You know, I've read the entire Bible and the whole Qur'an, and they say almost the same things about right and wrong. There's one difference: grace!"

"Wow, Dervish, that's incredibly insightful," I told him. Then I decided to point out his value to this God of grace. "Dervish, do you realize how much the God of grace loves you? Think about it, he guided you around the world so that you could know and experience his great love. Do you realize that?"

"Yes, I do. It's amazing." Dervish shook his head as if struck by the gravity of it.

"I mean, what are the odds of coming upon Ramy and that group of musicians who would welcome you in and give you the time and space to explore faith?"

"I know, I know" was all Dervish could say through a huge grin and glistening eyes.

Two months later, Dervish got baptized for his faith in Jesus, and I'm sure that God will use him as a tool of restoration for many others around the world in the years to come! But it all started because Phillip, Ramy, and other Christ-followers conveyed the message "You're valuable enough to be with. You have gifts God's given you to serve him—come join us."

Can you do the same? Can you demonstrate a love and value for people very different from you by including them and just *being with* them? Can you take risks for them to feel valuable using their gifts to serve with you? If that seems illegal in your church, just recall that your Lord took the risk to appoint Judas to serve as treasurer!

You Have Great Insight

Jesus pointed out wisdom from God even in people who did not believe in Jesus yet. One of the religious leaders, listening in on his co-workers trying to trap Jesus, gave an insightful answer about how our love matters more to God than all our sacrifice and offerings. Mark tells us, "When Jesus saw that he had answered wisely, he said to him, 'You are not far from the kingdom of God'" (Mark 12:34). Can you point out godly wisdom in others who don't believe in Jesus? "You are not far from the kingdom of God." Could you encourage your detractors if they said something that was wise according to the Scriptures? So many Christians think proving non-Christians wrong is the goal, yet Jesus sought to prove them right wherever they spoke truth.

"Why don't you guys have anything to help women suffering from sexual abuse or domestic violence?" Carrie* shot this accusation at Gary, one of our community pastors. "You know that this affects about one out of four women—and the church is not immune. Do you realize that?"

Gary knew Carrie had come to Gateway at the urging of her husband. She considered herself a liberal feminist, and in her own words, did not come to church to "get on the bandwagon." Christians actually repulsed her due to the hatred demonstrated toward her gay friends. Even through Carrie's bitter tone, Gary could see a trace of wisdom from God shining through the mud. He decided to point out that wisdom.

"You know, I think you're right. I think there probably are women here at Gateway suffering from sexual abuse or domestic violence, and I think God would want us to do something about it," Gary responded humbly.

That completely shocked Carrie; she hadn't expected to be validated. She had come ready for a fight. "Well, why don't you have any kind of ministry to help them then?" Carrie quipped.

"Sounds like something God would want us to do. I'll tell you what, why don't you help us figure out what that might look like?" Gary suggested.

Now Carrie was really on her heels. "Me, help start a ministry?"

"Well, you're not a follower of Jesus yet, right?"

"No—not at all!" Carrie retorted.

"So it's not like you could lead it, but you could help us think it through. And let me challenge you on this: While you're helping us consider how to minister to women, how about I help you explore what you believe about Jesus—maybe we can learn from each other."

Carrie agreed, and during the course of that year, not only did Carrie come to faith in Jesus, but a new ministry was born: Comfort and Hope! Three years later, Carrie did lead this ministry, which helped hundreds of women find healing and hope. Many others found faith in Christ through Carrie. But it started by recognizing "Your idea is not far from the kingdom of God—I think this is from God!"

Do you see how Jesus called out the Masterpiece in others, using grace and truth, united in love for the person? As we learn to be like Jesus, he will teach us to use the same tools in his restoration process with others. But in order to do this, we've got to let go of playing God, trying to clean people up by ourselves. We've got to learn to respect people's freedom.

QUESTIONS AND ACTIONS

1. Reflect on this: Do you tend to favor "speaking truth" or "giving grace"? How might you allow God's love to bring grace and truth together in your life? In your interactions with others?

2. Try this: Take a risk this week to love someone enough to speak grace and truth together in some of the ways we discussed (with the hope of seeing God's Masterpiece formed in them).

6

Respecting Freedom

Prince of Peace, Akiane Kramarik
www.akiane.com

Akiane* is a binary prodigy. She became a world-renowned artist and poet by the age of ten! At four years old, she sketched pictures of angels most adults could never draw. By the age of six, her oil paintings depicting people and nature equaled those of accomplished artists. But just as mysterious and beautiful as her artistic accomplishments is her self-proclaimed source of artistic creativity.

Akiane grew up in the rural countryside with two older brothers, all homeschooled by an atheist mom from Lithuania and an agnostic dad. The family never watched TV, never talked about God or religion, never prayed together, and had never gone to church. So Akiane's parents were dumbfounded when this four-year-old reminisced about meeting God and seeing extraordinary visions of heaven. Immediately after, she began to draw and paint and create poetry describing God, his loving, redemptive purpose for humanity, and the visions she had been given.

She believes God has commissioned her to use her art to lead people to love the Father, Son, and Spirit. Akiane's parents came to faith in Jesus through her visions and art. At age eight, Akiane felt led to paint a portrait of Jesus, whom she had seen in her visions. She searched to find a model on which to base her portrait, but could never find the right face. After a year-long search, one morning she prayed through tears of anguish, "I can't do this anymore, God. I can't find anyone by myself. I need you to send me the right model and give me the right idea."

The very next day, an acquaintance brought a friend over to the house. He was a carpenter! Akiane took one look at him and proclaimed, "This is he!" This eight-year-old's four-foot-tall oil painting of the resurrected Jesus and her canvas of Jesus praying, "Father forgive them," have now been viewed by millions worldwide, and her story has inspired many to faith in Jesus.[1]

I recently read a book by a pastor who claims his four-year-old, while undergoing surgery in which he almost died, also had visions of heaven and Jesus.[2] After multiple convincing facts the boy could not have otherwise known, the parents came to believe these near-death visions of heaven were real. For years after, whenever the parents would see a "Jesus painting," they would ask the son, "Did he look like that?" The boy would always say no and point out what was wrong with every one. . . .

Until he saw Akiane's painting!

God the Artist

God is an Artist. When I read Akiane's story, this fact, which should seem self-evident since he created everything, struck me in a fresh way! God works like an Artist! Artists love to provoke wonder and awe through the mystery and intrigue of their art. Just consider Jesus' love of parabolic teaching. If we fail to see the Master Artist behind all the beauty, mystery, and even the mess of humanity, we fail to understand how God works to create his Masterpiece in us and in others.

God is a painter—the origin of every color and every brush stroke of beauty you've ever witnessed.

God is a songwriter—the mathematical genius behind the melody's notes, the backbeat of every rhythm, the great lyricist behind every rhyme.

God is a sculptor—the creative mind forming brilliant galaxies and molding majestic mountains with a spoken word, sending the Big Bang into motion, sculpting beauty through nature in the medium of time and space. *really?*

But even more—God is a lover! "God is love," the Scriptures tell us, and he's the source of all love (1 John 4:7–11). As his crowning creation he designed free-willed creatures who *could* love God and each other. Only humans, of all creation, were shaped in the image of God with such ability to love. Jesus reiterated that love is *the* organizing principle of all God's creation (Matthew 22:37–40). But how does one create love?

Choose Your Medium

Whenever Akiane creates, she must choose a medium through which to create. If a sculpture is in her mind, she's free to choose bronze or copper, wood or marble as the medium through which to express herself. But once she has chosen, she limits herself by her choice. If she chooses oils on canvas, she has options of color that white marble doesn't afford, but she's limited to expressing in two dimensions rather than three. Every creator chooses a medium through which to create and then must work with the opportunities and limitations that medium presents.[3]

When God fashioned people in his image to love him, he chose the medium of free will in which to create. Love explains why God created in the messy texture of free will, and love explains why Jesus respected the free will of those he encountered. Love mandates that we learn to work with people's willingness as well.

Let's say you were in love as a single, but that love was not freely reciprocated. You could try to force love, I guess. You could hold that person hostage at gunpoint and try to make them say and do things that convey love, but we all know that's not actually love. That's forced obedience, slavery, which pales in comparison to love. Love cannot be forced. It must be free.

Once God chose to create creatures like us who could love, he limited himself by creating a world that could choose to reject or ignore our Creator and go against his will and spurn his love. Throughout the Scriptures, we see God using every human relational metaphor, vulnerably displaying a very real interplay of his heart with our free-willed choices.

This is what the LORD says: "I remember the devotion of your youth, how as a bride you loved me and followed me through the wilderness. . . . [But] my people have committed two sins: They have forsaken me, the spring of living water, and have dug their own cisterns, broken cisterns that cannot hold water. . . . I myself said, 'How gladly would I treat you like my children.' . . . I thought you would call me 'Father' and not turn away from following me. But like a woman unfaithful to her husband, so you, Israel, have been unfaithful to me," declares the LORD.

Jeremiah 2:2, 13; 3:19–20

God created people for a relationship more intimate than a bride and husband. And when the people he loves reject him, it feels like betrayal—like adultery—because of the passionate love he has for us. God wants your heart. That's what he wants from others. Not because he needs it, but because we need it, and he loves us!

He desires to give life that flows out of our inner being like living water. But he doesn't force himself on us. God works with our willingness. To cooperate with his restoration project, we cannot force others either, we must work with their willingness. We must take the approach of Jesus.

Condemnation Engineering

Most of us grew up under what Dallas Willard calls "condemnation engineering"—it's the way of the world.[4] If someone doesn't behave the way you would like, you subtly shame, cajole, manipulate, or condemn their very being until they work hard to conform, or else. Near and dear to the heart of the Pharisee is this system of working for something—earning and deserving, living up to the standard you control, punishment and rewards, excluding or judging those who can't live up. This makes up the life of a Pharisee—but it's also the system most of the world works under. It may produce conformity for a short while, but it doesn't change the heart of a person.

Condemnation engineering easily sneaks up on Christians. The modern-day Pharisee says to herself, "I don't do these wrong things, I do these right things, therefore I'm good in God's eyes." When the Pharisee looks at those who don't live up to her standards, she subtly communicates, "Unless you get your act together and work like I have to morally approximate these standards, God wants nothing to do with you."

109

This completely contradicts the message of Jesus. Jesus gives us mercy and sets us free from the treadmill of trying harder. He offers freedom and an invitation to Life in the place of condemnation. You know phariseeism has overtaken you when the way of freedom does not seem right or fair to you.

In one encounter Jesus had with the Pharisees, he said, "For the Kingdom of Heaven is like the landowner who went out early one morning to hire workers for his vineyard. He agreed to pay the normal daily wage [one denarius] and sent them out to work" (Matthew 20:1–2 NLT). Jesus went on to say that the landowner hired more workers all throughout the day, even as late as five in the evening, agreeing to pay them what was fair.

When it came time to pay them, he chose to pay the 5 p.m. workers first and gave them one denarius—a full day's wage for one hour of work! He gave the same to all the workers, including the first workers. The first workers complained: "'You have made them *equal to us* who have borne the burden of the work and the heat of the day.' But he answered one of them, 'I am not being unfair to you, friend. Didn't you agree to work for a denarius? . . . Are you envious because I am generous?'" (Matthew 20:12–15, italics mine).

Jesus points out that the system of Pharisees is one of superiority based on what you have or have not done. They resented those who had not worked as hard being treated equally! You can find this system in most families, social clubs, levels of management, and even in religious institutions—condemnation engineering, comparing, feeling superior based on what you think you've accomplished.[5]

A technology executive supposedly compared the computer industry with the auto industry, stating, "If GM had kept up with technology like the computer industry has, we would all be driving $25 cars that got 1,000 miles per gallon." Not liking this comparison, General Motors responded by releasing this statement, "Yes, but would you want your car to crash twice a day?"[6]

If your whole system is built on feeling good that you're better because you're smarter and you've worked harder, then God's gracious longing to lavishly do for all willing people what they can't do for themselves feels unfair. We want people to have to earn it and work hard for it, like we did! The problem is that condemnation engineering doesn't change hearts—it either produces outward conformity, or it makes people run from God, feeling he too condemns those who don't measure up.

I Can't Stand Her!

"She doesn't deserve a raise!" Christina thought as her co-worker boasted about her salary increase. "Why, Lord? Why do I have to work with such an immoral pagan who acts like a perfectionist with high work standards, then boasts about her low moral standards? I don't want to constantly hear about her wild-child party endeavors and sexual misconduct, and then watch her get a raise before I do. I can't stand her!"

Christina had grown up in the Bible Belt—Christianland—where people would dress nice to go out to Sunday brunch even if they hadn't been to church, so as to *look like* they went to church in the eyes of their churchgoing friends. Austin was so different. People didn't pretend to go to church. In fact, they didn't even pretend to be moral! Whenever Christina's co-worker Stacy would cuss or boast of her weekend escapades, Christina felt justified in making sure Stacy knew she didn't approve. She kept it subtle, but her disapproval could be clearly felt by Stacy.

The longer they worked together, the higher the silent barrier of differences grew. "I could feel Stacy's dislike for me increasing," Christina recalls, "but I also felt like I was right and she was wrong. I felt justified, even righteous. But I wasn't changing her. In fact, if anything I just provoked her to shock me with greater detail and more graphic language." Then Christina heard a series of messages about how Jesus treated his enemies and those who deserved nothing good from him.

"I started praying for my attitude at work," Christina recalls, "but I had to fight judgmental, critical thoughts that seemed to justify my behavior. In order to fight those thoughts, I started to pray *for* Stacy. God used those prayers to melt through my pharisaical attitude. Even then, I never dreamed I would one day call the co-worker I despised my friend."

Is God Impotent?

Jesus did not come forcing obedience or even morality—which is kind of disconcerting if you think about how much unethical, immoral behavior there is. When you ponder the extent to which we hurt each other with our disobedience to God, it raises a troubling question: "Why *would* God allow such horrendous freedom?"

You know, many people mistakenly believe that God's goal is to get people to do the right things and stop doing wrong things (as if this has somehow all gotten out of his control!). Pharisees try to assist God by forcing, cajoling, or shaming people to obey. But have you ever considered that if God's main goal is to get people to obey him, then God's pretty impotent?!

People regularly disobey God, and he seems to do nothing about it. In fact, God gives astounding freedom for people to completely go against his ways. Why? Why *does* God allow such horrendous freedom? We'd be much better off morally if God would restrict freedom—think of all the adulteries, murders, rapes, robberies, child abuse, hurtful gossip, devaluing lust, and uncaring greed that would be avoided. Think what a better world it would be if God just made us obey! So why doesn't he make us obey?

If we don't think deeply about this disturbing truth that God doesn't force moral conformity, we can easily become more pharisaical and less Jesus-like. If we don't see the beautiful, creative work he shapes in willing hearts, often through the most horrific, painful sin and brokenness, then we will fall prey to the forceful way of the Pharisees—it comes naturally!

God wants our hearts even more than our obedience. If God primarily wanted our obedience, he would just make us obey. (He doesn't need our permission or willingness to do that!) The reason he doesn't force obedience is love. He is creating eternally loving creatures in the messy texture of free will. God wants our obedience for sure, but obedience flowing from hearts that freely love and willingly trust him. To *all* who realize life is broken, they're sinful, and they need God's help, he gives *not* what they deserve, but living water that produces a fertile garden of fruit growing from the inside out.

Invitation to Life

John chapter 8 records an encounter Jesus had with a woman caught in adultery by the Pharisees.[7] (You have to wonder how they caught her "in the act of adultery." Can you say "peeping Pharisee"?) The text tells us they wanted to prove Jesus loved sinners enough to set aside the Law of Moses (and notice, they had confidence this would work because of the way Jesus regularly treated people like this woman!).

"The Law says she deserves death; what do you say, Jesus?" The angry mob shouted, stones in hand. Jesus didn't deny what she deserved, instead he pointed out what we all deserve:

"Okay, stone her to death, and whoever has no sin [whoever doesn't deserve the same according to the Law], you cast the first stone." They all slowly dropped their stones of condemnation and walked away.

Why?

Because Jesus caught them in their little game of condemnation engineering, trying to force moral conformity through a system of rewards and punishments. Jesus poetically reveals the system's fatal flaw—if we want everyone to get the rewards and punishments they deserve, *by God's standards*, we're all in deep doo-doo according to Jesus! (I'm paraphrasing—just in case you were tempted to condemn me for misquoting Jesus!)

God offers a different way to change our hearts—the way of freedom. The way of freedom respects, dignifies, values, asks questions, listens, and encourages willingness.

Jesus asks a question to the woman caught in adultery, "Did no one condemn you?"

"No," she said.

"And neither do I, now go and live a new way—don't keep muddying yourself up—go and sin no more."

Notice two things: Jesus didn't remind the woman caught in adultery that she'd broken the Ten Commandments—he didn't have to. Instead, he offered an invitation to life—a life free from condemnation with the freedom to choose a new path. But notice also, that's risky business. What if it didn't work? What if she went and did it again? He didn't even tell her how to "sin no more." Didn't his lack of commentary let her off too easy? He didn't even mention how wrong, how hurtful, how disrespectful her immoral behavior was to this man's wife—and to God. Isn't this approach too risky?

A false conclusion would be to think Jesus doesn't care about sin or sinful behavior. He cared to the point of laying down his life to free us from the effects of sin (Romans 8:1–2). Jesus didn't force obedience because he knew that's not actually the path to lasting change of heart!

Jesus respected the free will of those he encountered, yet invited them into Life, which quenches our deepest thirst in a way that makes muddy water unappealing. If we are going to be Jesus-followers who have the influence Jesus did on the world around us, we must do away with condemnation engineering and learn to respect free will and invite people into Life like Jesus did. But first we must understand the difference between the two.

Condemnation Versus Freedom

Paul contrasts the ministry of condemnation (which the Law without grace brings) versus the ministry of the Spirit (which brings freedom and life):

> The old way, with laws etched in stone, led to death, though it began with such glory. . . . Shouldn't we expect far greater glory

under the new way, now that the Holy Spirit is giving life? . . . For the Lord is the Spirit, and wherever the Spirit of the Lord is, there is freedom . . . [and the Spirit] makes us more and more like him as we are changed into his glorious image.

2 Corinthians 3:7–8, 17–18 NLT

The old way has to do with changing ourselves in our own power (and that just condemns us and leads to death). The new way of freedom has to do with our willingness to allow God's Spirit to restore his Masterpiece (more and more of his glorious image shining through).

Dallas Willard uses this helpful analogy: The ministry of condemnation tries to make peaches grow on an apple tree by tying peaches onto the branches. The ministry of the Spirit creates the inner heart of a peach tree that starts to naturally produce peaches—because that's the kind of person you are becoming.[8] Getting this straight is paramount for leading people to follow the Spirit of God. Do we see our role as getting people to stop doing wrong things, trying to fix them to look like we think they should look? Or do we see our role as valuing, respecting, pointing out God's good intentions, and encouraging their willingness to love and trust God fully? What really changes people?

Drive-by Invitation

Cheryl had grown up in church, but when she went off to college she fell away and fell in love with a guy who got her pregnant at age nineteen. They got married thinking it would make the situation better, and she had a son the next year. Listen to the email she wrote me:

Our entire dating relationship was completely unhealthy and that led to an unhealthy marriage. I felt desperate and lost. The next year I had an affair with a co-worker and filed for divorce not long after that. Emotionally I was torn to pieces. I was broken. I tried to seek help from my church home, but I felt like they turned their backs on me. I wasn't able to meet with anyone. People who I considered close friends wrote me off as a lost cause. I felt so condemned and alone.

I was driving down Brodie Lane to visit my parents [three years later], and I saw a sign that said "Gateway Church South." I felt like God was pulling on my heart telling me this is where I needed to be on Sunday morning. I knew nothing about your church, and I arrived skeptical that I was going to learn anything. Then I opened the bulletin and noticed the topic was on sex.

I listened to what you had to say about God's will for our sexuality, and I was so overwhelmed with emotion. Then you quoted the Scripture about the adulterous woman, and I felt just like her: humiliated and confused. But the second part of the verse where Jesus kneels beside her, full of compassion and grace, and tells her to go live a new life—in that moment I realized that I was forgiven and now is my time to move forward.

On my drive home I wept the whole way. For the first time in years, I felt God's love. I felt forgiven. I felt like I had met people who would take me as I am and help me grow into the woman and mother that God wants me to be.

If we are going to be Jesus-followers who have the influence Jesus did on the world around us, we must do away with condemnation engineering. We must learn to respect free will and invite people into Life—like Jesus did and still does!

On the last and greatest day of the festival, Jesus stood and said in a loud voice, "Let *anyone* who is thirsty come to me and drink. Whoever believes in me, as Scripture has said, rivers of living water will flow from within them." By this he meant the Spirit, whom those who believed in him were later to receive.

John 7:37–39, italics mine

Jesus offered an invitation to Life—to enter into a Life that wells up from within and makes the muddy waters of sin distasteful in comparison. But notice the invitation was to *anyone* who is thirsty. Thirst and a willingness to drink are the only requirements. Usually the thirstiest people have spent the most time in the desert, wandering around searching for water. What do we offer those people?

The Spirit of Freedom: Asking Before Telling

Many Christians today think their job is "telling" rather than "asking." We want to tell people "the truth"; we want to tell people "the gospel"; we want to tell people even if they don't want to hear. Jesus didn't do this. Jesus was asked 183 questions in the Gospels. He directly answered just 3, yet he asked 307 questions back.[9] Jesus provoked curiosity and willingness to hear by asking questions first. In John chapter 4, it says Jesus and his disciples were going through Samaria but stopped at a well at noon.

> When a Samaritan woman came to draw water, Jesus said to her, "Will you give me a drink?" (His disciples had gone into the town to buy food.) The Samaritan woman said to him, "You are a Jew and I am a Samaritan woman. How can you ask me for a drink?" (For Jews do not associate with Samaritans.)
>
> John 4:7–9

Pharisees despised Samaritans—their immoral behavior, their interracial marriages, their messed-up theology made them utterly shunned. Pharisees did not eat with, talk to, or associate with Samaritans. Samaritan women had an even lower value to Pharisees.

There were rabbis in Jesus' time who prayed every day: "I thank you, God, that I was not born a Gentile, a woman, or a slave."[10] Yet Jesus crossed racial, cultural, and religious boundaries to go to the Samaritans. Then he encountered this woman.

Jesus knew more than we do at this point. He knew all about her sketchy marital and sexual past—she had been divorced five times and currently lived with a man. Yet Jesus dignified her by asking her for a drink of water and engaging her in dialogue. She felt valued: "He's talking to me, a Samaritan woman? He's treating me with dignity rather than contempt?"

We should ask ourselves, do we cross society's divides to dignify people? Do we cross racial, socioeconomic, and gender divides to engage in dialogue? How about crossing lifestyle and behavioral boundaries? We can be like Jesus by asking questions, listening, and dialoguing rather than telling, fixing, and changing. Trust God's Spirit of freedom to guide you.

Listening for the Need

Jesus replied, "If you only knew the gift God has for you and who you are speaking to, you would ask me, and I would give you living water."

"But sir, you don't have a rope or a bucket," she said, "and this well is very deep. Where would you get this living water? And besides, do you think you're greater than our ancestor Jacob, who gave us this well? How can you offer better water than he and his sons and his animals enjoyed?"

Jesus replied, "Anyone who drinks this water will soon become thirsty again. But those who drink the water I give will never be thirsty again. It becomes a fresh, bubbling spring within them, giving them eternal life."

"Please, sir," the woman said, "give me this water! Then I'll never be thirsty again, and I won't have to come here to get water."

John 4:10–15 NLT

Jesus engaged her in dialogue about what was most important to her—he met her at her point of need. She needed physical water, that's why she was at the well, but Jesus knew she needed spiritual water that could quench her deep thirst to be loved, accepted, and cherished. So Jesus talked about what was on her mind—getting water, but also getting love!

If we're going to treat people like Jesus did, we must not only cross divides to dignify people by asking questions and dialoguing, we must listen deeply to try to understand their needs, their points of pain, their concerns. Pharisees just talk *at* people. Jesus didn't preach at her, lecture her, or even tell her what needed to change. He listened and cared about her needs, and prompted her spiritual curiosity.

As Christina kept praying for her mean, immoral co-worker, she began to get a new thought, "More than just praying for her, I need to *care* about her." Christina recalls,

I started looking for ways to serve my co-worker, which meant I had to take interest in her life and find out what she needed. I asked questions and listened a lot. I found out she had cats, and when she told me she was going to be out of town, I volunteered to watch her cats. When she came down with the flu, I brought her meals. When she got a promotion, I organized a celebration party with our co-workers—she was blown away. I could tell my newfound attitude was softening her attitude toward me. But what I didn't expect is that in the process of serving her, God opened my eyes to all the really good things about her that I couldn't see through my Pharisee-glasses.

While doing *Morph*, Gateway's spiritual formation path, one assignment had to do with listening to a non-Christian's deepest desires. I asked Stacy if she would let me ask her some questions about her hopes and dreams. In the assignment, you basically ask two questions: "What do you hope for in life?" and "What are your heart's greatest desires?" You cannot tell, preach, share your testimony, or do anything except ask clarifying questions, take notes, summarize, and feed back what you hear, encouraging those desires that align with God's. I listened and asked questions for over an hour, and when we finished, Stacy said to me, "I have never had a conversation like that in my entire life." She was glowing.

The following year, Stacy lost her boyfriend and was devastated. She came to me to talk about it, and she asked me why I had been so nice to her. That led to a deeper conversation about life and faith and the work Jesus was doing in my heart. As a result, she started coming to church with me, started seeking God, and found faith in him. This woman I could hardly stand, today, is not only a sister in Christ, but also my good friend. None of my disapproval changed her, but learning to value her and meet her at her point of need—that's what Jesus used to invite her into new life!

So Jesus engaged the woman at the well at her point of need, which was not just physical water, but spiritual water—she was thirsty to be loved. But she was trying to get that thirst met in broken ways. Jesus knew this, so once she indicated willingness ("Give me this living water"), he brought truth with grace in a way that shined a light on what was broken, but in hope rather than condemnation:

> "Go and get your husband," Jesus told her.
> "I don't have a husband," the woman replied.
> Jesus said, "You're right! You don't have a husband—for you have had five husbands, and you aren't even married to the man you're living with now. You certainly spoke the truth!"
> "Sir," the woman said, "you must be a prophet."
>
> John 4:16–19 NLT

She changed the subject, beginning an esoteric theological debate about the right place to worship. Jesus graciously went with the flow of conversation, gently steering back to her real need. He did this not to change her behavior, but to connect her to his life-giving Spirit.

Jesus never even told her to stop living with the guy she was using sexually for security, though this clearly was not his will for her life. He pointed out the broken, hurting places where God wanted to offer something better, basically saying, "It's not working too well for you, is it? Do you want something better?" Even though he pointed out the truth about her five divorces and current hookup, she didn't feel condemned. In fact, she ran into the village, telling everyone, "He told me all that I've done," yet with such hope for life, many found faith because of her.

Willingness Is the Key

Jesus worked with her willingness to help her connect to the only One who could change her from the inside out—to connect her to the Source of Living Water. See, when we try to change people by making them conform outwardly, it doesn't solve the real problem we all have—a deep spiritual thirst that, apart from God, drives us all to drink muddy water. Jesus knows that unless we have spiritually satisfying water that comes from God's Spirit, trying harder on our own spiritually dehydrates us. Paul told us to simply remain willing to walk with the Spirit, knowing that changes us:

> It is for freedom that Christ has set us free. . . . So I say, live by the Spirit, and you will not gratify the desires of the sinful nature. . . . If you are led by the Spirit, you are not under law. . . . But the fruit of the Spirit is love, joy, peace, patience, kindness, goodness, faithfulness, gentleness and self-control.
>
> Galatians 5:1, 16, 18, 22–23 NIV 1984

People change when they willingly follow God's Spirit in a moment-by-moment way.* God doesn't run over your free will; his Spirit works with your willingness. If this is how people change, not by trying to shape up and follow the law, but by following God's Spirit, then we need to be people who help others to willingly trust and follow the Spirit of God. That's our only job, not fixing or changing people, but encouraging them to see why God is good and that they can trust his Spirit to produce great things in them. Do you trust God's Spirit to do his part of producing fruit

*Soul Revolution is a book I wrote to help people learn to walk moment by moment with God's Spirit. It centers around Jesus' teachings his last night on earth and a 60-day experiment to show that Jesus really does what he promised when we actually abide in him.

in others, when you do your part (crossing divides to dignify, asking and listening, encouraging others to freely love and willingly trust a God who is good)?

Mark Buchanan tells about a riverside park in Guelph, Ontario, marked by large, intricate sculptures of dinosaurs, a man riding a bike, a woman and a child. Every year, the city drains the river and invites the community to scour the river bottom to clean up the refuse. They find everything imaginable: old tires, rusty shopping carts, beer cans, car fenders, even urinals. All get piled high into mountains of garbage lining the river banks. Afterward, the city commissions sculptors to make masterpieces out of the junk. What some see as trash, artists transform into ornate sculptures that beautify the banks of the river.[11]

Jesus uses the messy texture of free will, sin, pain, and even the junk of our lives to sculpt something new and beautiful. Listen to this email I got from a guy many Christians would discard or write off rather than cross divides to dignify, question, listen to, or encourage about anything. Sixteen years earlier, with newfound faith, he confessed to a student minister that he struggled with homosexual thoughts. The student minister's response was well intended, but Satan used it to condemn Sam and drive him away from his newfound faith and into a life he had struggled to avoid. But God is an Artist who sculpts beauty out of ugly things:

It is 1:24 a.m. on January 1, 2010, and I can't help but think that all signs point to the end of the world. Why, you ask? Because, for the first time in sixteen years, I am not drunk in a bar and looking for another man to help me ring in the New Year. I started 2010, shortly after midnight, sober and on my knees in my bedroom, thanking God for the blessings of the past year, asking for his guidance in the coming year, and offering every part of myself up to him as repayment for the gift that was given to me on the cross by his Son. This is such beautiful insanity, and I just wanted to share it with you. In one week, I will celebrate six months of sobriety. I actually look forward to church every Sunday. I have turned my same-sex attraction over to the will of God. I am plugged in with a small group of men who know about my past and actually CELEBRATE the perspective that can only be brought by someone who has experienced the darkest sides of life. I have people that rely on ME for guidance. I feel useful to both God and my fellow man, and I want to be more useful. I feel freedom!!

In Christ's Love, Sam

The Spirit of Freedom sets all willing people free, but he often uses pain and junk to do so. Are you willing to enter into people's pain and junk like Jesus did? If so, you'll experience him there with you, sometimes in surprising ways.

QUESTIONS AND ACTIONS

1. Reflect on this: When do you find yourself trying to fix, manipulate, or force change on people? How might this relate to the way you see yourself as less valuable than God sees you? How can you better respect the freedom God has given others?

2. Try this: If you've been doing these exercises, hopefully there are one or two people you've engaged in conversation. Asking respects freedom, so this week try asking them spiritual questions without telling (unless you're asked). Just keep asking questions and listening to see what God might be doing in their lives. Something as simple as, "Tell me about your spiritual background," can launch great conversations. Be curious without judgment and watch what God does.

7

Sharing Their Pain

The Suffering Servant
Photo: Curaphotography, Dreamstime.com

E veryone hurts; not everyone cares.
Within the first year of starting Gateway, I got an alarming email. I sat staring at the words on the screen, praying for wisdom as the gravity of the situation became clear. Lindi wrote:

> I have been attending Gateway for a little while now, trying to
> find some kind of purpose or hope. People say God is here,
> but I don't feel that, nor does it make the pain any less. My job
> as a hospice social worker is to comfort the hurting. But where
> do I go when I'm in the same boat? The church has never been
> there in the past, at least not for me, and yet I still hope. I wish
> I could tell you how terrifying it is to write. The fear of being
> known haunts me. During the past few months, I have been
> thinking about my own death and how to hasten it along. I am
> trained to recognize signs of suicide risk, and I am getting in
> pretty deep.

As the words ripped through my mind, I sat back in my chair, stunned. *Lord, what do I do? She's at the crossroads of life and death. Show her there's still hope. I don't have a clue what to say; you've got to show me.* I read on. Five years earlier Lindi had married her husband, trusting him with all her heart. Three years after that, she discovered an affair that ripped her heart in two. After nine months of separation and his many vows to be faithful, she trusted again and reconciled. Within a year, her husband committed adultery with still another woman. Lindi continued:

> I am able to recognize signs of abuse with my clients, but I was
> blind to the fact that it was happening to me. I am haunted
> by memories of things my husband said and did, and I can't
> make any of it go away. If the only person who claimed to
> love me could betray me in such a horrible way, how could I
> think anybody else would accept or care about me? I filed for

divorce last month, and now I feel a whole lot of guilt. What
does God really think about divorce? I have never felt so alone.
Enough. I already regret sending this, but I will. . . .

—Lindi

I felt a panic come over me as I finished reading. Again I prayed
for Lindi, and as I did, I found myself moved to empathy for this
woman I barely knew. I knew she'd come to Gateway claiming to
be agnostic, poking at others' beliefs, but now I could see through
this email the pain stabbing through her protective wall. She was
attractive and witty but stone-cold, I recalled, with a biting edge
that kept people at a distance.

Lord, what do you want to say to her? As I started to email a
reply, a passage of Scripture popped into my head—Hebrews 11—all
about God's heroes of faith. It's one of my favorite chapters, but has
nothing to do with suicidal hopelessness! I pushed the thought away
and kept writing. But the more I wrote, the more I felt compelled
to read Hebrews 11. I stopped emailing and read. As I got to the
last part of the chapter, about so many followers enduring horrible
suffering in faith, the thought kept coming to me: *It counted.*

But Lord, this isn't what she needs to hear! I prayed. *She doesn't
even have faith—she doesn't even believe in you. Why did I think
about Hebrews 11?* I decided to step out in faith and include it in
my reply. I wrote telling her why there's still hope, how God has led
her to our church for a reason, and that he loves her more than she
can imagine. I shared about God's grace offered in Christ. Then at
the end, in faith, I paraphrased the story of all the people of faith
who suffered and how God saw it all, witnessed all the horrors
they endured, and it counted in his eyes. I encouraged her to seek
God and let this count for something good.

She emailed back five days later:

Of all the things you wrote, the one sentence that I found
so very comforting was God saying, "But I saw what they

endured, and it counted." Why that means so much to me, I don't know, but it does. I remember asking my ex-husband what was my reward for forgiving his first affair. It seems as though there is no honor in "doing the right thing," yet maybe, if there is that God you speak of, maybe it means something to him. It is comforting to contemplate the possibility that he sees the turmoil that no one else can and that he cares and it does matter. That God would be worth checking out. Thank you for putting that in your letter.

—Lindi

I still get choked up realizing the amazing compassion of God, and the mystery of how he can use ordinary, messed-up people like me, and through our words and thoughts, convey his message of hope. Lindi continued to attend church and even began to attend a small group. I prayed that people would show her love by seeing past the sharp-edged cynicism that guarded her wounded heart. She had shared with me in other emails an even deeper source of her despair.

Having grown up feeling she didn't really deserve love, she would blame herself and heap condemnation on herself for everything. Her past haunted her with a vengeance. She would ponder her brother's suicide, and wonder what she did wrong to keep him from reaching out to her for help. Though she had been the victim of rape, she put the blame on herself, saying, "I should have fought harder. I should have screamed louder." She had lost a baby and felt she was the cause because she couldn't maintain proper weight during pregnancy. She felt angry with herself, scared, untouchable. Yet you would never suspect the current of pain that flowed beneath the surface of her tough, cynical exterior.

After the message one Sunday, Lindi decided to learn more about Jesus. She drove to Barnes and Noble and made her way to the Christian section. As she stared in bewilderment at all the books, wondering how to find the right book to help answer her questions, a man walked up and stood right beside her. She thought it strange the man would stand so close, but assumed he had a specific book he needed.

To Lindi's shock, the man reached out and pulled a book off the shelf right in front of her, then turned to her and said, "You should read this book," and handed it to her. She looked at him, wondering why a total stranger would do that for no reason, then looked down at the book in her hands. Curious, she opened it and glanced at the contents. When she looked up again a few seconds later, the man was gone!

She wrote me an email the next week. "Your God is continuing to show me things. I guess they are things necessary for my own healing. The signs are unavoidable." She told me of the "angel" at Barnes and Noble and said, "The book he gave me has helped me in ways I wouldn't have thought possible. Then your God sent another message," Lindi confided, "through a grieving widow tortured by guilt and anger. As I counseled her, she told me her husband had an affair eighteen years earlier. Now, after his death, she is struggling with all the regrets and guilt related to all the anger she carried for so long. After she left, I felt paralyzed by the impact of her words. It began to seem necessary and even comfortable to consider forgiveness."

A week later, Lindi wrote,

I am amazed at how far I have come in the past two months—from the depth of "the dark night of the soul" to a view of the light that is just now breaking through. God found it in his heart to save my life. It was what you wrote in one of your first letters that has stuck in my mind—that sometimes the greatest act of faith is simply hanging on until it gets better, and God knows what we're enduring and it matters to him. You have no idea what the simple act of writing those things to me did to help me take a closer look at your God. You have helped me see a God that I had never seen before—one who is compassionate instead of condemning. Today I bought a Bible

that I could understand, and finally, I prayed to your God and
he became my God.

—Lindi

⁴ Everyone Hurts; Jesus Cares

Everyone hurts; not everyone cares. But Jesus cares—of that you
can be sure. People like Lindi are all around you. God tugs at their
hearts, and many have a yearning to believe God cares, they are
loved, and their lives have purpose, but Satan uses their past pain
and wrongs to keep condemning them and lying to them about
God's intentions. But do we care? These places of brokenness and
pain often become the catalyst for faith when God's heart comes
through us.

Jesus entered into people's pain, hurt, and places of deep need,
and he showed them how much God cares. Picture what Jesus actually did the most: He spent morning to evening for three years
meeting people at their greatest points of pain and need! It didn't
matter to him if they believed in him yet or not; he started where
they felt the most need. If we want to treat people the way Jesus
did, we must do the same.

In John chapter 4, Jesus encountered a "royal official" while in
Cana (where he did his first miracle of turning water into wine).
This nobleman may have been a member of Herod's court, or more
likely a Gentile, pagan official. He didn't believe in Jesus, but he
had a desperate need. His little boy had been deathly ill, and now
the situation had gotten critical.

The royal official traveled from Capernaum to Cana because he
had heard that Jesus could heal, and he begged Jesus to do something before it was too late. Jesus said, "Go, your son will live."
Now notice, this man did not yet believe. It wasn't until after Jesus
cared enough to meet his desperate need that "he and his whole
household believed" (John 4:43–53).

How often do we get it backwards? We won't care or minister to people's pain or deep-felt needs until they believe. Yet Jesus' encounters show us the reverse order. While traveling along the border of Samaria and Galilee, ten lepers stood at a distance asking Jesus to have pity on them. He did. No strings attached. He told them to go show themselves to the priest as required by the Law of Moses, and they would be healed. As they went, the diseased, oozing sores that cursed them as untouchable outcasts faded away!

> One of them, when he saw he was healed, came back, praising God in a loud voice. He threw himself at Jesus' feet and thanked him—and he was a Samaritan. Jesus asked, "Were not all ten cleansed? Where are the other nine? Has no one returned to give praise to God except this foreigner?"
>
> Luke 17:15–18

Do we realize that Jesus still meets people at their greatest point of pain and need, even if they do not believe?

How many addicts overcome their addiction because of a "Higher Power" who gives them grace and strength to overcome when they simply admit they need him and yield their wills to his will? There's only one God like that! Do we believe he still heals even ungrateful, unbelieving people? If we do, we can meet people at their points of need and pain and show them Jesus cares, so that they will see his goodness and mercy and turn back, praising God.

Jesus Hates Me This I Know

Kevin approached me after a Sunday service and said, "I'm kind of embarrassed to say this in church, but every time I hear the word *Jesus* or see the word in the song lyrics, I think of a hateful person."

"Really," I said, astounded. "Maybe you're picturing humans who have not accurately represented him. Have you ever read the eyewitness accounts of Jesus' life?" I asked.

131

"No, I haven't," Kevin replied honestly. Weeks later he came back, saying, "I get it. Jesus is so different than what I picked up from Christians I've met."

How tragic that people far from God get the impression that Jesus has no compassion for the countless ways humans suffer. How many ways have we inadvertently conveyed that Jesus couldn't care less about people's pain and suffering, because they probably deserve it? Jesus didn't do this; the Pharisees did. Matthew tells us:

> Jesus was going through all the cities and villages, teaching in their synagogues and proclaiming the [good news] of the kingdom, and healing every kind of disease and every kind of sickness. Seeing the people, He felt compassion for them, because they were distressed and dispirited like sheep without a shepherd.
>
> Matthew 9:35–36 NASB

When Jesus encountered people, he had spiritual vision to see the river of hurt and pain flowing beneath the surface of those who drink and drug to numb the anger or hide the loneliness. He saw beneath the surface of people who get entangled in degrading relationships because they fear being alone. He could see through the shield of those who shut everyone out, terrified of being hurt again. He understood why people work themselves to death trying to prove they are worth something. Jesus could see that beneath all our adult pretense and posturing, hidden under the sands of time, are just little boys and girls, let down and confused, hurt and angry, wounded and afraid, rebelling and running from the only One who can ultimately make it better.

The word *compassion* in the original Greek language of the New Testament comes from the word *splagna*. It literally means "guts." Remember from English class the term *onomatopoeia*—a word that sounds like its meaning? *Splagna* sounds like your guts, doesn't it? Ever felt something so deeply it hit you in the gut? Maybe you heard tragic news, or someone hurt you deeply, something happened to a child or loved one, and you could feel it down deep inside, couldn't you?

Do you realize what Matthew 9:36 is saying? Jesus could *feel* the hurt and heartache, the disease and discouragement, the conflict and confusion of humanity. He felt our pain like a punch in the gut, and his compassion motivated action. He did something about it! He gave people a glimpse of God's kingdom—a preview of what God wants to do in every human life for all eternity—bringing healing, hope, and restoration. Is this the message we convey to a world in pain: "God cares, and he wants to bring something good out of it all, so turn to him, follow him; this can count for good"?

When Jesus felt moved in his gut by all the distressed, dispirited people, do you know what his solution was? To send you! Jesus said in Matthew 9, "The harvest is plentiful but the workers are few. Ask the Lord of the harvest, therefore, to send out workers into his harvest field" (Matthew 9:37–38). Then he sent them in answer to their own prayer! "As the Father has sent me, I am sending you" (John 20:21). What if we really did go into the world as "sent ones" doing what Jesus did?

Jesus sometimes seemed to have a divine advantage of knowing what was going on in someone's life. But if you observe his life and teachings closely, those insights came from the same Spirit who lives in us. Jesus was fully God, but also fully man. As a finite human, he had to do the same things we have to do: He had to *listen*—to God and people!

Do I Listen for People's Hurts and Needs?

While in Jerusalem, Jesus went to the pool of Bethesda. John tells us "a great number of disabled people" would sit by the pool, believing an angel would stir the water and the first person into the pool would be healed (John 5:3). Jesus got a prompting from the Father to notice one particular person. For thirty-eight years this guy had been confined to a mat. For years, he crawled hand over hand to be first into the water, only to have his hopes beaten down by someone faster, more able; he had no one to help him. Interestingly, *this* is the guy Jesus "sees" out of all the infirmed.

The text says, "When Jesus saw him lying there and learned that he had been in this condition for a long time, he asked him, 'Do you want to get well?'" (John 5:6). A strange question, don't you think? Why wouldn't the guy want to get well? But as we talked about in the last chapter, Jesus always works with our willingness, and he knows the truth: Sometimes we don't want to get well! Sometimes our infirmities, our addictions, our hated fears actually become comforting excuses we fear to live without. So he asks.

But notice, too, he had to listen and learn first! "Jesus saw him lying there and *learned*. . . ." As the perfect human, he stayed perfectly connected to God's Spirit and did whatever the Father was doing, but as a finite being, he had to listen and learn. "The Son can do nothing by himself; he can do only what he sees his Father doing" (John 5:19). Jesus had to listen to God's Spirit and to people's stories in order to do the works of the Father.

If we learn to listen to people and listen to the Holy Spirit, we too will know what the Father wants us to do. Jesus exhorts us, "Therefore consider carefully *how you listen.* Whoever has will be given more; whoever does not have, even what they think they have will be taken from them" (Luke 8:18, italics mine). We must cultivate the ability to listen and join God in his work. The more we listen and respond, the more opportunity we will get to hear and see and do his work. The less we respond when prompted, the fewer opportunities he will give us.

Listening is something I find many Christians are not real good at (myself included). We can sometimes be more like the Pharisees, who loved to be heard for their many words, but didn't listen to God or people. So as you're trying to be more like Jesus than the Pharisees, ask yourself: What is it like to listen with compassion for people's hurts and needs? How do I know that I'm doing it?

Airplane Blowout

Several months ago, I was flying to San Francisco for a leadership seminar. My flight was late leaving Dallas, so I was getting stressed realizing the seminar would be starting without me. I was the keynote speaker! I did a heart check and realized I was all stressed out but not consulting God about it at all. So I said, "Okay, Lord, I can't change this, so show me what you're doing. I'm available." I got rerouted on the next flight out.

I sat down in my aisle seat next to a woman in her sixties, who was squeezed between me and a young mom with a baby. Great! *Nothing like trying to prepare for a talk with a baby screaming in your ear.* I still had a bad attitude. Catching my thoughts, I said, "God, I'm being self-centered. Help me." Wrong thing to pray if you need some self-centered time to prepare! Just as we were taking off, *Boom!* We had a blowout.

Not the plane, the baby! The young mom started changing his diaper at 45 degrees. Ohhh, something was leaking! The sixty-year-old woman glanced at me with a look that said, "Oh, wow—she's really gonna do this?" Then she pitched in to help. Feeling guilty, I offered to help. So we all started working and talking, and I discovered the young woman was a single mom, this was her first baby, and diaper changing was new to her. No kidding! After we got the diaper blowout repaired, I told the older woman next to me, "You look like a diaper-changin' pro." That's all it took.

As I simply asked questions, took interest, and listened, she told me about raising three kids as a single mom working for Sam's Club. I found out her unmarried daughter just had a baby, so she gets lots of diaper-changing practice. I congratulated her as a grandmother, and she revealed that her daughter got accepted to Brown University, but got pregnant and moved home. I clued in and encouraged her, "Wow, you did a good job if she got into Brown. Was it hard raising them alone?"

I'm always amazed at how with a little encouragement and a few caring questions, people will tell you their life stories. Then you must listen for the need or point of pain to see where the Father wants to work. She opened up about how difficult life had been.

"Yeah, it's been hard all right. I finally had to leave my abusive, drug-addicted husband when he broke my nose in front of my eight-year-old son. All three were in elementary school, so I pretty much raised them alone. Unfortunately, my son followed his father down the same road until he kept stealing from me to buy crack. Toughest decision of my life, I finally called the cops on him. Third time, he took everything—what else could I do?" She shook her head, looking away, scrambling to find the tough outer mask she accidently dropped, revealing the pain it concealed.

There it was! That place of pain that God wanted to heal. I had a nudging from God's Spirit to listen more closely. I asked, "How's your relationship now?"

"Haven't seen him in four years. He went to jail. Got out and disappeared four years ago. He won't see me!"

I took a risk and said, "You know, I've seen God bring amazing restoration to many families torn apart by abuse or drugs."

"No—this situation's impossible," she quickly shot back.

"True," I said, "but nothing's impossible with God."

"No, this is impossible," she insisted. She still didn't know I was a pastor, but that opened up a deep dialogue about God, his intentions for us, how he allows us free will, and when we abuse each other against his will, God grieves over that. But I assured her, "God cares about you and your son, and he wants to bring healing and restoration if you will let him. But he doesn't force his ways on us. That's why you've felt so much pain. He doesn't force you or your ex-husband or son to do his will."

We talked about everything. Her anger and bitterness toward her ex-husband for turning her son against her, her guilt for sending her son to jail, her smoking addiction she hated but also didn't want to quit, why she had run from God for decades. We talked about God's grace offered in Christ, and how we can be made right with him if we're willing, and how he works with our willingness to restore what's broken. And after talking about all that, she said to me, "Do you think it was just a coincidence you sat by me today?"

I said, "No, it *definitely* was not a coincidence."

"You're not an angel, are you?" she asked.

"No," I assured her, "and I've never been accused of being one until today! But I did pray for God to show me where he's at work and let me join him, and he did! He cares about you, and he cares about your son and all you're going through. Let him help you." I gave her a book to jumpstart her faith, and I pointed her to our Internet campus. With tears in her eyes, she thanked me and hugged me as we parted.

People everywhere are distressed and dispirited, struggling through life, unsure if God cares. Jesus was moved in his gut with compassion and he cared, he met needs, he brought hope and healing. If you will listen long enough to the story of others to see their needs, their struggles, their concerns, and ask the Father to show you where he's working, you can be like Jesus to them.

Here's the second question we need to ask if we're going to be like Jesus to a broken, needy world of hurt: Do I demonstrate the heart of God?

Do I Demonstrate God's Heart?

I find most people have a very distorted view of God. We get the idea that God is big, powerful, and distant; somehow less loving, less kind, less personal, less caring or empathetic than we are. That's crazy! If you view God that way, do you realize the absurdity of that thought? God created us; we are lesser, he's greater. We cannot be more compassionate and caring than God no matter how hard we try. Yet hurting people don't often believe God feels our pain until someone, changed by God's compassionate love, demonstrates his heart.

Throughout the Jewish Old Testament prophets, God revealed his personhood and feelings:

He said, "They are my very own people. Surely they will not betray me again." And he became their Savior. *In all their suffering he also suffered*, and he personally rescued them. In his love and mercy he redeemed them. He lifted them up and carried them through all the years. But they rebelled against him and *grieved* his Holy Spirit.

Isaiah 63:8–10 NLT, italics mine

God suffers when we suffer. *God feels.* It *grieves* his Spirit when we turn from him and rebel and hurt each other. Yet in his love and mercy, he restores us if we are willing. Although he doesn't deliver us from all suffering, he does carry us through it if we let him. This is what Jesus demonstrated, not just in words, but also in the flesh. God feels our pain.

As we encounter people and listen for those points of pain where God wants to work, we must be careful to communicate and demonstrate first how God feels about their suffering or need. If we quickly try to fix, solve, or explain away the pain, we do more damage than good, and we inadvertently convey that God doesn't really care, and they shouldn't feel this way.

There's another encounter Jesus had when his good friend, Lazarus, died. Mary and Martha and their brother Lazarus had followed Jesus. The Bible says that Jesus loved Mary, Martha, and Lazarus, but he stayed away on purpose (John 11:5–6). So they were hurt, confused, grieving when Jesus didn't come in time to heal Lazarus.

God doesn't do things the way we would. He sees a bigger, eternal picture of what he's trying to do through all of life's brokenness. But he's not unmoved by our suffering. When Jesus finally went to see Mary and Martha, Lazarus had been dead four days, and everyone was grieving. Martha and Mary ran to meet him, but their hurt spewed out, "You could have healed him. Why? Why?" Mary fell at his feet weeping (see John 11:21, 32).

Now, here's the thing—Jesus would soon demonstrate God's restorative power. He was going to bring Lazarus back to life. It was going to be all right. Yet picture this: "When Jesus saw her weeping, and the Jews who had come along with her also weeping, he was *deeply moved* in spirit and troubled. . . . *Jesus wept.* Then the Jews said, 'See how he loved him!'" (John 11:33–36, italics mine).

Why did Jesus weep? He did not weep for Lazarus. He knew Lazarus would live. Jesus was deeply moved in the gut by *their* pain and grief. Jesus felt what they felt!

You're Not Alone

"God, why should I follow you if this is how you treat me?" I bellowed out my pain through a flood of tears, pounding my fist into the carpet as I finally was alone in my room and had space to grieve after my dad's funeral. He had been my rock, my best friend, my encourager, and I had just given my life to Jesus—yet he let my father die! Why?

I knew I faced a dangerous divide in the road of life ahead—the intersection of pain and faith forced a difficult choice—to follow God through this pain I didn't plan on experiencing, or to blame God for it. To trust God and lean not on my own understanding, or in my hurt to run from God and go my own way. This critical crossroads comes at some point in every person's life, and how we guide those we encounter who are facing the crossroads matters!

Some of my good friends could not even come be with me in my pain. They had good intentions, but poor execution. They didn't want to say anything "wrong" to make me hurt worse, and they felt bad and guilty that I felt such pain. So they stayed away. Don't make the mistake of running from people in pain just because you can't fix it!

But Randy and Karen came. They sat with me in my room and said nothing except this: "I'm so sorry. I just didn't want you to be alone." They wept!

Randy and Karen wept with me. They somehow felt what I felt. Randy knew Christ and led me to faith. If he had tried to tell me, "God will work all things for good in this," I would have shut down. But like Jesus, Randy just wept.

Randy and Karen simply cared about the pain and hurt I felt from a broken world. They didn't explain that "you reap what you sow," and my dad smoked, so he reaped cancer. True—but not compassionate. They didn't try to solve the mystery of why God didn't answer my prayers of faith to heal my dad, or how this all works as part of a bigger picture (and it does), but right then, I wouldn't have cared at all!

They wept. They didn't really even know my dad, but something about the God they knew moved them to feel the brokenness and pain of life with me—and their tears showed me that God actually cared. I wasn't alone. Jesus wept.

After their visit, I said to God, "If I go back down the path of life without you, there's no hope for anything good to come of this. But I'm hurting so badly, so please, if I follow you, will you be my Father?" In that moment, the pain didn't leave, but I felt a comforting presence—like somehow, I wasn't alone in my pain. Years later, I came across this verse, "A father to the fatherless, a defender of widows, is God in his holy dwelling" (Psalm 68:5), and I realized that God gave me that thought, *be my Father,* to comfort me and turn me to him in my pain.

When people are in pain—hurting, grieving, struggling—don't be a Pharisee! Pharisees try to quickly fix it or defend God's sovereignty, but they cause people to feel more alone. They give trite, platitude answers because they want things in their control, and messy emotions are uncontrollable. Jesus didn't do that.

As Jesus demonstrated, God does allow pain and suffering as a wake-up call to a sleeping world—a world that falls into a godless bad dream and needs to be shaken awake sometimes. The brokenness of life reminds us we need God—we need his kingdom to fully come. Jesus showed us a partial picture of what his kingdom coming looks like—the transformation of death, disease, hunger, and hatred into life and love—but until that fully comes, God feels what we feel and wants to carry us through it to the other side as stronger people.

When you meet people in their pain or brokenness, and you serve them, doing what you can to meet their needs, sitting and just feeling the sadness or the grief with them—you remind them that God cares. That was the message Jesus conveyed.

Do I Inflict Pain for God's Sake?

A Christian woman brought her unbelieving friend up to talk to me after a service where I shared my story of how God met me in my pain. "My friend has some questions for you. We went to my home church, and they told us that everything that happens is God's will. God is sovereign and nothing happens apart from his will, good or evil, but you seem to be saying that's not the case."

Her seeking friend butted in, "If it was your God's will for my bastard stepfather to sexually abuse me repeatedly from child-hood, then have my mom side with him and kick me out to live with my drug-addicted dad I'd never met, I want nothing to do with him."

Hit pause!

What do you say to a person who has deeply felt the hurts, pains, and evils of this broken world? I find that in the name of defending God's sovereignty and glory, some people inadvertently inflict more pain and lead people away from the God of Jesus, who entered our suffering to deliver us through it. What do we say about God's will to people in pain?

If you study the Scriptures, you'll find a tension, a paradox revealed. One hundred thirty-one verses in Scripture talk about predestination, free will, or both (I've listed them in appendix B for your own study). Ninety-five speak of God's sovereignty (predestination, election, foreknowledge, his perfect will cannot be thwarted), but seventy-three talk of human free will (we must choose, receive, decide, our choices can align with or go against God's will, and they even affect God's will and feelings). We err and do damage when we refuse to embrace this paradox God has revealed—both are true.

From our finite viewpoint, both cannot be true: If God knows all events in advance, then I cannot have free will. If my father raped me, God knew that would happen, so that must have been his will. Yet God makes it clear in Scripture these acts of evil are against his will. Personally, I find resolution to this paradox by realizing God does not exist bound by one-dimensional time as we experience it. If God exists in two or three dimensions of time, his sovereign foreknowledge and our free will can simultaneously exist. (See appendix B for further explanation.)

Why do I bring up this long-debated, heated argument of sovereignty versus free will? Because not everything that happens is God's will. If it were, why would Jesus teach us to pray for God's kingdom to come, *his will to be done*, on earth as in heaven? (See Matthew 6:10.) If God's will is always done on earth already, why pray this?

In the name of defending God's glory and sovereignty, we can convey to people in pain that this is God's will, but evil choices are never God's will! He can use them to accomplish his ultimate will, but when we convey that evil deeds are God's will, we act like the Pharisees whom Jesus confronted:

> Woe to you, because you load people down with burdens they can hardly carry, and you yourselves will not lift one finger to help them. . . . Woe to you experts in the law, because you have taken away the key to knowledge. You yourselves have not entered, and you have hindered those who were entering.
>
> Luke 11:46, 52

Common thinking in the religious circles of Jesus' day said, "If someone suffers, either they did something to deserve it, or their parents did something wrong." Jesus was quick to correct this still common lie. When he encountered a man born blind, his disciples asked, "'Who sinned, this man or his parents, that he was born blind?' 'Neither this man nor his parents sinned,' said Jesus" (John 9:2–3).

Two tragedies happened during Jesus' ministry, and when he encountered people trying to figure out who was to blame, he revealed an important understanding that we must gain about all human pain and suffering.

> About this time Jesus was informed that Pilate had murdered some people from Galilee as they were offering sacrifices at the Temple. "Do you think those Galileans were worse sinners than all the other people from Galilee?" Jesus asked. "Is that why they suffered? Not at all! And you will perish, too, unless you repent of your sins and turn to God. And what about the eighteen people who died when the tower in Siloam fell on them? Were they the worst sinners in Jerusalem? No, and I tell you again that unless you repent, you will perish, too."
>
> Luke 13:1–5 NLT

Jesus showed us two important truths about pain and suffering: First, don't quickly assign blame or declare tragedy or evil done as direct punishment for sin. Jesus makes it clear that's not always how it works. Second, God does allow these tragedies and the evils of human choices for a time and for a purpose. They *generically* serve as a warning to every human to turn to God.

The hurts and pains, tragedies and evils remind us all that this life is temporary. It's not heaven, it won't last forever, and it's broken and rebellious against God. God allows suffering because he knows there's something *much better*, and something *much worse* possible. God knows the reality of life where his kingdom fully comes (heaven), and the reality of life where God is fully absent (hell). And often, it's only when life gets painfully out of our control that we awake from our slumber of thinking we're God, we're in control, and life is supposed to go according to our will. Pain and suffering are a *generic* call to repent—to change our minds and turn 180 degrees back to God, so we won't perish (something far worse than physical death), but instead live forever with God.

But even though Jesus knew this greater purpose of pain and suffering, he demonstrated God's ultimate kingdom ways by meeting deep needs, healing disease, comforting the distressed, offering to remove the worries and burdens and anxieties that sit heavy on the shoulders of humanity. "Come to me, all you who are weary and burdened, and I will give you rest" (Matthew 11:28). Jesus demonstrated that all this pain and suffering, though necessary for a time, is not God's will ultimately.

This is the message we can bring to those suffering and in pain: "The evils done to you were not God's will, and none of this suffering and pain is ultimately God's will. All that God did through Jesus made a way for us to reconnect to the One who cares, who has compassion, who experiences our suffering and wants to carry us through it to make it count." (See appendix B.)

Am I a Wounded Healer?

Shane♦ and Erin♦ moved to Brazil to work among impoverished communities. After sixteen years of marriage, Erin confessed to an affair six years earlier, and it devastated Shane. During this time, God led them to Mont Serrat Church in Porto Alegre, Brazil, which happened to be doing a series, "No Perfect People Allowed." This started them on a path that healed their marriage during a very painful year of recovery.

A year later, Shane and Erin publicly shared their restoration story at several churches they had helped start. Rafael, a big-time, bad-dude drug dealer, heard about it, tracked Shane down, and told him, "Shane, I'm going to kill my wife and her boyfriend, but I heard of your story, so I came to talk to you first." Shane shared his own brokenness over his wife's unfaithfulness and told him how God was teaching him through the pain and restoring their marriage. Shane pointed him to the forgiveness and love God offers us, so we can become wounded healers for others. Today that drug dealer is clean, no longer dealing, and even though his wife left him, he forgave her and continues to follow the way of Jesus—all because of a wounded healer.

Jesus became our wounded healer:

> He was despised and rejected by mankind, a man of suffering, and familiar with pain. . . . He took up our pain and bore our suffering. . . . He was pierced for our transgressions, he was crushed for our iniquities; the punishment that brought us peace was on him, and by his wounds we are healed.
>
> Isaiah 53:3–5

If we are to be like Jesus to a broken, hurting world, we too must become wounded healers.

As we tell our story, even the broken, vulnerable parts—especially the broken, vulnerable parts—and the way God has carried us through, we point others toward the same hope. Can we share our own brokenness, hurts, pains, and confusion with a world that doesn't believe? It is often the solidarity of the human condition that opens the door for a person to hear about a God who can make it all count. Then we will find an open heart wanting to hear the message of Christ. But what exactly is that message, and how do we best convey it like Jesus did? Be careful not to twist Jesus' message into a pharisaical one.

QUESTIONS AND ACTIONS

1. Reflect on this: When someone is hurting, what is your natural reaction? Why? How willing are you to let others into your pain or failures, and how might this affect how you treat others who are hurting?

2. Try this: Pray this week that God will lead you to one person who is hurting (you'll see them everywhere if you start to see through the eyes of Jesus). Practice moving toward one hurting person to simply care, be with them in it, and tell them that God cares.

8

Sharing Jesus' Good Message

Boom Box Jesus, Michael Johnston
www.mikejohnstonartist.com

A number of years ago when we first started Gateway Church, we had some cracked tile in our house. I was naïve enough to believe Home Depot, "You can do it; we can help." Not only could I *not* do it, I cracked more tile. So I hired a guy to come replace the tile. Tom came on Friday, my day off. He brought two little kids with him, who started playing with our kids. I decided it would be smart to learn how to lay tile, so I watched Tom and asked questions.

As Tom talked, I mentioned how neat it was that he could take his kids with him on jobs. He told me, "Yeah, sometimes it's not real good for business though—doesn't look professional. But I have to in the summer because they're out of school."

"You a single dad?" I asked.

"Yeah, their mother left us last year." I could tell from the tone of his voice that Tom was still reeling.

"Man . . . I'm so sorry," I tried to imagine what that would feel like. "What happened—how could she leave such beautiful kids?"

"Said she just couldn't take it anymore. Ran off with another guy." I realized *this guy's got to be hurting badly.*

"That must be really hard" was all I said. With that, Tom stopped working, and for the next thirty minutes, he poured out his heart about the mistakes he realized he'd made as a husband, and how worried he is about trying to raise three kids alone—how his thirteen-year-old daughter is pulling away from him, and he doesn't know how to love her and discipline her at the same time. And mostly I just listened, asked questions, and thought, *I'm glad I'm not paying by the hour.* (Compassion is a learned trait!)

Then, he said this (and you've got to understand, he doesn't know I'm a pastor yet): "I don't know what you believe about God and all, but as bad as things are getting, I wouldn't be surprised if the end is near . . . you know, lights out."

So I asked a question I often ask, "What's your spiritual background, Tom?"

He said, "I'm not really the religious type—never really gone to church or anything, but I think about it. What about you?"

I'm thinking, *Oh man, I'm gonna floor the poor guy, but here goes*: "Actually, I'm the pastor of a new church here in town." I explained a little bit about how the church welcomed people like him, who still had questions about God. Then as we continued talking, he said, "You know, I think about God a lot. I think about what might happen when it does come to an end—what would happen to me?"

I asked Tom, "If you could know without a doubt that you would be safe with God, that God forgives and adopts every willing person into his family, and that he actually wants to help you in this life with these struggles, would you be interested?"

He said, "Yes."

Now let's push the pause button for just a second. Put yourself in my place. What would you tell Tom?

The Gospel of God's Kingdom

Jesus told his followers, "This gospel of the kingdom will be [proclaimed] in the whole world as a testimony to all nations" (Matthew 24:14). All followers of Jesus must be prepared to help people understand this "gospel of the kingdom." But what is the gospel, and what is this kingdom? How do we translate this into relatable language today?

The original Greek term translated "gospel," *euangellion*, comes from *eu*, "good," and *angellion*, "message" (our term "angel" means messenger). It literally means "good message," "good proclamation," or "good news." Ironically, our word *evangelism* comes from this word. In most post-Christian countries, I find the word *evangelism* does not sound like "good news" at all to most people. Somehow, we have miscommunicated the heart of the gospel.

We don't use the term *kingdom* regularly, but it implies a ruler and a realm where the will and ways of the king are done. God's kingdom is where God's will and ways are done. That happens fully in heaven, and one day it will come fully to earth; but for now we pray "your kingdom come, your will be done, on earth as it is in heaven" (Matthew 6:10). In other words, a taste of eternal Life can come to earth through all who allow God's kingdom will and ways to flow through their lives. And this Life (life in God's kingdom) lasts forever. So the gospel of the kingdom is good news about Life with God.

About a year into his ministry, Jesus had healed and delivered so many people from all kinds of suffering, people in need flocked to him: "The people were looking for him and . . . tried to keep him from leaving them. But he said, 'I must proclaim the *good news of the kingdom of God* to the other towns also, because *that is why I was sent*'" (Luke 4:42–43, italics mine).

Because we are "sent ones" on mission with him, Jesus had a priority that we cannot neglect. "As the Father has sent me, I am sending you" (John 20:21). Like Jesus, we must care for the physical needs *and the spiritual needs* of people equally! We must tell them the good news about God in both word and deed, for that is why we are sent.

Fixing or Farming?

I got this email from Edward in Dayton, Ohio:

> I've been a believer for a long time now, but I've often had a hard time sharing my faith. After reading *No Perfect People Allowed*, I've realized it was my approach: I would often try to "fix" the person rather than listen to them, accept them, and then show them the difference God's grace makes in a life.

He went on to tell me about a Bible study he'd started with others exploring faith, and he found even a Wiccan girl was willing to come and explore faith with his new approach.

150

What keeps many of us from telling others about our faith is thinking our job is to fix or change or "convert" someone. Paul explains that's not our job: "I planted the seed, Apollos watered it, but God has been making it grow. So neither the one who plants nor the one who waters is anything, but only God, who makes things grow. . . . We are co-workers in God's service" (1 Corinthians 3:6–7, 9).

We get to co-labor with God in his harvest (your part matters!), but you can't cause growth, change hearts, or force repentance, and when you try, it's anything but "good." We can plant seeds and water, but then we must *leave the results up to God*.[1] Sometimes we plant the first seeds, sometimes we water along the way, sometimes we get to see a person take the first step of faith. Jesus assured us each part matters: "The harvesters are paid good wages, and the fruit they harvest is people brought to eternal life. What joy awaits *both the planter and the harvester* alike! . . . I sent you to harvest where you didn't plant; others had already done the work" (John 4:36–38 NLT, italics mine).

Communicating the Gospel

What I've typically seen in a generation devoid of much knowledge of God or the Bible is that it often takes six months to a couple of years for a person to find faith. It's a process. And it usually requires a community of Christ-followers and a "come as you are" learning environment (as we'll explore in part 2). But first, what is the message we convey along the way, and how do you lead someone to faith when the time is ripe?

As I re-looked at every instance where Jesus or his followers (throughout the New Testament) shared the "gospel," or "good news," I found no formula. There is no formal, repeated definition for the gospel. However, I did see creative expressions of three distinct "themes" that can serve as an outline for us. I've seen thousands of people far from God respond and follow Christ when they understand these three themes, conveying good news not just to the head, but to the heart as well. Here's a summary of these themes that we will look at in more depth:

1. **There is good news about *God and Life*!** God created us for loving relationship with himself and others, and he is available to lead us into the Life we long to experience (an eternal quality of life that comes from the inside out).

2. **There is good news about *Jesus*!** Jesus' life, death, and resurrection opened the way for us to know that God does not condemn us, but forgives our sins, so that we can walk into Life with his Spirit, who helps us become all he intended.

3. **There is good news about *our part*!** God has removed every barrier between us and God except one: our pride (our free will)! We can humbly choose to *turn* and *trust* God (repent and believe) to experience his forgiveness purchased by Christ, and to find guidance into Life by his Spirit.

Let's look at the ways we can follow Jesus in creatively expressing these three themes to help our friends and neighbors find faith in a good God.

The Good News About God and Life

I was talking to a contractor responsible for installing all the granite countertops and sinks in one of the largest high-rise hotels in Austin. He was telling me what a nightmare the job had been. He ordered and cut all the countertops to the specs on the plan, but when they began to install them, nothing fit right. The countertops all had to be re-cut since the plumbing wasn't coming out of the walls to line up with the holes in the granite. It was a mess! It was costing money and causing tension between workers because fingers were pointing about who was right or wrong, and no one could work together.

Finally, they discovered the problem—the center line in the building was marked one inch off true center. He explained that they build the shell, then mark the center line on every floor, then the contractors build out the interiors according to plan off that center line. Until they got the center line right, they couldn't really work together to build what the architect intended.

Jesus gave us his center line from which everything else must be measured. Remember when the expert in the law asked Jesus, "What must I do to inherit eternal life?" Jesus replied, "What is written in the Law?" He answered, "'Love the Lord your God with all your heart and with all your soul and with all your strength and with all your mind'; and, 'Love your neighbor as yourself.'" Jesus told him, "Do this and you will *live*" (Luke 10:25–28, italics mine).

This is the center line of the message of Jesus. God invites us into Life—"to live" an eternal kind of life that centers on learning to *truly love God* so he can lead us to *truly love others*. If we fail to convey this clearly, we are clearly missing the point! *The gospel is all about restored relationship that restores relationships.* And that starts with God.

If you study Jesus' encounters telling the "good news of God," he offered an open invitation to Life with God. His message was less about salvation *from* sin, death, judgment, hell—though these are real and he talked about them as we will see in the next chapter. But his main focus was salvation *into* Life in God's kingdom, now and forever. We can live within the good reality of God. The invitation is to *everyone* who will come.

Listen as I paraphrase every encounter where Jesus talked about the goodness of God and his invitation to Life. And notice how Jesus spoke to the head (giving understanding about God's ways) but even more to the heart (with word pictures, stories, and analogies that connect people to the heart of God). If you reach people's minds but not their hearts, they will have understanding without motivation. If you reach their hearts but not their minds, they will have passion without direction in how to grow.[2] Jesus spoke to both.

To Nicodemus, a Pharisee, Jesus invoked curiosity by talking about a Life that comes from God's Spirit like a new birth, truly coming alive. "You can't see this life of the Spirit physically just like you can't see the wind, but you can see the effects of it." Then Jesus told him, "God loves the world so much, that he gave his only Son so that people would not perish without God, but live now and forever with him in his kingdom (the realm in which God's will and ways are done). God does not stand ready to condemn, but sent the Son to save (to restore all willing people in right-relatedness to their Creator). All who trust in God's Son will not be condemned but will live eternally" (John 3:1–21, my paraphrase).

In his second encounter, Jesus told the woman at Jacob's well, "If you only knew the gift God wants to give you, and who I am, you would ask me and I'd give you living water—a water so good, you will never thirst again! If you ask me, I'll give you something that will become like a natural spring in your soul, welling up and bubbling over with Life—not just any life, but life of an eternal quality." Jesus indicated that this life of love that comes from true worship of God would satisfy her soul's deep craving that her serial broken relationships would never satiate. "The love you've craved is the gift God wants to give you!" (John 4, my paraphrase).

Even when speaking to those "wanting to kill him," Jesus offered Life! "Whoever hears my word and believes him who sent me has eternal life and will not be judged but has crossed over from death to life" (John 5:24). He offered this Life to his enemies, saying, "Yet you refuse to come to me to have life" (John 5:40). No one was out of reach of God's good invitation, even those who hated Jesus and wanted to kill him. Jesus implored, "I say these things so that *you may be saved*" (John 5:34 NASB, italics mine).

In his final year, Jesus told a large crowd, "Do not work for food that spoils, but for food that endures to eternal life, which the Son of Man will give you. . . . I am the bread of life. Whoever comes to me will never go hungry, and whoever believes in me will never be thirsty" (John 6:27, 35). Jesus invites people to feast on a spiritual Life that's so good it satisfies our deepest spiritual hunger and quenches our parched souls like living water.

This offer of Life comes from living by his Spirit (a critical point often missed). At the last Passover before his crucifixion, "Jesus stood and said in a loud voice, 'Let anyone who is thirsty come to me and drink. Whoever believes in me, as Scripture has said, rivers of living water will flow from within them.' By this he meant the Spirit, whom those who believed in him were later to receive" (John 7:37–39).

Paul explained later that this Life welling up from God's Spirit produces "love, joy, peace, [patience], kindness, goodness, faithfulness, gentleness and self-control" (Galatians 5:22–23). The whole world runs after these things. But they think external plans, or possessions, or people will quench this thirst and satiate this gnawing hunger for a Life that *only comes from within* by God's Spirit. Do you see? That's what we must help people understand.

God invites people into the very Life they grope and grab to possess from external things that only leave them empty-handed. Life only comes by his Spirit from the inside out—this is the "so what" of the gospel in relation to us all, as we will see in the pages that follow!

You Can't Oversell God's Goodness

You can't *over-convey* to people the "goodness" of God and his intentions for them through Jesus. Mark tells us everywhere Jesus went, he proclaimed the good news of God, saying, "The kingdom of God has come near. Repent and believe the good news!" (Mark 1:15). Because this language does not translate well, we can miss the "good" that people experienced with Jesus and might accidentally convey something completely different.

Whenever Jesus announced that God's will and ways have come near, people were healed of horrible disease and suffering; others were set free of oppressive bondage. Those who observed Jesus often tied healing closely with talk about God's kingdom: "Jesus went throughout Galilee . . . *proclaiming* the good news of the kingdom, and *healing every disease*" (Matthew 4:23, italics mine). Again and again, healing and freedom from bondage accompanied news of God's kingdom (Matthew 9:35; 10:7–8; Mark 6:12–13; Luke 9:2; 9:6; 9:11; 10:9; 11:20).

Imagine how "good" the mental association with this King would be—to see God restore all that's broken and messed up! And when Jesus sent his followers out, they "went from village to village, *proclaiming* the good news and *healing* people everywhere" (Luke 9:6, italics mine).* You will never over-convey how *good God is* or how *good his intentions are* for broken, sinful, hurting people! He healed their worst diseases and removed their worst burdens, so your words will probably fall short in conveying the full extent of God's good intentions.

Jesus used metaphor, simile, and analogy to convey God's goodness and his invitation to Life, and we should find ways to do the same: "The thief comes only to steal and kill and destroy; I have come that they may have life, and have it to the full [the fullest life possible]" (John 10:10). To those stressed, weary, and worn down by life (which are most people these days), Jesus said, "Come to me, all you who are weary and burdened, and I will give you rest. Take my yoke upon you and learn from me. . . . For my yoke is easy and my burden is light" (Matthew 11:28–30). All who receive him, John tells us, are adopted into his family as his children (John 1:12), and Jesus said, "The one who comes to Me I will certainly not cast out" (John 6:37 NLT).

Love, adoption, security, stress-free living, burden-free responsibility, joy from within, a soulful peace, worth, value, and guidance from his ever-present Spirit lead us into overflowing Life, *and* forgiveness from *all sin* and freedom from *all condemnation* too! That's the Life in God's kingdom we invite people into! We're not selling fire insurance to keep people out of hell; we're inviting people into Life with God as his children, and of course none of his children will ever be cast out.

You can't overcommunicate God's goodness. But you ought to try!

---

*I'm not saying proclaiming the message has to be accompanied by miraculous healing. I've seen many find faith and only once did healing accompany it, and I had nothing to do with it. But don't miss conveying God's goodness that accompanied Jesus' message. This goodness will eventually restore all things for all who trust in him.

Translating "Good"

When my wife and I first moved to St. Petersburg, Russia, we understood very little and studied Russian four hours every morning. If a Russian had come to us announcing "great news" that we had been chosen by then president Gorbachev to experience life with him and all its perks in the kingdom of Russia, that might have been an amazing invitation. But at that point, if someone didn't translate the invitation from Russian into English, we would have missed our opportunity simply because Russian was a foreign language.

In the same way, the first theme of God's goodness must be translated into language people can understand. Words like *kingdom*, *repentance*, and *saved* sound odd and uncommon to most people. It's like we're speaking a foreign language, Christianese, when we talk about being "justified," "sanctified," or "redeemed." These terms are important, but we must understand the truth of God's message enough to translate them into language ordinary people can understand. (See appendix A for translating Christianese terms.)

Why would someone turn from the only semblance of life, love, and security they know (apart from God) and turn to God if they don't believe he's good or has good intentions toward them? Jesus used creative language and many analogies to paint an accurate picture of the Father's goodness in terms people understood: "He runs to the prodigal son with open arms," "He gives good gifts to his children," "He values you more than many sparrows," and "He longs to protect you like a mother hen gathers her chicks under her wing." Sure, he also spoke in parables, provoking either opening or hardening of hearts, but he painted vivid linguistic pictures of God's goodness too.

We should do the same. Apart from sin itself, the greatest barrier to belief is an inadequate view of God's goodness. In order for people to turn and trust God with their whole lives (repent and believe), they must hear that he's trustworthy and really will lead them into Life.

Hope for the Hopeless

The very thought of God or church brought waves of shame and condemnation washing over Shae. *What should I do?* Her brother had called to invite her to church, but she didn't want to face those overwhelming feelings of failure. *Three failed marriages by age twenty-seven!* The thought crashed against Shae's conscience, *Even in our no-fault-no-harm divorce culture, my failures provoke gossip and judgment. I can't imagine how much worse church people will treat me!* Yet running from the painful reality was not helping.

"I knew I needed help," Shae recalls. "I just didn't know where to turn to find hope. I was stuck and lost, but hiding it well. My brother knew my story, and he wasn't a Christian but trusted this church, so I started attending. From the messages and from the people I met at Gateway, I started to get the sense that I didn't have to hide my past. I started to believe that God would actually take me 'as is,' and love me enough to help me! I found hope hearing others talk about this life that God produces from within. Slowly but surely, I found myself coming out of the shadows of hiding, and wanting to trust God more and more to lead me into this life he promised."

After about eight months of listening, learning, hearing about God's goodness, experiencing Christian community in a small group, telling her story and finding love and acceptance and hope for a path forward, Shae got baptized, marking her decision to follow Christ fully. "I realized I had a horribly wrong view of God, thinking God was so disappointed in me he really did not want anything to do with me until I could get my act together. The problem was, I couldn't get my act together without him—I just didn't understand grace."

That happened over a decade ago. I've had the privilege of watching Shae grow in faith, then lead a small group where others found faith and grew strong in Christ. I watched God heal her from the inside of the struggles that kept tearing apart one marriage after another. I had a front-row seat to see God root his love and

Summary

Good News About God and Life

As you tell people about the good news of God's kingdom Life, get creative and tell of the goodness of God *you've seen*. I try to keep it simple with something like this: "God created you for himself—for a love relationship with your Creator. You can't even imagine the extent of God's great love for you. He's the Source of love, and he's the Source of every good thing you've ever experienced—that's reality! There's nothing good you've experienced that didn't come from God. He wants to lead you into the life we are all searching for—a life of love, joy, peace, and purpose. It doesn't come from the outside, but from the inside. It's something God produces within us as we do life with him. And it's not just about you. He wants to lead you to learn how to truly love other people with his kind of love. But here's the thing: He doesn't force his will or ways on you. You must be willing."

security deep in her soul as she trusted him, and he's led her into this promised Life of love that has kept her marriage to a wonderful Christian man growing strong for ten years now!

The Good News About Jesus

The good news that God's Life is accessible to all is only possible because of the good news *about Jesus* (the King of this in-breaking kingdom)! Here we need to explain that *Jesus' life, death, and resurrection opened the way for us to know that God does not condemn us, but forgives our sins, so that we will walk into Life with his Spirit, who helps us become who he intended.*

This is the point where Christians often misconvey the "so what" of the gospel to those without faith. Jesus was crucified to pay for our debts, so that we could be set right with God to live with him now and forever. Entire books have been written on the significance of Jesus' work on the cross. The cross demonstrated God's justice and mercy.

We all hate the evil of this world when it hurts us or our loved ones. We demand justice. In fact, we even curse God for not wiping out all the evil that causes us pain. But we rarely consider justice from God's point of view. If every evil act is rooted in a simple act of treason against God—playing God and wanting "my will be done" instead of "God's will be done"—then the line between good and evil runs through every human heart. If God destroyed every root of evil, he'd have to wipe out you, me, and every human.

God hates the evils that hurt us more than we do, but he also loves us who do evil. On the cross, God's hatred of evil and love for humans met once for all time. "God presented Christ as a sacrifice of atonement, through the shedding of his blood—to be received by faith. He did this to demonstrate his righteousness . . . so as to be just and the one who justifies those who have faith in Jesus" (Romans 3:25–26). The price of justice in God's economy is the greatest price a human can pay—death. Not just physical death (separation from our earthly life) but spiritual death (separation from our Creator's Life). God himself paid the price his justice requires to set things right (for righteousness to be done), so that all who want to turn back to God can be justly forgiven and restored in right relationship with God. Peter says it beautifully: "Christ suffered for our sins once for all time. He never sinned, but he died for sinners to bring you safely home to God" (1 Peter 3:18 NLT). God is triumphing over evil one willing human heart at a time.

But some people will say, "Why Jesus? Why was the cross necessary?" If God wants to forgive, why not just forgive? But you can't "just forgive." Think about it. If you gave me your new $55,000 BMW to drive, and I didn't drive carefully like you asked, but I totaled your new car, I would owe you a debt, wouldn't I? I would owe you the full price of the car—$55,000 to make it all right again—to restore righteousness to your world. What if I said to you, "Well, why don't you *just forgive* me that debt?" Could you really JUST forgive? No! If you forgave me my debts—cancelled out the charges against me, it would cost YOU $55,000. Forgiveness is never free—someone must pay in order to restore things to the way they were supposed to be.

Why was the cross of Christ necessary? That's what it cost God to "just forgive" you, and me, and everyone who commits treason against the Creator by ignoring God's will and ways. But Jesus' work on the cross did so much more than clear our debts so that we could one day be with God in eternity. His work made it possible for God to live with us today as we live by faith.

Faith is a simple act of trust! We don't have to clean up our lives first; we don't have to prove we'll straighten up and fly right. "It is by grace [God's unmerited good will and favor] you have been saved [set right related to God], through faith [a simple childlike relational trust]" (Ephesians 2:8). But why?

Ephesians 2:10 goes on to say, "so that we can become his Masterpiece, restored in Christ Jesus to live out all he planned for us long ago" (my paraphrase)—that's the point of grace: full restoration of his Masterpiece! The "so what" for today is that we can stop running and hiding from the only One who can lead us into Life!

So often, we make the gospel about fire insurance: "So you'll escape hell and judgment" (very true—praise God), "So your sins will be forgiven" (very true—praise God), "So you can be justified, sanctified, and glorified and one day be with God in heaven" (wonderful—praise God). But the gospel helps us live a changed life NOW! If people don't understand *how*, they might buy fire insurance, but they won't buy into fully trusting God's guidance. As a result, they never change! Here's why.

In Romans chapter 7, Paul talks about the struggle we've all felt as we try really hard to change on our own *without God's help*. Here's his color commentary: "I do not understand what I do. For what I want to do I do not do, but what I hate I do. . . . For what I do is not the good I want to do; no, the evil I do not want to do—this I keep on doing" (Romans 7:15, 19 NIV 1984). Have you ever vowed, sworn, or committed yourself to "stop doing something" or "be better next time," only to find yourself doing it again without flinching?

You have this bad sin-habit and vow, "I'm gonna break it this time." But in your own power, you can't seem to do it. You fail again. Then you get on this cycle of guilt and shame—beating yourself up over it, vowing to try harder next time. And when you fail again, you sink even lower, feeling a greater weight of condemnation heaped upon you. We go around and around and around—until finally some of us just give up. We give up on God because we *mistakenly* think he is heaping guilt, shame, and condemnation on us while we try harder and harder only to fall harder the next time around. (This is where most people live, by the way!)

But look at what else Paul says: "Now if I do what I do not want to do, it is *no longer I who do it*, but it is sin living in me that does it" (Romans 7:20, italics mine). This is profound. What he's saying is that we all have this sin nature that is not a part of who God intended us to be—we inherited it.

We grow up, and we respond to this inherited tendency of humanity to go our way instead of God's way. That's what sin is—living by our kingdom will and ways instead of God's kingdom will and ways—and it's natural, it's habitual for us. But it keeps us from doing life with God, the Source of Life. That's why Paul says, "Oh, what a miserable person I am! Who will free me from this life that is dominated by sin and death? Thank God! The answer is in Jesus Christ our Lord" (Romans 7:24–25 NLT).

See, Jesus helps us off this sin-cycle of failure . . . shame . . . trying harder . . . failing again. Because as Paul explains, "There is now *no condemnation* for those who are in Christ Jesus" (Romans 8:1, italics mine). So what God did through Christ's substitutionary payment for our wrongs is deliver us from condemnation. If you've told God, "I want what Jesus did to count for me," it will count, and you can know you are not condemned.

As awesome as that is, avoiding condemnation is not the end game. God wants to bring full restoration to our lives. He wants to help us become all that he created us to be. But apart from God having access to our hearts and minds—that will never happen. *We can't become who God intended without God leading our lives.* God does what he does in Christ, "[*so that*] the righteous requirements of the law might be fully met in us, who do not live according to the sinful nature but *according to the Spirit*" (Romans 8:4 NIV 1984, italics mine).

If we're willing to receive what Jesus did for us, we can know that even as we fail, he doesn't leave us or condemn us. That allows us to open our minds to God's Spirit, even as we are failing or falling—as we are getting squeezed in life—because that's where we need help the most. God causes the growth! But if we are afraid God condemns us, we will hide from the only One who can change us from the inside out. See it?

That's why Paul goes on to say:

> Those who live according to the sinful nature have their *minds set* on what that nature desires; but those who live in accordance with the Spirit have their *minds set* on what the Spirit desires. The *mind* [*controlled* by] sinful man is death, but the *mind controlled* by the Spirit is life and peace.
>
> Romans 8:5–6 NIV 1984, italics mine

The good news about Jesus is that his death and resurrection paid the price, once and for all, to reconnect us to the Source of Life. Now, we can stay connected in our minds to his Spirit, even as we're failing and falling, and he helps us grow through it to become all God intended. This is the "good news" we need to convey.

Run to God

For her whole life, Sarah had been running—she ran from God, knowing she wasn't living as he would want. She ran from guilty feelings caused by the sexual relationships she kept plunging into in hopes of finding love and security. She ran from a deep shame that told her she was dirty, scarred, damaged goods because of the sexual abuse she had endured . . . so Sarah ran. But she kept running to people and places that just multiplied the pressures and pain. Finally she found herself with nowhere left to run. And she ran to God. Listen to what she emailed me:

I spent my whole life feeling guilty, not knowing that God was a loving God and forgiving, so I ran from God and ran to things and people that weren't good for me. I was so very fearful. Grasping for solutions through alcohol, drugs, abusive relationships, for years I found myself digging a deeper hole of loneliness and despair. I was broken, distraught, financially devastated when my boyfriend abandoned me five months pregnant.

A friend invited me to Gateway. God blessed me with angels through Gateway who helped me get on my feet. They helped with my move, childcare, and temporary housing. I was accepted and loved as a single mom without being judged. Gateway became like family! I got involved in a small group that comforted and supported me and led me to the Lord. I also got connected with other single moms, and I chose to volunteer to serve other single mothers who needed help. God used your Wounded Heart[3] course to heal me from the sexual abuse in my past. Then God blessed me in 2005 with a marriage to a godly man who is wonderful to me and my 3-year-old daughter. We have now had a second child together.

With all this support, I chose to go down the path with God. To my surprise, the pain, resentment, anger, and hurt lifted. I was able to forgive and let go by allowing God to be the center of my life. You see, John, everyone that has known me for years says they are shocked that out of all the adversity I've had, I was able to cope and turn that adversity into all the wonderful things that are now happening in my life! *I tell them it is not difficult if you turn your life over to God and let God lead your life.* Now, instead of running from pain and suffering, I choose to turn to God, and then turn and help others.

Summary

Good News About Jesus

After explaining that God is good and has good plans for us, I will say something like this: "But God does not force his will or ways on us, and the truth is, we live most of life thinking about our will and ways rather than God's will and ways—right?" (Most people will admit this.) "And truthfully, everything we hate about life comes from ourselves and other people ignoring God's loving will and doing what they think is best. This is what the Bible calls sin and it separates us from God. But God does not stand ready to condemn us for our sins. He sent Jesus to die on the cross to pay the debt we owe, so that we can know we are not condemned, but set right-related to God now and forever. That way we will stop running and hiding from God and instead let him lead us. This is what it means to truly love God, to let God *be God* of our lives by doing life with him at the center, and letting him lead us to truly love others. But he won't force you; he needs your willingness."

Then I will often ask a very important question that I asked Tom that day: "Is there anything that would keep you from opening your heart to God's forgiveness and leadership made available through Jesus?" You'd be amazed at how many people say, "No, not really."

The Good News About Your Part

What do people need to do to be set right with God and begin this Life with his Spirit? The good news we convey is that *through Christ, God has removed every barrier between God and people except one: our pride (our free will)! You can humbly choose to turn and trust God to experience his forgiveness and guidance into Life by his Spirit.* But what does that really mean?

Jesus and his followers proclaimed, "The kingdom of God has come near. *Repent* and *believe* the good news!" (Mark 1:15, italics mine). These words show up again and again: "repent and believe." But what do they mean? Again, if they are just Christianese terms that don't translate, people can miss the point.

In Jesus' day, "repent," *metanoeo*, literally meant "to change your mind about something." Presumably, it meant to turn from thinking one way to a new way of thinking. It apparently became a military term used to change direction; when "repent" was called out, the soldiers would turn 180 degrees and head the other way.[4] I find the word *repent* needs translating today in order to mean what Jesus' hearers would have understood.

In simplest terms, "repent" means I turn from my will and ways to follow God's will and ways. "We all, like sheep, have gone astray, each of us has turned to our own way; and the LORD has laid on him the iniquity of us all" (Isaiah 53:6). I explain to people that we must turn from playing God and seeking our will and ways only, to letting God *be God* of life, seeking his will and ways first. That's the heart of repentance—to change our minds about where Life will be found (not my will, but your will be done, Lord).

Turn and believe! People asked Jesus, "What must we do to do the works God requires?" In other words, tell us what God requires. Here it is: "Jesus answered, 'The work of God is this: *to believe* in the one he has sent'" (John 6:28–29, italics mine). To believe is all we must do. But why? What does that do?

Belief, faith, and *trust* are all synonyms. You can't have a relationship without trust. That's why faith is so important to God. What relationship with God requires is to believe, to have faith in, to trust in God. We turn from self-centered trust to God-centered trust in this good news—that God does not condemn, but forgives, and enters life with us to help us as we trust him more and more. Jesus conveyed this central idea his last night on earth:

> As I have loved you, so you must love one another. By this [everyone] will know that you are my disciples [followers], if you love one another. . . . *Trust in God; trust also in me.* . . . I am the way and the truth and the life. No one comes to the Father except through me. If you really knew me, you would know my Father as well. From now on, you do know him and have seen him. . . . It is the Father, living in me, who is doing

his work. . . . I tell you the truth, anyone who has faith [trust] in me will do what I have been doing.

John 13:34–35; 14:1, 6–7, 10, 12 NIV 1984, italics mine

The goal is relationship—loving God by trusting him and his Messiah, so he can lead us by his Spirit to love one another in a new way that reorients our little self-consumed worlds. Jesus invites us into this deep mystery about God. At the center of the universe is a relationship of self-surrendering love between Father, Son, and Spirit, who want to continue expanding their kingdom of love through those who are willing.

Praying With Tom

After I talk about God's goodness and his invitation, I almost always ask the question I asked Tom that day: "Is there anything that would keep you from opening your heart to God through Christ?" If they say, "Yes—what about evolution?" or get stuck on less-central issues like, "Do you really believe Adam and Eve were real people?" I try to help them not focus on all these tangential issues but first answer the question "Who is Jesus and what will you do with him?" I will try to give them books to read or messages to listen to, but I will also suggest this: "Look, if there is a God who created you, he knows all your thoughts already. So just start asking him honestly to reveal himself to you (but be open to him doing it on his terms, not yours). Tell him if he's there, you want to know him. Then see what he does—stay open." I've seen God fulfill his promise in amazing ways: "You will seek me and find me when you seek me with all your heart" (Jeremiah 29:13).

When I ask if anything is keeping them from opening their hearts to Christ and they say, "No, there's nothing really stopping me," then I ask, "Would you like to pray with me and open your heart to Christ? All it takes is a humble, willing heart." If they don't want

Summary Prayer

Good News About Your Part

"Lord, you love Tom more than he can imagine, and he wants to know that he belongs to you, now and forever. You are here, you know our deepest thoughts, and you love us anyway. Hear Tom's heart.

[Then I'll say], "Tom, just tell God in your own words, *'Thank you for loving me and paying for all my sins. I want what Jesus did to count for me.'* [Then I pause to let him pray.]

"'Lord, come and lead my life, teach me how to love others as you love us.' [I pause again to let him pray, and then I close.]

"Thanks, God, for drawing Tom to yourself, and for assuring us through Christ that we will never be condemned, and you will never leave us. Now help us both become more and more of who you created us to be. Amen."

Then I suggest baptism as a way to publicly mark the new decision, and I encourage him to invite friends who don't know Christ to hear about his decision. I remind him that he's entered into a relationship, so now the goal is to grow in trust and faithfulness to God.

to pray with me, I encourage them to go home and tell God their decision. Then I talk through what they can pray.

I always tell them, "It's not so much the exact words, it's the attitude of your heart that God looks at." After all, the thief hanging on a cross next to Jesus simply said, "Jesus, remember me when your kingdom comes" (see Luke 23:42). That was enough. There's no formula because it's about the heart.

If the person wants to pray with me, I tell them, "I'll pray and then you can pray the same idea in your own words—just tell God you want what Jesus did on the cross to count for you, for your sins to be forgiven and for his Spirit to lead your life." Then we pray.

There's nothing more exciting in life than getting to be in the divine delivery room, watching God bring new life into a human heart, knowing you got to co-labor in the changing of an eternal destiny! Don't ever let fear or self-concern keep you from loving another person enough to help them experience the greatest news on earth. So that's the good news. Some of you may be asking about now, "But what about the bad news?" We'll consider that in the next chapter.

QUESTIONS AND ACTIONS

1. Reflect on this: How prepared are you to explain the good news? If you don't feel prepared, use the text in boxes in this chapter to think over what you could say to people who need faith.

2. Try this: Pray for an opportunity to tell someone about the good news, and when the opportunity arises, be bold this week. If you've been doing these exercises with a co-worker or neighbor, maybe the ground is fertile to plant this seed.

9

Hardened Hearts and the Hammer of Truth

Christ Driving the Traders from the Temple, El Greco (1570–75)
Photo: Album/Art Resource, NY

My friends Steve* and Karen* decided to walk the streets of Austin regularly, praying to see what God would have them do in his city. People from every walk of life congregate on South Congress the first Thursday of each month for music and a street festival. As Steve and his friends walked the busy, crowded streets past one vendor after another, they approached a group proclaiming, "God's judgment is coming, and he will demonstrate his wrath against all sinners who do not repent. You are a sinner—repent or you will go to hell." A man from this group stuck a tract in their hands. Steve took the tract, thanked him, and explained that they believed in Jesus as their Savior. The man was so relieved to hear the news, his whole countenance changed.

A few vendors down, another group stopped them, saying, "You're lost and going to hell unless you repent of your sins." Steve told him he just got the message, and asked if they were with the guy down the block. "Oh no, they don't believe anything like we do," and he explained the theological differences that set their groups at odds.

Steve and his friends continued walking and praying but didn't make it to the next block without a third, then fourth warning, all from different Christian groups, telling them they are sinners condemned by God and need to repent and trust Christ or face judgment. Steve tried to hand them tracts from the others, but they didn't want them.

Steve later said this to me: "Nothing any of them said was theologically off—technically—but they just didn't come across like Jesus in the New Testament."

When Bad News Is Good

Jesus said the Pharisees were "technically correct" doctrinally, but missing God's heart: "Practice and obey whatever they tell you, but don't follow their example" (Matthew 23:3 NLT). Some Christians believe that to accurately represent the gospel message to a fallen world, we must first make sure people understand the "bad news" that they are sinful and condemned and face judgment; otherwise they won't feel the need to repent and trust the "good news" about Jesus saving them from their sins.[1]

So far, we've seen that Jesus' approach to a broken, sinful world did not start with bad news first, but truly wonderful news first. Without meaning to, this bad-news-first "gospel" leaves people with a message that says, "If you accept Christ you are now saved from hell, but still doomed to trying harder, failing, and attempting to live worthy of God's grace on your own power." It doesn't lead people to fully trust a loving God to lead them and change them. See the irony? This bad-news-first approach produces a gospel and life of sin management! But there is a time for the "bad news."

In Jesus' encounters, he did speak hard words. But we need to understand the context and timing. He talked about the "bad news" regarding judgment and hell, but he reserved the "bad news" as a warning for those who rejected or resisted his good invitation. Sometimes human pride and depravity so harden the heart that the only hope of restoration is to take out the hammer of truth.

Jesus challenged the masses. He said provoking, shocking statements to differentiate who was truly seeking from those who were not, but the hammer of truth and warnings of judgment usually came only *after* repeated rejection of the good news. The bad news comes to the hardhearted! That was Jesus' approach. Let's look at how Jesus encountered hardhearted people and used the hammer of truth, and see principles we can follow in our own encounters with hardened people. First, with those who persist in unbelief.

Hard Words for Persistent Unbelief

We tend to think Jesus' hard words were directed at the immorality of his day, yet only two times does Jesus address sin personally with someone he encounters. Once with the woman caught in adultery: "'Neither do I condemn you,' Jesus declared. 'Go now and leave your life of sin'" (John 8:11). The second time was with the disabled man at the pool of Bethesda who had been bound to a mat for thirty-eight years. Jesus healed him, and then he found him in the temple and said, "See, you are well again. Stop sinning or something worse may happen to you" (John 5:14).

Weird, of all the sinning people Jesus encountered (thieves, prostitutes, greedy religious leaders), this is the only guy to whom Jesus says, "Stop sinning," and this guy was mat-bound! How much sin can you do on a mat? But Jesus knew something about the heart, which is the real issue of sin that people miss. The root of all wrong actions is a heart that persistently turns from God and his ways. What people hate most about this world comes from each of us going our own way, thinking it's no big deal. That's what we must fully embrace, and then help people far from God see when sin blinds them.

As you will see in part 2 of this book, creating environments where non-Christians can hang out in loving Christian community and explore faith is critical, but at the same time, we can't expect those who are not Christ-followers to act like ones! How should Christians deal with the persistent sin patterns of nonbelievers? Jesus' encounters give us guidance. Only after persistent unbelief does he confront.

As we have seen already, Jesus treated the mud of sin as foreign to the Masterpiece he wanted to restore. As long as people responded to his offer of restoration, their sin was not the issue (recall Jesus made no mention of Zacchaeus's thieving practices, the sexual sin of the woman at the well, or the prostitute's past because they were turning from it to God). But when people had persistently heard the good news of God's offer of Life, seen demonstrations of God's love, kindness, and healing, yet persisted in hardhearted refusal to believe, then Jesus confronted them with hard words. But only after persistent hardheartedness!

The first time Jesus spoke to nonbelievers with the hammer of truth came after *two years* of ministry! He taught, loved, healed, and displayed miraculous signs for over two years, when finally, "Jesus began to denounce the towns in which most of his miracles had been performed, *because they did not repent*. . . . 'It will be more bearable for Sodom on the day of judgment than for you.'" Yet even with his hard words of pending judgment, he followed immediately with the hope that some would still turn to God, inviting people from the same crowd, saying, "Come to me, all you who are weary and burdened, and I will give you rest" (Matthew 11:20, 24, 28).

As we love and serve and share our faith with neighbors and co-workers and those who don't follow Christ, we must show the same patience Jesus demonstrated. However, I find that after months or years of hearing the good news with little movement, a person might need the hammer of truth to break through a hardheartedness keeping them from responding to God. Sometimes, they won't see no matter what we do.

How Great Is That Darkness

I could relate to Jeff because we had a lot in common: We were both engineers by degree, both loved to surf, and both had wrestled with intellectual struggles before coming to faith, only Jeff still struggled after a year and a half of hearing the message and hanging around church. At lunch one day, I asked him what held him back from trusting in Jesus. He didn't see why Jesus wasn't just a good teacher and why Jesus needed to die to forgive him. Why did he need forgiveness? He wanted some sign from God before he would believe.

I challenged him to read *Mere Christianity* (to see his need), but at the same time to start praying every night for God to reveal himself, but on God's terms, not Jeff's! I implored him to stay open to how God might show himself. He agreed. Three months later, Jeff approached me on a Sunday after I gave a message on forgiveness.

"This is really weird," Jeff said. "This week, I had a dream about my ex-wife." His ex-wife had divorced him and hurt him badly. "It was a vivid dream," Jeff continued, "and in the dream, we were friends again. But the weird thing is, the next day I was downtown pulling out of my parking space on Congress Avenue, and as I looked up—there she was! I hadn't seen her in two years, yet there she was walking across the street directly in front of my car. And I'll admit, my first instinct was to step on the gas."

I thought, *Oh no, my first murder confessional.*

"I wanted to kill her," Jeff said, "but I didn't. And then this weekend, here you are talking about forgiveness. Isn't that a weird coincidence?"

"Jeff," I said, probably looking dumbfounded, "don't you see it? God's trying to show you something about your need for forgiveness and your need to forgive!"

He said, "No, I just think it's a weird coincidence."

I tried to point out to him that God was revealing himself by showing Jeff the hurt and unforgiveness keeping him from experiencing God's love. He needed God's forgiveness so God could help him forgive and be healed and set free. He didn't see it at all! Not long after that, he stopped coming to church altogether.

As a Warning

In Luke 10, Jesus sent seventy-two of his followers to different towns to tell the good news. If the people of a town reject you, and will not respond to your message, Jesus said, "go into its streets and say, 'Even the dust of your town we wipe from our feet *as a warning to you*. Yet be sure of this: The kingdom of God has come near'" (vv. 10–11, italics mine). We don't use that language, but there comes a time when a hardhearted person will not respond, you've done all you can after lots of loving persistence, and at that point you must "wipe the dust from your feet," and stop trying to convince him. Otherwise you just become a noisy gong. They get it, but don't want it.

This does not mean we become unloving or condemning. Jesus rebuked his disciples who wanted to "call fire down" to destroy the Samaritans who rejected Jesus (Luke 9:54–55). We can still be friends, love and serve them, but we give a last warning and back off talking about Jesus. It takes Spirit-led discernment to know when it is time to warn and back off. Sometimes this strong warning opens their eyes.

Joshua kept coming to our church for over a year as a young single, admittedly agnostic. We create space for people like Joshua to explore God, but Joshua's real interests seemed to be in exploring women. When I heard from several single women that Joshua had been aggressively, suggestively hitting on them, and even ran his hand up the dress of one of the women, I knew it was time for strong words.

I told Joshua we wanted him hanging out with us, continuing to explore faith, but his aggressive hitting on women and sexual advances would not be tolerated. If he was willing to cease and desist, he could stay and keep exploring faith, if not, he could not stay at our church.

I really expected that to be the last I saw of Joshua, but to my surprise, God used that strong shaking to wake Joshua up. He not only apologized and stopped hitting on women; he got serious about seeking God and came to faith in Jesus that year. Joshua has been a faithful, growing follower of Jesus and a leader in our church for nearly eight years now!

For Jesus, persistent rejection of his invitation to Life warranted hard words in hopes of changed hearts. As we find courage to love people who seem stuck, God's Spirit will sometimes lead us to speak hard words of warning in hopes of turning lives around.

Hard Words for the Religiously Hardhearted

Jesus aimed most of his verbal bullets of "bad news" *not* at the "sinners," but at religious people. If you study the encounters of Jesus chronologically,* during the first two and a half years of his

---

*I used Robert Thomas and Stanley Gundry's A *Harmony of the Gospels* (San Francisco: Harper & Row, 1978) to study Jesus' ministry chronologically to research this book.

ministry, his eyewitnesses record him speaking hard, confrontational words only eight times! Six of those eight times Jesus directed hard words at the Pharisees or religious people who should have known better. This is significant!

Jesus spoke another twenty-two confrontational or challenging words during his *last year* of ministry. Half were directed at the Pharisees. So two-thirds of all his confrontational words came in the *last year*, after people had heard the good news, followed him for years, seen God's healing, life-giving power, and yet remained hardhearted. Jesus escalated the confrontation after years of persistent invitation! We should take note and follow Jesus' ways. If we miss the timing and context, we can easily misunderstand Jesus' hard words as something routine to do in every encounter. That was not the way of Christ.

Jesus didn't hesitate to confront directly the hardness of heart of the religious leaders, who claimed to know the Scriptures and follow God. But only twice did Jesus force his will; both were when he physically drove out the money-changers in the temple at the beginning and end of his ministry. In driving out the money-changers, Jesus attacked the Pharisees' authority.[2]

Jesus confronted the religious leaders who diligently studied the Scriptures, but refused to come to him and learn from him. He warned them that Moses' very words they claimed to live by would judge them on the last day! (John 5:45). Jesus felt righteous anger when the Pharisees got legalistic on technicalities of right and wrong, yet showed no love or mercy for a broken man. Their hearts were far from the heart of God (Mark 3:1–6; 7:5–8). Jesus called out their secret sins, the pride and hidden pretense that blinded them to the truth and made them hypocrites (Matthew 15:1–20; John 8–9).

And near the end, as their hardheartedness intensified, Jesus faced down the Pharisees, accusing them of being nicely painted tombs that looked good on the outside, but were filled with dead, rotting greed and self-indulgence inside. He scolded them for loading people down with impossible burdens but not being willing to lift a finger to help, putting barriers in the way of people who wanted to seek God and enter his kingdom, shutting the door in peoples' faces who tried to turn to God, and making converts but turning them into twice the sons of hell they were. Ouch! (Matthew 23). They accused Jesus of being demon possessed when he exhibited power over evil, and he warned them sharply:

> I tell you that everyone will have to give account on the day of judgment for every empty word they have spoken. For by your words you will be acquitted, and by your words you will be condemned. . . . The men of Nineveh will stand up at the judgment with this generation and condemn it; for they repented at the preaching of Jonah, and now something greater than Jonah is here.
>
> Matthew 12:36–37, 41

Jesus warned his followers to be on guard against this form of religiosity. This same principle applies when we form Networks of Christians serving the world, or organize in classes, small groups, or church gatherings, and we start to see religious wolves in sheep's clothing prowling around. You will find people who talk a good religious talk, but don't walk with God or demonstrate fruits of his Spirit. They cause harm to people and the mission of Christ. When you see this, like Jesus, you must speak deliberate and confrontational hard words.

Date Rape in Jesus' Name

We had a situation where a woman came to faith in our church, got into a small group, and started to grow, then met a very "nice Christian man" who talked a lot about Jesus and his faith and finally won her trust enough to go out to dinner with him. He ordered wine for them, they had a nice dinner, and the next thing she remembers, he was forcing himself on her in his apartment.

She told her small group leader, who followed Jesus' prescribed path for handling sin accusations like this (see Matthew 18), and together they confronted this man. He denied it and said it was consensual, so the leader took the issue to one of our staff members who spiritually led the small group leader. Together they confronted him again and discovered he had actually come from another church.

Doing a little detective work, the staff member not only discovered similar accusations at the former church, but they pointed him to a website connected to this man. The website charged a fee to teach men how to get sex from vulnerable women (including using the "forget pill" and other date-rape drugs).

When our staff member confronted him with these facts, he did what every hardhearted person we confront typically does. He denied it and accused us, saying, "It's not your business! You're not a 'come as you are' church." To which I always answer, "You can come as you are—but not swinging a baseball bat at people's heads. When your sin hurts others, and you're not willing to walk with God and us in accountability, we have to love others enough to protect them from you."

When he refused to walk with us in accountability or get counseling for his brokenness that drove his sexual addiction, we told him he could no longer come to any of our gatherings unless he came willing to walk a path of restoration. She pressed charges, and he ran.

Tough Love

When those claiming to follow Christ do unethical or immoral things that hurt others or themselves, we must speak truth in love. When it appears they continue in stubborn hardheartedness, we must follow Jesus' instructions in Matthew 18:15–17, which says confront them in love to win them back, and if they refuse, bring two or three to confront them in love. If they still refuse, tell it to the leadership of the church. And if they remain hardhearted, tell them to leave until they agree to walk a path of restoration. The goal of increasing confrontation with the hammer of truth is to crack the outer shell that sin and pride build up around people. But again, the ultimate goal is always restoration.

Recall that even when speaking hard words to the Pharisees who wanted to kill him, Jesus offered Life. He warned them, saying, "The time is coming when all the dead in their graves will hear the voice of God's Son, and they will rise again. Those who have done good will rise to experience eternal life, and those who have continued in evil will rise to experience judgment. . . . Yet it isn't I who will accuse you before the Father. Moses will accuse you!" (John 5:28–29, 45 NLT). But he said these hard words "so that you may be saved" (John 5:34 NASB).

We have had small group leaders who have discovered verbal or physical abuse from a husband toward his wife and children. In one case, the leader followed Jesus' example and confronted the husband by speaking hard words in truth and love. As a result, the man admitted his problem, got counseling, and healed from the abuse that had passed down many generations.

Sometimes love must be tough. Love does not sit by and watch people self-destruct or cause harm to others, and sin always does damage! I explain it like this: One little molecule of water can't cause much harm, can it? If I throw a drop of water at you, no big deal. But when one little molecule bumps into another, into another—the cumulative momentum of all those little molecules together can form a tsunami that could wipe out an entire nation's coastal population!

When we fail to trust God's words and ways, when we say, "I know what's best and doing my will doesn't hurt anybody," it's like saying, "One little drop of water doesn't hurt." But we're discounting the cumulative destructive force of one little sin after another building momentum in a society until lives are destroyed. Ironically, no one ever traces it back to that one little droplet of free will rejecting God's will.

Before speaking hard words, I sometimes explain that sin is self-abuse—trading God, the Source of Life, for something destructive. Trading joy for a buzz and a hangover, trading selfless love for sex with strangers, trading true security for the endless chase for more. God hates sin because he loves people. He hates to see it spread from person to person and generation to generation like a growing tsunami.

Hard Words of Discipleship

So as we've seen, Jesus took out the hammer of truth to challenge nonbelievers persisting in unbelief, and he confronted hardhearted religious people, but he also challenged one last group with hard words—would-be disciples. To those following him, Jesus said challenging words as he headed to Jerusalem during his last months on earth. We should take these hard words to heart.

> If any of you wants to be my follower, you must turn from your selfish ways, take up your cross daily, and follow me. If you try to hang on to your life, you will lose it. But if you give up your life for my sake, you will save it. And what do you benefit if you gain the whole world but are yourself lost or destroyed? If anyone is ashamed of me and my message, the Son of Man will be ashamed of that person when he returns in his glory and in the glory of the Father and the holy angels.
>
> Luke 9:23–26 NLT

This is a radical statement! They knew to take up a cross meant the Romans would hang you on it. Jesus says, "You want to follow me? Really? You want to be great? Really? You want to be part of a groundswell of loving action that changes our world and lasts for all eternity? Really? Then every day, you've got to die to self and live for me. You've got to *die daily*." It's a daily practice that reorients how we view ourselves and what we're here to do.

If you find yourself holding back from talking to others about Jesus because you're kind of ashamed to be thought of as "one of those kinds of people," pray, "Lord, help me die to this pharisaical need for approval. Help me love people by not being ashamed of you, the Source of their very life!"

Jesus warns those who follow him that it won't be easy. People who reject him will reject you, and even your own family members may treat you like an enemy. Hardheartedness blinds people. Still, we must be faithful and leave the rest to God.

It's Not You They Are Rejecting

I sat across the table from Jake at the swanky restaurant he had picked. Jake and his family had been coming to our church for about a year. We'd had them over to our house. We'd been to their house several times, and I considered Jake a friend. Though we had spent numerous conversations discussing faith in Jesus, why Jesus was more than just a good teacher, and how God had good things in store for Jake and his family, still Jake clung to his amalgamated Buddhist/New Age beliefs that there really is no right or wrong, and maybe even the things we call evil are actually good in the end.

I finally understood why he persisted in these beliefs that resisted the notion that he needed Jesus' death on the cross to pay for his sins: Jake was doing cocaine and much, much more with their twenty-year-old nanny who lived with them.

I had come to really love Jake and his wife and kids, and it killed me to think of the destruction and devastation building like a volcano beneath the surface of his life. I thought about Jesus' words, "Light has come into the world, but people loved darkness instead of light because their deeds were evil. Everyone who does evil hates the light, and will not come into the light for fear that their deeds will be exposed" (John 3:19–20). Jake's beliefs formed a hard shell around his hardening heart to protect him from facing the hammer of truth about the evil he was doing.

In love, I confronted him since he was a friend and had been attending our church regularly. I told him I knew what he was up to. He denied it and then made light of it, so I warned him of the destruction I had witnessed adultery cause in other families. He seemed callous to my warnings, so I escalated the confrontation to remind him that God sees and knows everything, and one day he will die and stand before his Creator to give account, and if he persists in pushing God away, God will let him have his way. But that means eternal separation from all that's good. I told him again that God is willing to forgive and lead him forward, but he's got to turn from this and turn to God.

That was the last conversation I had with Jake. He cut off our friendship, but I feel like I loved him well. I did not follow the path of least resistance—what was easiest or most convenient for me. I spoke hard words in hope that my love for him would save him from a lot of pain, now and eternally. I still pray for Jake when God brings him to mind, but as far as I know, he still has not turned to God. It's hard to watch people reject your message. It hurts! But we must remember it's not really about us—it's God whom they are rejecting.

Great Cost, Great Reward

Mark chapter ten tells us that after three and a half years with Jesus, on their way to Jerusalem, the twelve got in a fight over who deserved to be greatest! Jesus knows he's headed into the hurricane; the religious leaders now have hell-bound determination to crucify him. Yet his disciples, like many of us, are primarily following Jesus so he can help *them* be successful. They wanted God to do their will, not join God in doing his will. They wanted to be great, significant; they wanted their lives to matter. There's nothing wrong with that. You should want your life to really matter. But Jesus took out the hammer of truth to break through the plastic shell of hollow success.

"Whoever wants to become great among you must be your servant, and whoever wants to be first must be slave of all. For even the Son of Man did not come to be served, but to serve, and to give his life as a ransom for many" (Mark 10:43–45). Jesus doesn't chastise them for wanting to be great, or wanting their lives to be significant, but they needed a reorientation to truth.

What's the path to greatness? Our world says greatness comes from moving up. Jesus says, "You want to be great—good! Move yourself down to serve—better yet, become a slave to all! Then you'll be great."

But we don't really believe Jesus. These are hard words.

We may believe *in Jesus*, but we don't *believe Jesus*—we don't trust that he's telling the truth. In fact, most of us don't even consider that he *might be* telling the truth! That one day, when his kingdom comes fully, those who are greatest for all eternity will be those who held nothing back from serving God by serving others, never ashamed of Jesus or his message.

On that same trip to Jerusalem, Jesus told them:

> I assure you that everyone who has given up house or brothers or sisters or mother or father or children or property, for my sake and for the Good News, will receive now in return a hundred times as many houses, brothers, sisters, mothers, children, and property—along with persecution. And in the world to come that person will have eternal life. But many who are the greatest now will be least important then, and those who seem least important now will be the greatest then.
>
> Mark 10:29–31 NLT

What if Bill Gates said to you, "Become a servant in my kingdom. That means you must let go of the enjoyments and possessions of your current life; you won't get any recognition or reward; it'll be hard, thankless work; at times it will feel like nobody notices, nobody cares; and people may reject you and look down on you for being my servant. But if you will become the lowest servant in the kingdom of Microsoft for five years, I will make you the greatest in Microsoft. You will be like an adopted heir, sharing all the glory that comes with being greatest in my kingdom."

Now *that* we can understand—right? Who in their right mind would not humble themselves and give up everything to become a servant with that kind of promise? You're not giving up anything in reality—you're making a wise choice to *gain everything*! Jesus promised you something so much greater than that, yet we don't believe it! We don't believe Jesus.

If we did, we would live to serve, and love, and make Jesus known everywhere and with everything: serving people at work, serving our families, serving our neighbors, boldly inviting people into the Life Jesus offers, dying to self that worries about the approval of people, dying to greed that spends all our thoughts on getting more rather than giving more.

Here's where Jesus' restoration project often gets delayed even with those who claim to follow him. So I want to challenge you to begin to pray a prayer of surrender: "God, I open my hands to serve you and others, wherever I am, with all I've got. Make me bold to serve not only their physical needs, but also their spiritual needs as I love them and unashamedly invite them into Life with you."

With that simple prayer of willingness, God will allow you to share in the greatest work in history, and he gives you back so much more than you ever give. In the next section, we'll start to get practical about how you and your friends can network together to make a Jesus-like impact in your world.

QUESTIONS AND ACTIONS

1. Reflect on this: Do you struggle to speak hard words when they are needed? How might this be the most loving thing you could do for a person? What hard words might you need to hear?

2. Try this: If there is someone you know who is stuck, pray for courage and go to them in love speaking the hard words of truth. Point out the Masterpiece God wants to reveal and ask them to respond to him.

ON MISSION WITH JESUS

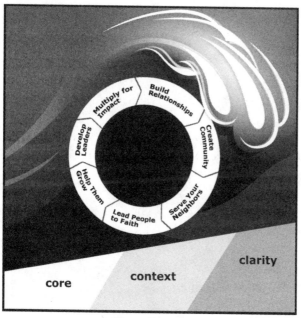

Wave of Impact

I love waves. There's something mysteriously beautiful and majestic about a wave. I grew up surfing and experienced the awe-inspiring power of this invisible energy rolling through the ocean, creating a playground of adrenaline for us teenagers. It's easy to underestimate the power of a wave. When my dream finally came true and I landed a trip to Hawaii, I was determined to surf the famous breaks I had only read about in *Surfer* magazine.

I'll never forget paddling out about 300 yards to the reef that first day. The closer I got, the more I realized how much I had underestimated the size and power of these waves. When I finally reached the break, all I could think about was how to get back in alive! My sudden reverence and awe for the power of waves was not unfounded. A cleanup set came in (surfer talk for a series of huge waves) that cracked my board in half and pinned me to the reef. I found myself praying to a God I didn't yet believe in!

Waves can have enormous power! But what makes a wave powerful? Even a monstrous North Shore wave is actually made up of many small circular movements of tiny little water molecules all working together. Huge waves grow from little ripples caused by a steady, consistent breeze that keeps building and building. Each little molecule of water doesn't move very far, but as a wave moves through water, the wave's energy gets transferred from one water molecule to the next, moving together in a circular motion under the surface, allowing the power and impact of the wave to grow. The longer the wind can move across more and more molecules of water, and the longer the molecules of water work together in a growing circular motion, the greater the impact of the wave.

What does this have to do with us? It has everything to do with us. I believe God desires to make a huge wave of impact in this world *through you*. Jesus once described the way the Spirit of God works like the wind: "The wind blows wherever it pleases. You hear its sound, but you cannot tell where it comes from or where it is going. So it is with everyone born of the Spirit" (John 3:8). God's Spirit is like the wind blowing across the hearts of those who willingly follow Jesus. If we follow the Spirit's direction, little ripples of simple life-on-life investments, serving, growing, working together can build into a huge wave of impact. God can start a ripple effect that goes out from you and a small group of friends to change the lives of thousands.

Once we have our hearts right, holding a Christlike attitude in our minds toward people we encounter, it's time to go on mission with Jesus. Whereas part 1 of this book looked at the *attitude* of Jesus, part 2 will look at the *actions* of Jesus as he sent people out on his mission to encounter and restore the world around him.

Regardless of the style of church you are currently in, you can be a part of starting something that impacts the world around you. All you need are a few friends within your church who get the principles we've been talking about and are willing to go on mission with Jesus and each other.

I will walk you through the formation of a Network of people serving, growing, and reaching the world with the impact Jesus had. The Wave of Impact diagram (the figure at the start of this chapter) will serve as a framework for the chapters in part 2. A Network starts small, with a co-missioned core group of at least three. From there we will talk about how that small *core* can begin to understand your *context*, pray for a focused *clarity* (a vision of whom to love and serve), and find ways to begin building relational momentum with your neighbors or co-workers or the people God puts on your hearts.

We will explore how Jesus built relational momentum by going to parties, by meeting needs, and by creating inclusive, loving community. He then equipped and sent seventy out to do the very ministry he had been doing. You will read stories of Networks across the globe, which by doing these small movements over and over, have grown into Waves of Impact of 25–70 people who are engaged relationally, growing in small groups, and serving those around them; many of those served have started following Jesus as a part of that Network.

We will talk about the three elements of contact most people need in our post-Christian world to find faith: befriending one Jesus-like person, meeting a "tribe" of Christians they like, and having "come as you are" learning space. With the intersection of these three elements, which Networks can create together, you will be amazed at how many people far from God start to follow him and serve with you. You will hear it in the stories from around the world.

We will look at Jesus' underlying plan of life development, lived out in growing and equipping those who would lead this movement called the church. You will catch a vision for how your life can impact thousands, simply by investing in a few in the same way Jesus did. And finally, we will look at how gathering for worship and teaching can accelerate this Wave of Impact to give birth to new Networks. You'll be amazed at what God can do through ordinary people. To begin with, meet Bryan and Amy, a *Brady Bunch* family with six kids, two careers, and no plans to do anything extraordinary, but God had greater plans for them—just like he does for you!

10

Ordinary People
Doing Extraordinary Things

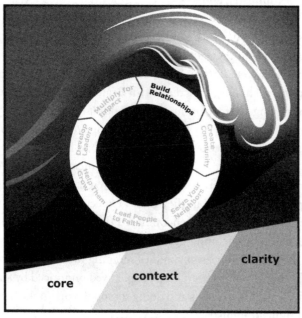

Wave of Impact

B ryan Stallings* sat in the store he managed, lost in thought. It wasn't the phone business that preoccupied his mind. He and Amy* had only been married four years and had enough on their plate already—two careers, six kids from previous marriages, negotiating a *Brady Bunch* lifestyle. *How can we take on anything else, Lord?* Bryan prayed silently.

Yet he and Amy agreed they had to do something. They had both tried to start ministry initiatives at the Missouri church they attended, but the feeling they got was that their lives had been too messy for ministry, and it was best left for the professionals. They could volunteer at the info counter or serve in other ways, but real ministry required degrees and expertise. Nobody specifically said those words, but they got the message.

That's when it started. They had volunteered a few years earlier to serve Thanksgiving dinner for Branson's working poor. As Thanksgiving approached and they couldn't find the ministry that organized the dinner, Bryan felt a prompting. *You serve the dinner.* It was that distinct Holy Spirit nudging he had begun to recognize since starting to follow Christ five years earlier.

Bryan and his family responded and catered a turkey dinner that fifty people attended, but they didn't expect the ambush of their hearts as they personally encountered the plight of the working poor. The overwhelming gratitude people showed them, mixed with the painful stories of families scraping by to feed their kids, caught them by surprise. These people lived unnoticed by society, living in run-down motels and doing seasonal work in the Branson entertainment industry.

That day at the phone company, Bryan called Amy and both decided they had to do more. The family made sack lunches for those fifty families and delivered them that week to the motels. The next few weeks, over and over they'd hear, "Thank you so much! You know, the family in room 224 could sure use this right now too." With that simple step of faith in obedience to God's Spirit, Bryan, Amy, and their girls soon found themselves making 150 sack lunches a week as word spread.

Bryan's family found it very gratifying not only to meet physical needs, but also as they befriended these forgotten people, they found God doing something in their own hearts—growing them spiritually. The word spread, and more meals were needed. Bryan and Amy began to recruit others to join them, and after a year, Jesus had multiplied that first sack lunch like the fish and loaves into 11,000 lunches assembled and delivered with love by the many volunteers they had recruited.

The more Bryan and Amy got to know the working poor, the more they saw regular, struggling people, many of whom had real interest in God but felt that churches would only judge them. Bryan read *No Perfect People Allowed* and got a vision for meeting spiritual as well as physical needs. They started an "investigative" spiritual discussion at the motel, showing short videos and discussing them in one of the rooms. Soon people overflowed into the hallway.

They started watching our Internet campus and realized our Sunday service could create "come as you are" learning space for the people they served. The back room of a local Denny's soon became the place they met for breakfast, and Gateway's Sunday service was piped in on a large-screen TV for more than forty people who showed up each month with growing spiritual interest.

By year two, their volunteer base grew to seventy people serving 20,000 meals a year! One volunteer, Scott, loaned his bicycle to a homeless motel patron so he could ride to a job interview. The bike got passed around to several people before returning to the owner. Realizing that his bike had been ridden fifty miles, Scott felt God prompt him to meet this need for transportation. Bryan and Amy invited churches to donate used bicycles; soon thirty bikes had been donated and were circulating among the motel workers, providing much-needed transportation.

Meanwhile, Amy still worked for a tourism company and Bryan managed the cell phone company, but their ministry kept growing. Amy says looking back, "I felt prompted to go part time at my job so I could devote more time using my organizational gifts to serve this effort we named 'Jesus Was Homeless.' I probably never would have quit, but when layoffs happened, part-timers went first. Now I can see that God was providing a way to expand."

With Amy now able to give full time to her kids and the Jesus Was Homeless ministry, God provided another miracle. A building became available, rent-free, in which they could bring the Network of volunteers who weekly made meals into one "kitchen," the bicycle ministry into a space they call "the garage," and provide a "living room" like space to launch a weekly Sunday gathering for people exploring faith—a spiritual home for the homeless! Bryan and Amy are seeing the church raised up out of a forgotten culture of working poor; many are finding faith, serving others, and connecting in smaller groups to grow deeper in the way of Christ. All it took was one step of faith, following the Leader.

Follow the Leader

The last times Jesus appeared to his followers after the resurrection, he empowered this diverse group of ordinary fishermen, tax collectors, former prostitutes, and 120 others to do extraordinary things *by his power*! Jesus told them:

> All authority in heaven and on earth has been given to me. Therefore go and make disciples of all nations, baptizing them in the name of the Father and of the Son and of the Holy Spirit, and teaching them to obey everything I have commanded you. And surely I am with you always, to the very end of the age.
>
> Matthew 28:18–20

Don't think for a minute that Jesus expected this group of 120 people to help every nation follow him in their generation. He intended them to equip others who equip others, just like he had modeled. And life by life the torch has now passed to you and your Christian friends.

Have you ever considered that Jesus fully expects you as his follower to do the same things he did? Do you realize that you can make disciples (learners and followers of Jesus) by leading them to faith and baptizing them? And do you know that you can teach others, especially those you help lead to faith, to observe all the things Jesus commanded?

Jesus didn't commission professionals to lead others to faith and teach them to fully follow Jesus; he commissioned *all his children* to participate in the family restoration business. I know it may not feel "legal" for you to do these things as an ordinary, imperfect Christian, but I'm not the one who said it—Jesus did.

You can do it—you know why? Because all authority has been given to Jesus . . . and he's always with you! And it's not up to you! It's up to him. It's not by your power, but by his. It's not by your ability, but by his. That's what you must remember. When the risen Jesus appeared to his followers in Jerusalem, forecasting the promised Spirit, he said, "You will receive power when the Holy Spirit comes on you; and you will be my witnesses in Jerusalem, and in all Judea and Samaria, and to the ends of the earth" (Acts 1:8). God has been doing extraordinary things through ordinary people for 2,000 years because his Spirit is always with us and gives us power along the way.

Jesus expects to do the same through you. The only question is whether you believe him and will trust him to do *in his power* what you could never do alone. That won't feel comfortable or easy. It will stretch your faith, but you will experience the adrenaline rush and intimacy with God that only comes by co-laboring with the Lord of the harvest. You don't need to change jobs, go to seminary, or move overseas to the "mission" field. You just need to look up and see what Jesus sees.

Right after Jesus helped the woman at Jacob's well find faith and taste living water, the disciples returned from lunch with a sandwich for Jesus. "Rabbi, eat," they urged. "I have food to eat that you know nothing about," Jesus replied (see John 4:31–32).

I feel we need a commercial break for Christian maturity here. I've been shocked over the years at the number of Christians who have come and gone through our church, wanting to be a part of a church really making a difference in the world, but then getting frustrated and contentious because they felt they needed to *be fed* by a particular way of teaching and *they needed* more worship in a style they liked. Yet they didn't serve with their gifts, help others find faith, or teach others to observe all Jesus commanded. That's not maturity, that's the immaturity of a spiritual adolescent. I fear our churches get stuck in spiritual adolescence.

We need to learn the Scriptures, we need to worship together, but at some point (usually within a few years) spiritual growth gets stunted if you don't learn to eat the spiritual food Jesus ate:

> "My food," said Jesus, "is to do the will of him who sent me and to finish his work. Don't you have a saying, 'It's still four months until harvest'? I tell you, open your eyes and look at the fields! They are ripe for harvest. Even now the one who reaps draws a wage and harvests a crop for eternal life, so that the sower and the reaper may be glad together."
>
> John 4:34–36

Jesus offers you an invitation into his work, gathering fruit that will be more rewarding than anything you've dreamed of accomplishing thus far, because it lasts forever! All this may terrify you because you feel so inadequate, and if it does, good! That's right where God wants you to be—fully dependent on him. Like the Lord told Paul, "My grace is all you need. My power works best in weakness" (2 Corinthians 12:9 NLT). So instead of running from weakness, challenge, or even persecution, Paul welcomed them as a reminder to draw strength from the Lord: "For when I am weak, then I am strong" (v. 10 NLT). So keep it simple. Jesus made it simple.

The night before his crucifixion, probably walking toward Gethsemane, Jesus picked up a branch and said, "Guys, see this branch?

A branch doesn't have to stress and strain to bear fruit, it just stays connected to the vine, and fruit grows naturally. I am the vine; you are the branches. If you simply stay connected to me, you will bear much fruit. Apart from me, you can do nothing!" (John 15:5, my paraphrase). Jesus has all authority. He is always with us by his Spirit. As we simply learn to listen to those quiet promptings in our conscience to do his will and participate in his kingdom work, we will bear much fruit. He will produce spiritual vitality within us, and a wave of impact in the world through us.*

So remember, you're not doing this alone. He will lead you and guide you because it's his work. And he wants you to do this work with others. So the first thing to pray and ask the Lord of the Harvest is, "Lead me to those you have co-missioned to do your work with me."

Build a Co-missioned Core

When Jesus first commissioned the twelve and then seventy others and sent them out to do the exact ministry he had been doing, he sent them two by two. Jesus' small group formed a support system as they moved from a season of equipping into a season of ministry. As you go on mission with Jesus, it will be important early on to find a co-missioned core group of three or four other Christians to work with you.

Together, using your diverse gifts, you can begin building a Network of people who can serve others and grow a vibrant Christian community out of the culture around you. This can happen no matter what church you attend. You and a few friends can begin to be the church to the world. That's what I hope to help you see in the remaining chapters of this book.

*If you are not confident about how to stay connected, listening and following his Spirit moment by moment, I wrote Soul Revolution: How Imperfect People Become All God Intended to help you learn to do this one thing Jesus said was most important of all.

You can't do it alone. So begin praying and talking to others from your church or Christian group, keeping this in mind: "Just as our bodies have many parts and each part has a special function, so it is with Christ's body. We are many parts of one body, and we all belong to each other. In his grace, God has given us different gifts for doing certain things well" (Romans 12:4–6 NLT). God still has a body through which to do his work, and it's made up of you and others willing to listen and respond to the head of the body, which is Jesus (Ephesians 4:15–16). Look around for a few Christians who have compassion and a vision for the broken, hurting world around them.

Imagine if you could get a small group to start meeting and praying, "Lord, send us into your field. Show us the physical and spiritual needs you see. Lead us to be your body doing your work together." And imagine that nucleus growing as you serve people around you, throw parties and invite those you work with or live near, create "come as you are" learning spaces where people can explore faith, help others not only follow Christ but discover their gifts and deploy those gifts to function together as a loving body! Imagine small groups forming to help people grow in faith intentionally from finding faith to fully following Christ. Imagine a day when fifty to seventy people feel like one big, extended family, many who came to faith, some still in the process, others who joined as co-missioned Christians, and together you're seeing Jesus change the world around you life by life by life! Feel impossible? "All things are possible with God" (Mark 10:27).

As you meet other potential co-missioned Christians, talk to them about this vision and challenge them to meet for six weeks to talk and pray about going on mission with Jesus and each other. You may want to read this book together and discuss next steps through each chapter. Then explore your unique contributions.

Do you know what your gifts are? "Now about the gifts of the Spirit, brothers and sisters, I do not want you to be uninformed" (1 Corinthians 12:1). God doesn't want us to be ignorant of the gifts he's given us, but the truth is some of us don't really know what they are. You need to help each other discover and deploy your gifts. Do a spiritual gifts assessment together and talk about the unique gifts God has given each of you, the life experience you bring (both positive and negative experiences become restoration tools in the hands of the Master), and the things you get passionate about. Two free online gift assessments you can use are listed in the notes at the end of this chapter.[1] We find that several roles need to be filled for a healthy Network to emerge out of the culture.

First, a Network Leader will typically be a person with gifts of leadership, or apostleship (like a spiritual entrepreneur who likes starting new things). You might be the catalyst God uses to build the co-missioned core team, but you might not have the best gift mix to lead the Network in the long haul. Pray for that person who typically rises to positions of leadership in business, or has entrepreneurial vision to see what could be, or organizational leadership to help a team work together. It should be someone who can create fun or give direction in front of twenty to fifty people. The role of the Network Leader over the long haul will be to keep the vision fresh and empower and lead a smaller core team to help every Christ-follower in the Network connect in groups to grow, and be empowered to use their gifts to serve.

A Small Group Leader will be another necessary role, as you will want to connect people into small group contexts of three to twelve people to equip them to follow Christ and eventually to spiritually develop others. People with gifts of shepherding (pastoral gifts) or teaching, and secondary gifts of leadership or administration (organizational abilities) are best suited for this role, although other gift mixes also do well. The Small Group Leader will help each person connect into her or his small group to grow spiritually, then develop Christ-followers who can connect and develop others in a multiplying way as the Network expands.

You will want someone to fill the role of Serve Leader. Because the Network is to function like Jesus' body serving the spiritual and physical needs of the world, the Serve Leader will help new people discover their gifts and get plugged into serving opportunities.

Because this person will champion the cause of mobilizing the body to serve, the following gift mix works well in this role: someone with gifts of mercy (a person who passionately seeks justice for the marginalized or oppressed), or gifts of evangelism (someone who longs to see those far from God served, loved, and told about God's grace), or administration (a person with organizational ability to help people discover their gifts and coordinate well-organized serving projects).

Other roles will emerge as the Network grows, like someone to lead worship and someone who is the connector/host type who welcomes new people, gets people connected, and coordinates communication as the Network grows. But a Network Leader, Small Group Leader, and Serve Leader should minimally form the co-missioned core. If one of these is not you, pray for the Lord to bring others into your core to fill these roles.

It is important that this core group not only be gifted for their roles, but have spiritual character like Paul outlined for Timothy as he built a team of people to see the church raised up out of the culture (1 Timothy 3). A summary of those spiritual qualities can be found in the notes at the end of this chapter.[2]

Exegete Your Context

Gregg* and his wife, Helen,* looked out across the Australian outback night sky in awe of God. Their neighbors had just left a lively night of conversation that felt like God's Spirit had set them on fire. Gregg thought about the miraculous way this group had formed. His daughter gave him *Soul Revolution* to read, and while he did the experiment of abiding in Christ for sixty days, God gave him an idea: "Invite your neighbors over and show Gateway's Internet church service, and then talk about it."

I'm a pig rancher, not a pastor, Gregg thought. But he also realized their neighbors, all living on large ranches in southern Australia, had no church or real community, so Gregg responded. Ten or so neighbors had been meeting for months, growing spiritually in ways they had never experienced. The message that day asked people to look around the world God has put them in and ask, "Lord, what do you see? What do you want accomplished? What should we do about it?"

After watching the service, the group started talking about the needs around them. Gregg mentioned the prison and how he had been visiting prisoners and giving them copies of *Soul Revolution*. Someone else said, "I've had this desire to start a camp on my ranch for troubled kids. I've just never acted on it." Gregg mentioned the prisoners' kids and how they needed support.

"I've got four-wheelers and all kinds of fun gear on my ranch that kids would love," another person offered.

"And what if we could minister to the wives too?" mentioned a woman in the group.

Since then, Gregg and Helen have set up a way to employ ex-convicts on local ranches to give them jobs and hopefully a spiritual foundation to start a new life. God is using this group of Australian ranchers to change the lives of prisoners and their families in their community. And it all started by praying to see what God sees and wants done in the world around them.

Once you gather a co-missioned core group of at least three people, begin to exegete your context. Exegesis has traditionally referred to exploring and understanding the biblical text by making observations, exploring the historical situation, asking lots of penetrating questions, and then seeking to interpret the significance and meaning for today. In a post-Christian world, we need to exegete the context and culture around us along with the biblical text to bring the two together.

Begin prayer walking the world that God has you in already. The Great Commission Jesus gave you could literally be translated, "As you go . . . make disciples." In other words, God has you where you are for a reason. As you go throughout your day, ask the Lord to show you the needs or opportunities that he sees with those you work around and with neighbors you live near. Ask him who the modern day "widows, orphans, and foreigners" are—those often forgotten or marginalized that God wants his people to care about.

As a group, spend several weeks praying to have eyes to see what God sees as you go through the day. Write down observations, opportunities, needs, or struggles in the world around you. Then come together and discuss what God shows you.

I play soccer Sunday afternoons with people from all over the world. Driving through the neighborhood near the soccer field, I started to notice how many Indian and Asian families were walking or playing in the park. As I got to know the people I played soccer with, I found out many lived in that neighborhood. We had started a Network in that neighborhood, so I asked the leaders if they had noticed what I had noticed. I was so encouraged to find out that some of them had already exegeted their context very well.

They informed me that many Indian Dell employees live in that neighborhood, and that Dell was the largest employer in Bangalore, India. They also found out that most foreigners living in America will *never* be invited into the home of an American, and many feel very alone and isolated. Knowing this, Sandra started an International Women's Club to bring women together to learn about each other's cultures and support each other in the challenge of living in a foreign land. This has opened great opportunity for spiritual conversations with people of different religions from around the world because Sandra saw a need through the eyes of Jesus and began to meet that need.

Clarify Your Vision

Once you begin to "look up and see the harvest that's ripe," you and your core group can begin to clarify your vision. Ask "Whom has God called us to serve?" Maybe it's your neighbors, or a particular group of people, twenty-something singles downtown, or maybe an immigrant population. Think of ways to engage and serve the people God puts on your heart. (For worksheets to help you clarify your vision, and other next step resources for core and Network building, go to www.mudandthemasterpiece.com.)

A huge mistake many Christ-followers make is to go and serve others, but never build real relationships with people far from God. It is possible to go and serve and yet never see the people around us become followers of Jesus. Often that's because we fail to build relational momentum.

QUESTIONS AND ACTIONS

1. Reflect on this: What might God want to do through you and a few others if you were fully willing? Does this scare you or excite you? Why?

2. Try this: Begin praying for two or three other people who could potentially join you to form a co-missioned core group. Invite them to read and discuss this book with you as a first step.

11

Create Relational Momentum

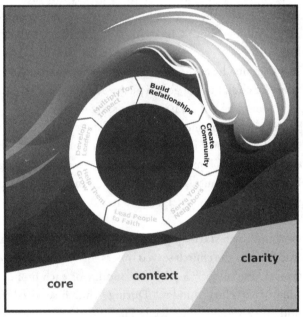

Wave of Impact

Donna grabbed another beer as Shanna poured a frozen margarita. "We met this couple down the street," Donna informed her good friend Shanna, who lived in their San Antonio neighborhood. "Really nice people—they invited us to their church. Said it was a 'come as you are' church, and I think Ryan and I might try it."

"Well, just don't try and drag us into anything like that" was all Shanna said. Shanna and Tim had only been to church twice in their lives, both times for weddings, but past experiences and the little they knew about Christians had put a bad taste in their mouths.

"They're gonna be at the party," Donna responded. "Just meet them. They're cool. I'm not gonna push you to come with us. I just thought it would be nice to have friends to go with."

When Steve and Joanne showed up, Shanna and Tim did meet them. As it turned out, Tim and Steve had a common love—Xterra off-road bike racing! Tim and Steve spent the evening sharing stories of off-road wipeouts. After that night, Tim and Steve started riding together regularly. Then came a few dinners where all three couples hung out together.

Donna and Ryan started attending Rockhills Church regularly and loved the way the church served others. Instead of meeting for their typical Sunday service, the first Sunday of each month they would have "ServeFirst Sunday." During "church service" they'd meet and go serve people in need. Tim and Shanna soon joined Donna and Ryan, Steve and Joanne, and others, serving people in need by throwing an inner-city block party. Several months later, Donna and Ryan accepted the invitation to join Steve's Rockgroup (their small group) meeting in the neighborhood.

Meanwhile, Tim and Shanna were finding themselves making more and more friends among these Christians, realizing that Steve and Joanne and the other Christians they met were normal people who struggle with life just like they do, yet also had something life-giving about them that was attractive. They still had no desire to attend church, but they found themselves feeling a part of the relational Network with these "church people." After about four months, Steve asked Tim after a ride one day if they wanted to come check out the Rockgroup that Donna and Ryan were attending. To Steve's surprise, Tim hesitantly said, "Maybe so."

Tim and Shanna were really nervous about attending this Rockgroup at first. Tim later admitted he was afraid they'd "go all Jesus" on him and be like Ned Flanders on *The Simpsons*. But they overcame their fear and went.

Steve recalls, "That first night, Shanna shared with everyone that she can't even conceive of God as a loving Father because she was born out of a one-night stand and was abused as a child. Tim shared that his father became a born-again Christian about two years ago and that he's asked him to 'leave them alone' about that. There was obviously a lot of pain and bitterness in their past. We didn't try to fix it; we just listened and let them talk."

On their way home that night Tim looked at Shanna and said, "Wow, they didn't try and force Jesus on us. If it stays that way I think I can keep going."

They not only kept going, but started attending church as well, learning more about this God Steve and Joanne followed. It took months of learning, reading the Bible for the first time, and making friends with a number of Christians, but fourteen months after that first party, Steve baptized Tim and Shanna as followers of Jesus in their own hot tub!

Tim recalls, "The love and support we received from our new friends, like when our baby went to the hospital and Steve showed up—that floored us. The guys I met with on a regular basis made a huge difference in my coming to faith. I was able to voice my doubts and fears and not be judged or made to look stupid."

Now Tim brings his friends, and Shanna brings her mom, who doesn't believe yet, but is exploring faith and serving on the church BrewCrew, serving coffee every Sunday.

The Post-Christian World

Tim and Shanna illustrate how people tend to find faith and become the church in a post-Christian world. It is not enough for one Christian to befriend and share her faith with another person. That worked in a culture that was mostly Christian, where most people grew up with a background knowledge of and respect for the Bible, mainly needing the central theme of grace clarified to decide whether to follow Christ. However, in today's post-Christian context, people often need the intersection of three elements in order to find faith and become the church:

1. A friendship with someone who truly acts like Jesus—listening, caring, serving, and talking openly about faith in a non-pressuring way. (We talked about this in part 1.)

2. Relationship with a "tribe" of four to five other Christians whom they enjoy hanging out with and who make them feel like they truly belong (the focus of this chapter).

3. A "come as you are" learning environment where they can learn, usually for six to eighteen months, about the Way of Jesus. (We will discuss this in chapter 13.)

When all three of these elements intersect the lives of those far from God, it's amazing how many people find the love and grace of God and bring their network of friends and family along with them. You will begin to see more and more people, once far from God, now following Christ and leading others to do the same. But first, we must build relational momentum.

Europe, Canada, Australia, South Africa, and much of the United States and even South America face post-Christian barriers to people finding faith. It requires relationship and learning to overcome these barriers. In a post-Christian context, most people do not really know much about the Bible or the life-giving Way of Jesus, but there still exists an awareness of Christianity (usually this awareness comes only from negative media or bias about

Christians). Honestly, it would be easier in some respects to reach a culture with zero awareness of Christianity than have to overcome negative stereotypes left in the wake of dying churches, but post-Christian is where much of the world lives.

In order for people of post-Christian cultures to become followers of Jesus, they must get to know multiple Christians willing to be open about their own struggles while also demonstrating the hope and fruit of the Spirit-filled life. When non-Christians encounter Christians who act like they never struggle, have all the answers, and suggest quick fixes for every problem, they quickly see through the pharisaical pretense and want nothing to do with that kind of faith.

But seeing people who try to love but struggle, who face real setbacks and need encouragement, who get tempted but ask for prayer and support, and who are learning to stay connected to God's Spirit alongside a loving spiritual community—that's what the whole world longs for, and that relational momentum draws people to Jesus. But how does a fledgling core group of Christians build relational momentum?

Build Relationships Where You Live

Jesus' Great Commission tells us to "make disciples" (learners and followers of Jesus) by first helping them identify with the Father, Son, and Spirit through faith and baptism, then helping them "observe" (not just know) all Jesus commanded (Matthew 28:19–20 NLT). But the context is "as you go." God has you where you are for a reason. Maybe you hate your job, or struggle with the city you're in, but maybe that would change if you started to ask, "Who are you drawing to faith around me, and how can I love and serve them as I go?"

Most of us have at least four, some as many as ten, people we interact with regularly who are either not following Christ or are disconnected from his church. Start noticing as you go. As a co-missioned core group, make a list of the people God has already

211

put in your life, and simply begin to pray for them. Steve said, "Joanne and I live with an 'adopt our block' mind-set. Our goal is to actually get to know our neighbors, pray for them, care for them, live life with them, and then when the opportunity comes up, share Jesus with them."

Matt in San Diego read about an important sociological principle in a book called *Refrigerator Rights.*[1] All people long for the kind of friendships and belonging where you feel so comfortable that you could go over to a neighbor's house, open the refrigerator and get a drink, and never feel weird about it, and they could do the same at your house. Interestingly, if you never invite your neighbors into your kitchen, or go into theirs, the relationship will stay at a friendly surface level for years. So inviting neighbors into your kitchen opens the door for a kind of belonging that everyone longs to experience.

Jay and Jen, along with a Network of people from Matt's church in San Diego, threw a "meet your neighbors" party at their condominium pool. There was a great turnout, and as a result of the party, the next week Jay ran into Emily and Mark, stopped and talked, and invited them over for dinner. Mark was agnostic and really hostile toward Christianity. Mark later reflects, "If you had invited me to anything 'church,' or if I had even known the party was church, we would have been gone."

But Jay and Jen had them over for dinner, and friendship grew as Jay introduced Mark and Emily to other Christ-followers in their circle of friends. Emily was a believer, but had shelved her fledgling faith ever since dating and marrying Mark. Jay and Jen had opened their home and built trust enough that Mark agreed to check out Jay's small group and attend church with Emily because he liked the people. Relational momentum was building.

Emily started growing in faith and Mark started openly exploring faith, because, as they put it, "We had never had friends like this before, people who actually cared, listened, built you up rather than tearing you down—people we trusted!" Refrigerator rights spread as Emily began to interact with Alex and Karen across the street. The pool party sparked relationships among many isolated neighbors. Alex and Karen's families lived in New Zealand and Puerto Rico, so they longed for close friendship as well.

Because Emily and Mark were experiencing a level of loving relationship among these church people, it felt natural to invite Alex and Karen to attend some of the church gatherings with them, even though they did not "do church" or follow Christ. The day Alex and Karen came to church, Matt spoke on refrigerator rights. That evening, Alex and Karen went over to Emily and Mark's house, told them how much that message moved them, and opened up about struggles they were having and how that's what they were longing for—refrigerator rights.

As your core group begins to simply build trusting, caring friendships "as you go," thinking about how to give refrigerator rights to people far from God, you will see relational momentum begin to build. Refrigerator rights go deeper than access to your food. It's about a willingness to invite someone into your personal space, your real life, even your struggles—to let them see where you really live.

Not everyone will find faith. Alex and Karen did end up coming to church and connecting in a small group, but underlying marriage struggles caused an ugly divorce before they ever found faith, and both moved away. And this is an important sidenote: Building relational momentum only happens as you allow the weeds and wheat to all grow up together, knowing God will sort it all out in the end (Matthew 13:24–30).

Jesus created relational momentum as he invited people to come and see where he was staying. It says after spending the day with Jesus, Andrew brought his brother, Simon, to meet Jesus. Jesus invited Philip to come with him to Galilee; Philip immediately invited his friend, Nathanael, who was skeptical. Philip's invitation to Nathanael mirrored the words of Jesus, "Come and see" (John 1:35–46).

Stuff You Enjoy

A great way to build friendships with people far from God is simply doing stuff you enjoy with people outside your church. I love soccer. I've played my whole life, and so when I started thinking about how to serve people around me and build relationships, I decided to coach my son's soccer team with my wife's help. One of our neighbor's kids joined our team, and we got to be friends with Cindy and Jeff and their family. This led to a lot more time together on and off the field and around the neighborhood. After months of relationship building, Cindy and Jeff and their family started attending our church, then got in a small group, then found faith.

Cindy enthusiastically shared with the other parents at practices about our church, especially encouraging Kathy to come. Kathy started listening to messages on the Internet because she struggled with alcohol and impatience and wanted help. Over the next few years, Kathy and Alejandro and their whole family found faith. Cindy also introduced us to Sandra and Grey down the street. Having grown up in England, they wanted their son to play soccer, so he too joined our team. As we became friends, both Sandra and Grey had resistance at first to the message of Jesus, but when they hit some struggles the next year, they reached out to us for help. As a result, Sandra came to faith, and Grey and I had some great talks about Jesus before they moved back overseas.

David and Trina were the parents of Ryan, a boy I ended up coaching from age eight to twelve. David was easy to get to know. He loved to joke around and was a life-of-the-party kind of guy, crude and rude but totally funny, and super successful managing a global high-tech sales force. Kathy and Alejandro, Cindy and Jeff, and another couple who started coming to our church all got to be friends with David and Trina.

One day I asked David, "What's your spiritual background?" He gladly told me about his horrible experiences with organized religion from a young age as he grew up in Europe. David felt it horribly wrong that beggars could go hungry right across the street from a huge, ornate cathedral, and decided it was all hypocrisy. I agreed with him that God cares about the plight of the poor and wants all people to love him by serving others.

Because several of the parents on the soccer team had already come to faith and had told him what our church service was like, David and his family started attending. This led to much more sideline chatting about messages, and jokes about God and religion, but also increasingly real conversation among this group of soccer moms and dads. David was learning about the way of Jesus with his family, and his eyes were opening to God's goodness.

When David and Trina hosted the team at their house for one end-of-the-year soccer party, I noticed a tap coming out of the refrigerator. David let me know unashamedly that he liked his beer . . . a lot! It was his one vice.

I asked David, "So where are you at with God?" He said, "I think I believe in God now, I'm just not sure about Jesus." I asked if he'd be up for a breakfast conversation about it, and he said, "Sure." At breakfast, I asked what it was about Jesus that tripped him up. He just didn't understand why you had to believe Jesus was more than just a good teacher. I told David that God created him to do life in loving relationship with God and others, and I explained why Jesus not only showed God's character in a form we could comprehend, but also paid to make a way for anyone to turn back to God and be forgiven. I challenged David to read Scripture and begin to openly pray for God to reveal himself, but on God's terms.

A year later, I heard he'd been promoted to national sales manager of a company moving him to New Jersey, so I requested one last lunch. I said, "So, David, we haven't talked about faith in a while. Where are you at with Jesus?"

His words dropped my jaw. "I'm in" was all he said.

"You're in?"

"Yeah, I'm in, man! You know, after our last meeting I started thinking about what you said, and then I did that *Soul Revolution* experiment with the church and started realizing that God's been trying to get my attention for a long time. He's been giving me all these good gifts, blessings, jobs, a wonderful family, but I just didn't realize it was God. I wasn't being thankful, so I started being thankful, and at the same time Trina and I both decided to get in shape and stop drinking, and I guess somewhere along the way enough of my struggles got answered."

"So you believe Jesus was the Son of God?"

"Yep."

"And you've told him you want what he did to count for you—to have his forgiveness and leadership over your life?"

"Yep. I think I want you to baptize me before I move, but I really wanted Trina to do it with me, and I'm not sure she's ready."

The next month, I had one of the highlights of my life as I baptized David, Trina, Ryan, and his little sister, too, as followers of Jesus!

Over the ten years we coached, I figured out twenty adults and kids we met through soccer started following Christ as part of our church! Find ways to build relational momentum with neighbors, co-workers, or just with people doing what you love to do—coaching soccer, riding mountain bikes, jogging, golfing, watching football. But then you need to go beyond that to create loving community with Christians, inviting non-Christians to belong and experience life with Jesus.

Aware As You Work

We can join the Father in his work even as we work. After Jesus healed the mat-bound guy at the pool of Bethesda, the Pharisees accused him of breaking the Sabbath. Jesus responded by saying, "My Father is always at his work to this very day, and I too am working. . . . The Son can do nothing by himself; he can do only what he sees his Father doing" (John 5:17, 19). We too were meant to work with an awareness of what the Father is doing, and join him in his work.

Paul understood this when he pointed out to idol worshipers in Lystra that "[God] has shown kindness by giving you rain from heaven and crops in their seasons; he provides you with plenty of food and fills your hearts with joy" (Acts 14:17). In other words, God got there first! God had been there at work, giving good gifts, filling their hearts with joy, drawing all people to himself even though they didn't acknowledge him yet. As we go about our work, do we see where God is working in order to join him?

Paula came to faith in our church after years of atheism. The wounds from a father whose only attention came when he got her drunk and molested her as a teenager kept her alcohol dependent to numb the pain. She got sober through trusting a Higher Power who forgives, gives us second and third chances, and loves us enough to help us do what we can't do ourselves as we surrender our will to doing his will only.

Paula joined my small group, and I had a chance to show her that the Higher Power she experienced healing her was the God Jesus revealed—there aren't other gods who do that! She came to faith and started following Christ.

Paula works doing developmental home therapy with kids. One of Paula's clients was a four-year-old named Luke, who had nearly died several times in the hospital due to complications at birth. He required ongoing therapy. Luke's mother, Shelly, had become friends with Paula over the year of therapy, and one day Shelly opened up to Paula about something troubling her.

"I'm concerned about Luke," Shelly began. "He's been having strange dreams or imaginative ideas, but I don't know where they could have come from."

"What kind of strange dreams?" Paula asked.

"When I tuck him in for bed at night, he keeps telling me he wants to go and play in the fields with Jesus again. I asked him about it, and he insists that when he was in the hospital, Jesus came to get him and they would run and play in these beautiful meadows. As you know, his father's a doctor, and Andrew thinks it's a hallucination. I just can't figure out where he even heard about Jesus. We have never been to church, talked about Jesus, or let him watch anything on TV about Jesus. How did he come up with Jesus?"

Realizing that God might just be at work behind the scenes, drawing this family to himself through the near-death experience of this child, Paula told Shelly what she had been learning about Jesus. God used that conversation to set Shelly and Andrew on a path of exploring faith. They started attending our church, and a year later, after learning about Jesus, they came to believe and follow him.

Where is God already at work in the lives of your co-workers, or those you live near or interact with throughout your day? Pay attention and join God in his work. Then invite people into loving community.

Establish Loving Community

I play soccer on a men's indoor team, and it serves as a great way to build friendships with people from around the world. However, I've also noticed that a relational norm (a kind of social contract) gets set after a while, and if the norm has nothing to do with deeper talk about life and spiritual matters, friendship can go on for years without ever engaging with faith issues. To overcome this glass ceiling, it is important to establish loving community among Christians that others can be invited into. Real relational momentum happens when your Christian friends become their friends too.

You see this happening with Jesus and his friends. As a group, they attended weddings together, accepted invitations to dinner at people's houses, went to festivals and other places people gathered, and Matthew threw a party so that all his "sinner" friends could meet Jesus. Jesus provided better wine after they drank all the wine at the wedding. Yet Jesus never sinned.

Jesus got a bad reputation among the religious elite precisely because he and his followers made ways to hang out with the "gluttons, tax collectors, and sinners." Can we hang out, even with those sinning, without sinning ourselves? Can we bring light and life into places where God's good gifts get corrupted and abused, so that relationship and faith can bring restoration and a better life? To do this, we need a way to invite people from their world into loving community in God's world.

You can accomplish this in a variety of ways. Starting small groups with believers who also know how to create space for nonbelievers to explore faith is an excellent way. As you heard in several stories previously, this is a very effective way of engaging relationally and spiritually, as long as the culture of the small group reflects the soil in which exploring people can find faith (No Perfect People Allowed was written to help groups form this culture).

But often an intermediary stage of building loving community is needed. "Party with a purpose" is something we encourage Networks of Christians to do regularly, so that you can all invite your friends who don't follow Christ to begin to interact and get to know your friends who do. Jay's condo pool party, dinner parties, or game-watching parties are examples. Again, until someone gets to know a smaller "tribe" of Christians that they like, they don't often find faith and become his church.

Theresa* and Greg* met with three other couples and formed the co-missioned core of a new Network in their neighborhood. As they began to pray about needs of their neighbors, thinking about ways to party with a purpose, one guy piped in and said, "I watch football every Sunday afternoon. I have a big-screen TV and room for a crowd—I'll open my house for everyone to bring friends to watch the game after church."

Greg and I play soccer together with a lot of the same guys. From hanging out on the soccer field, he invited friends to come watch the game, and our international soccer friends met our Christian football watching friends and soon dogs and cats were living in harmony together! Okay, maybe not, but relationships with multiple Christians creates the environment where an invitation into a small group or church event feels safe because "these people are my friends."

Some Networks have formed "moms at the park" meetups. Moms with young kids in one Network from Gateway invite other moms to meet at a park weekly. Relational momentum is built as they support each other in how to survive and thrive during this challenging stage of life. From there, spiritual conversations can grow and small groups can form where invitations are not scary—again, because these people are all friends.

As you form small groups in the early stage of Network life, make sure they remain open to people discovering faith. There's a time to close groups for deeper equipping, but always have a few groups stay open in a Network. (We'll talk more about this in chapter 14.) It's really important for the Christians in the core of your Network and the early small groups to allow questions, doubts, struggles, or "sin issues" to come up and not try to quickly answer, fix, change, or solve them. Try to get rid of Christianese (see appendix A) or explain the terms in normal ways. You can talk about what you believe and what the Bible says with integrity; just respect those who are not yet convinced, and you'll be amazed at how God does the rest. Listen to how relational momentum carried Leigh to the point of faith:

> I had tried Hindu meditation retreats, Unity churches, and very New Agey churches searching for truth. It felt too nebulous. Gateway wasn't like that. It was clearly a Christian church, but I felt that if God led me to Gateway, maybe there was something I needed to understand about Jesus.
>
> Still, on the inside, I was kicking and screaming intellectually. I didn't want to be exclusionary. I didn't want to start quoting Scripture at people. I didn't want to feel like anybody else was wrong. I didn't want to be like "those Christians." I have very liberal friends. If I had anything to say about Jesus, except that he was a teacher among many, I would be labeled a freak.
>
> But I was looking for a community of people who cared about each other, and I could sense that with Gateway. So after a month, I got involved in a moms' group. I had a real attitude, but whenever I'd come at them with my issues, I didn't get an attitude back. I sensed genuine humility from the leader, who constantly encouraged me to be myself and question openly. She welcomed me like a friend and tried to understand my point of view while explaining the Bible's point of view with integrity.
>
> I didn't know anything about the Bible except I had been told it had been changed over the years, a book of myths. I was walking my son in the stroller one day, and I remember praying

to God, saying, "If there's really something to this Jesus thing, I'm gonna give you thirty days, and I'll just focus on Jesus. If this is what you want for me, come lead me and guide me." I started reading the Bible for the first time, and I know it was the Holy Spirit guiding me, because I not only understood it, I couldn't get enough of it. I couldn't wait to read more about Jesus every night. I kept giving God thirty-day extensions to convince me.

During that time, the church did a series called "Prophecies of the Messiah." Those messages changed everything for me. That was the key to my intellectual resistance. Not long afterward, I worked through the pre-baptism study, and that's really when I understood the grace of God offered in Christ. I asked him into my heart and my life.

It takes time and patience, but relational momentum and a loving community where those exploring faith can belong before believing are critical. If belonging before believing seems wrong, just remember that Judas belonged to Jesus' small group and never believed, and not only that, Jesus appointed him to serve as treasurer. Encouraging members and even nonbelievers to serve with your Network is our next focus as the wave of impact builds to see the culture become the church.

QUESTIONS AND ACTIONS

1. Reflect on this: Do you have a group of Christian friends who can create loving community and include people far from God? If not, how might you go about forming this kind of community?

2. Try this: Set a date to try one of the ideas you read about, or come up with a new idea that you and your friends can do with your friends who are not yet believers.

12

Serve Your Neighbors With Your Neighbors

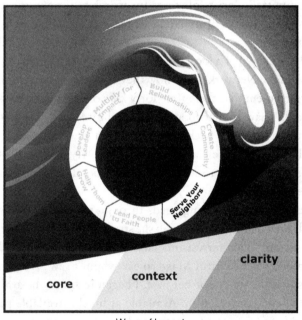

Wave of Impact

R ebecca had personally experienced the healing power of loving community and people serving her at her point of need. She got into a small group and was growing, so doing the same for others came naturally. Rebecca joined a growing Network of Christ-followers in Round Rock and quickly caught the vision for serving people God put in her path.

This Network of about thirty people, some connected in small groups, some still exploring faith, all worked together to have greater impact. They gathered monthly with a growing core group of committed Christ-followers for worship, time in the Word, and sharing stories of impact. From there they would plan ways to serve.

The principal of a local elementary school was extremely grateful when the Network asked how they could serve her school. She informed them that there were forty kids on free-lunch programs who didn't have enough food to eat over the weekend. The Network began to pack forty backpacks of food each week to serve these families in need. They launched other ministry initiatives as they seized opportunities to serve, and they responded to needs arising in the neighborhood.

Rebecca started seeing needs through the eyes of Jesus. She recalls how that changed the job she struggled with into a purposeful mission. "Jennifer was my cube neighbor at work," Rebecca explained. "A beautiful Masterpiece whom I saw struggling to withstand the weight of her past. I began to simply be available. Available in conversation. Available at lunch. Available period. I would try to respond to some of her interests and be engaged where she was in life.

"After a couple of weeks of simply loving and listening, I asked Jennifer if she wanted to go to church with me. Her response was, 'No way! Church people are mean. Why would I ever do that?' It was clear that Jennifer didn't like church or church people."

But Rebecca continued to take an interest in Jennifer and to serve her in any way she could. Meanwhile, Rebecca noticed her neighbor Nick's yard getting overgrown week after week. Nick managed a nightclub on Sixth Street, Austin's younger, hipper version of Bourbon Street. He would often come out on his front porch.

Rebecca struck up a conversation and discovered that his wife, Ashley, had been fighting cancer for several years, which explained why Rebecca rarely saw her. Nick did his best to get his wife transported to and from Houston for chemo, all the while keeping life going for two preteens and managing a bar. That explained the overgrown yard too.

Rebecca started mowing their yard whenever she mowed hers. During a serving project one Saturday, some of Rebecca's friends from the Network joined in mowing Nick and Ashley's yard and repairing their broken fence. Several weeks later, Ashley and Rebecca had a deep conversation, and out of the blue Ashley asked, "Can I come to church with you?"

Rebecca recalls God's amazing timing: "The message Sunday was about testing and trials and how you're not alone. It was amazing to see God draw Ashley to church for that message, which completely spoke to her heart and met her at her point of need. We went to dinner on Wednesday night. Ashley opened up about her struggles and just how powerful Sunday was. She said she still had no idea why the words just popped out of her mouth . . . 'Can I go to church with you?'" Seeing a Network of Christians serving them at their point of need started Ashley and her family on a journey toward faith.

"I asked Jennifer if she wanted to come serve with me," Rebecca recalls. "One of our unchurched neighbors needed help painting a garage. Jennifer said, 'Sure.' After serving that Saturday, Jennifer asked, 'Were those your church friends? They were pretty cool.' I told her they were, and again asked if she'd be interested in coming to church, reminding her it's a 'come as you are' church. Again she said, 'No!'

"It's in a bar in Round Rock this Sunday," Rebecca added. Gateway was piping their Internet service into two sports bars on Sunday mornings. (The bar owner in chapter 1 got us two sports bars for free!)

"Church in a bar? Yeah, I'd do that!" Jennifer surprisingly replied.

Jennifer not only liked it; she kept coming. Rebecca introduced her to others. Hearing Jennifer loved organic gardening, another Gateway person invited her to serve in our community garden, growing fresh produce for our food pantry and for refugee families. During that time, Jennifer and Ashley both started following Christ and got into Rebecca's small group.

To Serve or Be Served

To serve or be served? That is the question for those who claim to follow Jesus. Which do we go to church to do? Recall that Jesus said, "The Son of Man did not come to be served, but to serve, and to give his life as a ransom for many" (Mark 10:45). So what does it mean to follow Jesus? And if God intends his church to function together as Jesus' body (Romans 12:4–8), what would that look like? I believe any church can form Networks of twenty to seventy people who look together for opportunities to serve the spiritual and physical needs of their neighbors in ways that turn the world upside down!

A Network can start out of one small group, a Sunday school class, a singles' group, or out of a children's ministry serving kids and the network of relationships those kids and families know. The sky's the limit! A Network could birth out of a women's or men's ministry, around musicians and artists serving other artists, or simply one willing Christian who gathers a co-missioned core that begins to love and serve their neighbors together.

Jesus met needs wherever he went—he helped parents distraught over their children's self-destructive tendencies, he healed physical problems, he fed the hungry, he helped spiritually distressed people find hope, he gave relationally outcast people friendship. And he taught his followers to do the same.

We must start here as well—simply seeing people's greatest need and serving them in that area of need. This requires relationship, listening, and caring to discern a person's greatest need. But as we go on mission with Jesus, he will show us the needs he wants to meet through us individually and together as his body. And as you can see from the stories I've told, serving together and inviting the world to serve with us creates relational momentum.

From a small nucleus of a co-missioned core or one small group, you can grow into a Network of seventy people serving spiritual and physical needs, as you watch others find faith and join with you. As you exegete your context to consider what the needs are in your area, also consider trying what our Round Rock Network did, called "soul storming."[1]

The goal of soul storming is to see what the intersection might be between the unique needs of the world around you, the passion God's put on each heart, and the unique gifts and experiences that together can serve as his body to meet needs. Jason Heriford, author of *Soul Storming* and a member of our Round Rock Network, encourages groups first to take one night for "heart storming."

Each person writes out an answer to the question "What really breaks your heart about what you see around you?" Think about your neighborhood. What's broken there? Think about the places you travel or things you know of in your city or area—what would God want restored? Think about the people around you. What's most broken in their lives? What would it mean to see God's kingdom come to restore what's broken? To do this exercise effectively, you probably need to first spend time prayer walking, exegeting your context, and learning about your area because often we don't see the broken things God sees.

At the next meeting, give each person time for "life storming." Answer this question: "What gives you life or what's shaped your life that you have passion for?" What do you love to do? If you had no fear, and all the resources needed, what would you do?

What things have happened to you in life that give you a passion for helping others in the same situation? Maybe it's overcoming an addiction and you're passionate about helping others break free. Maybe you suffered abuse and would love to help others heal. Maybe you felt worthless as a kid and passionately want to give value to kids who feel abandoned or unwanted.

Finally, have each person take their lists home and rank the top five things that break their hearts and the top five life passions. Then at the next gathering, give each person ten minutes to share his or her top fives. Take time afterward to discuss what God's Spirit might be showing you as a Network. Where might you serve together? What should you try? How could your different gifts and experiences support one another as you serve your world?

For instance, one member of the Round Rock Network talked about the struggles of childhood and a passion for kids in crisis. That led another person to mention the Texas Baptist Children's Home in her area, which later sparked an idea borne out of three people's passions. Today a team of people minister to families in crisis at the children's home; one guy uses his passion for music to teach kids free guitar lessons, another with a passion for animals does pet therapy with kids as well as the elderly, and a garden team has beautified the place.

In another Network in South Austin, Josh* recovered from a cocaine addiction and has a passion for sponsoring people through recovery. Any Network member meeting an addict connects the person to Josh. Mykel* and Sheeri* have a passion for strengthening marriages and have experience leading seminars, so I suggested they have their Network host a five- or six-week "Making Marriage Great" workshop as a way to serve families in their neighborhood with so many marriages in crisis.

Everyone needs a cause to serve. Networks can find causes to serve together in an ongoing way in order to bring God's kingdom restoration to what's broken in the world around us. As we individually see needs, we can bring the needs of people to the Network.

For instance, our Cedar Park Network had a member who discovered a family in crisis in the neighborhood. This family's elementary age son developed a rare disease insurance wouldn't cover, and it wiped the family out, yet the child still needed treatment. The Network rallied and put on a carnival in the park for the neighborhood in order to raise funds for the treatment. As a result, that family had their financial burden eased, and they started attending Network events, serving others, and exploring faith. And the whole neighborhood saw the church in action through this local Network. This is how you will see your little core begin to grow and grow. But one word of warning: It is possible for us to serve people in a way that actually hurts.

When Serving Hurts

Our Downtown Singles Network stumbled across an interesting phenomenon. Last summer we had a heat wave and the temperature hit 100 degrees for 100 days. On one particularly hot evening, the Network decided to pass out bottles of ice-cold water. Free water—how could you go wrong on a 108-degree evening? But people wouldn't take it! Some just said, "No thanks." Others asked, "What's the catch, what do you want?" One lady got so angry, she slapped the bottle of water out of the person's hand and stormed off. They struggled to give out free water.

The next week, they tried a very different experiment. Everyone in the Network was handed a cardboard sign that said in bold letters on the bottom, "Just Love Me." Each person was challenged to write on the sign three reasons they believe people struggle to love them, their character flaws or failings that make them hard to love. Then they were to go to complete strangers in downtown and explain that they were doing an experiment about love.

They were given instructions to tell people, "These are the reasons I'm hard to love. Would you be willing to take a sign like this and write your three reasons you're hard to love? If you will, then we can trade signs and if I encounter a person who is hard to love like you, I'll pray for the ability to love them anyway. You can do the same with my sign."

The shocking realization: It was easier to get people to trade character flaws than to take ice-cold water!

I believe there's an important lesson buried in this experiment. When people we encounter sense a "handout mentality" in our service, it does harm and turns people away. When we encounter people with humility and recognition of our own brokenness and need, people can receive from us and are drawn to us.

Churches can send out missional Christians in droves to serve "those people." But if "they" never become "us," I'm greatly concerned that we may be doing more harm than good to Jesus' mission. Jesus restored not only what was physically wrong, but also what was spiritually and relationally wrong. That's the invasion of God's kingdom we should seek.

Who Are the Poor?

Our attitude has huge implications when we serve marginalized or economically impoverished people. Steve Corbett, a professor of economics and community development, notes that when poor people explain their poverty, they talk about shame, inferiority, powerlessness, humiliation, fear, hopelessness, depression, social isolation, and voicelessness—almost never do they talk about material lack!

People with means think of poverty materially: lack of food, money, housing, transportation, and jobs.[2] Inadvertently, this creates a handout mentality of the "haves" helping the "have-nots," of the "fixed" serving the "broken," of the "powerful" serving the "powerless," of the "Pharisees" serving the "sinners." The relationship is imbalanced. Serving out of a "one-up, one-down" posture does not help and can actually hurt. If we as the church serve "them," but "they" never become the church, something's relationally wrong.

Corbett gives the example of "helping" a person by paying his electric bill. But what if that person's fundamental problem is not a lack of money, or an inability to earn money, but a poor view of God and himself that keeps him sabotaging job after job? In this case, giving money does more harm than good. A better and more costly solution would be for your church to develop a relationship with this person that says, "We are here to walk with you and help you use your gifts and abilities to be all God created you to be, and even help you serve others." That's the difference between relational serving and handout-style serving.

Handout serving is fairly easy, and it feels pretty good, but it doesn't *do as much good as is needed*. Not if restoration of God's Masterpiece is the goal. Relational service costs: "If you *spend yourselves* in behalf of the hungry and satisfy the needs of the oppressed, then your light will rise in the darkness" (Isaiah 58:10, italics mine). "Spending yourselves" means investing relationally and materially. Most of the problems of humanity are relational problems at the core.

Understanding that we all suffer from poverty will reorient our service to be truly helpful. Corbett points out that God created us to relate to God, self, others, and creation under his kingdom will and ways. "Because [these] four relationships are the building blocks of all human activity, the effects of the fall are manifested in the economic, social, religious, and political systems that humans have created throughout history . . . the systems are broken, reflecting humans' broken relationships."[3] As Bryant Meyers, a Christian development specialist, says, "Poverty is the result of relationships that do not work."[4] This realization is critical for all who desire to help others.

Who are the poor? asks Corbett. "Due to the comprehensive nature of the fall, every human being is poor in the sense of not experiencing these four relationships in the way that God intended."[5] We suffer a *spiritual poverty* of intimacy with God, causing some to deny God's existence, or like the Pharisees, to put material greed and positional power above God.

We suffer a *poverty of being*, where people don't see God's intended Masterpiece in themselves or others. For some that leads to a "god complex" of superiority as the powerful, wealthy, or righteous and good, compared to those who suffer an "inferiority complex" as the poor, or helpless, bad or outcasts.

We suffer a *poverty of community* where self-centeredness, abuse, or exploitation divides people. And we suffer a *poverty of stewardship* over God's creation where people get lazy or feel no purpose for their work, or become workaholics and use the stewardship God's given them only to serve themselves.

We are all poor and broken people. Development experts note that trillions of dollars of Western aid has had little impact in impoverished nations because of a failure to recognize the relational foundation of poverty. When the wealthy, powerful, or "righteous," who might suffer from a *poverty of being* (feeling superior), try to "fix" the needy person's problem, it exacerbates the poverty of both parties! This doesn't mean giving money to serve impoverished communities causes problems, as long as the money is used to relationally empower those in need.

Recall, the root problem materially poor people have is feeling inferior and hopeless, rather than feeling like a valuable Masterpiece God wants to restore to do the good works he intended. The poor don't feel relationally empowered to use their God-given gifts to find solutions that last, and the powerful stay stuck in their "poverty of being," feeling superior about "doing good" but not seeing the harm being done.

This applies to all areas of "poverty." When we come across as superior, it does more harm than good. Until we embrace our mutual brokenness, our serving will likely undermine the good God wants to do in seeing his restorative kingdom come.

Homeless to Helping

Sledge. The name fits the look—a former Army Special-Ops soldier with a purple heart. The tattoos bulging from his arms tell the story of a war that has become more spiritual than physical. Ben Sledge♦ came to Gateway a mess. While he was still in Iraq, Ben's wife had an affair and left him. When he returned home, a friend in Austin offered a couch and brought him to Gateway. People met him at his point of need, loved him, and served him, and Sledge decided to follow Jesus.

Four years later, Sledge and his friend Jordan♦ began to meet and pray about starting a college Network. They met college students and invited them to serve others, then formed a small group to spiritually grow these students. The Network grew that first year to about sixty students, meeting in four small groups, serving at Church Under the Bridge for homeless people. That's where they met Jason, a young man in his twenties living under the bridge.

Jason had moved to Austin from Portland because, as he put it, "I got in with the wrong crowd and had been kicked out of just about every place I'd stayed. With nowhere to go, I came to Austin but ended up on the streets." Jason was invited to come to the Network small group, and he accepted the invitation.

Mattias♦ drove over and picked up Jason. During the small group, Jason felt accepted and treated as a real person, even though he wasn't sure what he thought about God. Mattias offered Jason his couch instead of having to sleep on the ground, and for the next few weeks, Jason couch-surfed between several houses of those in the small group. Jason kept attending the small group every Tuesday night and became friends with many in the group.

One of the guys Jason stayed with got him a job with Josh (the guy in our South Network who sponsors people coming out of drug addiction). They also found a car Jason could use to get to and from work and got him clothes he needed for work. Sledge was getting married, but opened his house to Jason for the two months before the wedding.

Jason told Sledge, "Man, I feel so blessed. Whenever I feel down, I have friends to talk to. When I have needs, you guys meet them. I don't feel like I deserve any of this. You guys give to me and expect nothing in return." He was wrestling with what it means to follow

Christ, because he had seen people living it. The combination of relationship, love, and serving needs in a way that sees the Masterpiece waiting to be revealed motivated Jason to enroll in college. He now lives with Mattias and is working full time, paying rent, attending the community college, and serving others with the college Network because he was served relationally, not just materially.

One of the ways to keep serving "eye to eye" rather than "one-up, one-down," is by encouraging others to serve with Christians. As Bryan and Amy have seen with the Branson Network and Jesus Was Homeless ministry, getting people you once served serving others raises their sense of dignity and worth. This empowers them to follow Christ and become more of what God intended.

The Three-Legged Stool

Just as a three-legged stool depends on each leg, God restores his Masterpiece in people when three elements work together:

(1) They are befriended by one Christ-follower demonstrating the *attitude* and *actions* of Jesus.

(2) They meet a Network of Christians who include them in loving community and service.

(3) They have "come as you are" learning space.

With all three elements working together, it's amazing how God restores his Masterpiece life by life by life. But people need space and time to "come as you are"—even with sins, struggles, questions, and doubts—to learn about the way of Jesus long enough to decide if they will commit to fully follow him.

That's the rest of Rebecca's story (from the beginning of this chapter). Rebecca has seen amazing healing, growth, and restoration as God's Masterpiece, and she feels called to full-time ministry. She continues to serve and lead others to faith like Jennifer, Ashley, and Shelly. (I received a picture last Saturday night of the baptism of Shelly, a woman Rebecca helped lead to faith.) Now Rebecca leads a small group for these women to grow deep spiritual roots. What I didn't tell you is that . . .

Four years ago, Rebecca felt suicidal when her five-year lesbian relationship blew apart in her face! For more of Rebecca's story, turn to the next chapter.

QUESTIONS AND ACTIONS

1. Reflect on this: How often do you find ways to serve others? How might you serve the people God has already put around you—at work, where you live or go to school, or in your own home?

2. Try this: Come up with a serving project with a few other Christians and consider inviting friends who may seem far from God to serve with you.

13

"Come As You Are"
Learning Space

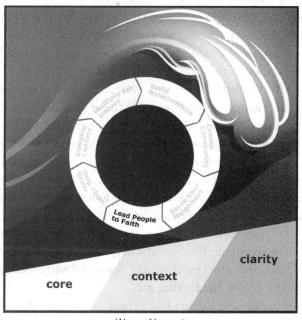

Wave of Impact

Rebecca was thankful to be on the road escaping from Austin, escaping from all the mistakes of the past year, escaping to Tennessee to find space to breathe. Space to reflect on the past year, the past decade. Space to figure out how she had ended up so broken, so alone. Alone on the path she thought would bring happiness.

She grew up in a Christian home and tried walking the straight and narrow, but in college another voice stalked her. A voice pushing her down a path she thought she couldn't resist. No matter how hard she ran, she could never seem to evade its chase, and now the knife stabbed deep into her wounded soul. "How did I get here? I feel so lost, so confused, so alone." The thoughts swirled like a tornado of destruction winding through Rebecca's mind.

The tears blinded her as she drove onward. She put in a CD one of her students had given her. God spoke to her through the words of the second song, reminding her of the love they once shared. Through tears of hope Rebecca cried out, "God, set me free. If you'll take me back, I'll follow you out of this mess, but you have to show me how."

The next week, Rebecca found herself back in Austin at Gateway Church. When it was announced that the following week's message would be on same-sex attraction, her heart started pounding with fear mixed with hope. She searched our website and listened to one of the messages online for clues of what might be said. She listened to another and another until she had devoured twelve messages in twenty-four hours. She emailed me.

Amy, Renee, and Robert had agreed to tell their stories that weekend of coming from the gay lifestyle to faith in Christ, and the journey God led them on toward sexual wholeness. They had not tried to change, but they simply followed God's Spirit step-by-step and he led them into something better than they had imagined. As we sat in my office, one by one they all backed out. I understood their fear, but I felt prompted to read Rebecca's email to them:

I saw your topic for next week. I'm thirty-four and for the last ten years, I've been in same-sex relationships. I grew up in a very legalistic church. My mom took us every time the doors were opened. I led Bible studies and mission trips, I was the perfect Christian girl—perfect smile, perfect prayer, perfect everything . . . on the surface.

Underneath were the wounds left behind by a broken, imperfect family combined with the wounds from a sexually twisted world. The mix of wounds proved to be the perfect breeding ground for me to seek love and affection in a same-sex relationship. In college, I dated guys and was even close to engagement, but I couldn't even lie on the couch beside him without feeling creeped-out thinking about the past. I gave up trying to be straight and became a closeted lesbian for the past ten years. If I'm honest with myself, I don't want to live my life without God. At the same time, I don't want to live my life alone, and there doesn't seem to be much room in the middle.

I'm writing to tell you I'm going to attend your service on same-sex relationships. I know you will say it's wrong and not what God intended. My fear increases every day, knowing the turmoil and hopelessness hearing that will produce. Will you tell the hypocritical Christians to show a little love and compassion? The life of a gay person is hard and feeling the hate only makes us run further away from God.

—Rebecca

After I read that email to Amy, Renee, and Robert, they all changed their minds. That weekend in faith rather than fear, they boldly proclaimed what God was doing in their lives. Rebecca was listening attentively:

Listening to Amy and Renee gave me hope that I could break out of my cell. I saw that they had been in the exact same cell, they broke free, and they were reaching back to help others find their way out. I often sit in amazement at the thought that they could have remained silent.

What I found that day was hope. Hope that I didn't have to figure it out; I just had to walk with Jesus and trust him. Hope was step one, but hope needs help. As I listened to message after message, I realized I needed spiritual friends to walk with me. I prayed for them, and they came. I got in a group that helps people struggling from all kinds of sexual brokenness walk toward healing and wholeness. I realized I wasn't alone.

I met Karin, who became my cheerleader and introduced me to others who accepted me, loved me, and supported me. God used Karin's gift of encouragement to motivate me to take steps two and three out of my cell toward community. Learning the teachings of Jesus and processing them in community, I was able to identify the two lies that had kept me locked up— an illegitimate view of God and an illegitimate view of myself.

Over the next few years, Rebecca grew stronger as she experienced healing, wholeness, and increased freedom. She began serving others like Jennifer. God used Rebecca's Christlike love, combined with meeting other Christians, to open Jennifer up to learn. But Jennifer needed time to learn about the way of Jesus. That started in the sports bar that day. After that, Jennifer came weekly to church with Rebecca while continuing to do things sporadically with the Round Rock Network. After about four months of listening and learning, Jennifer got into Rebecca's small group. Eight months later, Jennifer got baptized as a follower of Jesus.

Time to Learn

By now, hopefully you can see the commonalities in so many of these stories. Not only does a person from our post-Christian world need to encounter someone with the heart of Jesus and meet several Christians loving and serving like Jesus, they also need time! They need time to learn and understand the way of Christ because they really don't know much more than hearsay. We can't expect people to clean up their lives before learning about God and his restoration process. They need space to come "as is" and learn without pressure, where it's okay to have doubts, questions, and struggles as they grow in the knowledge of the Lord.

Kathy and I led a team of ten American college students who all moved to Russia for one year right after the fall of seventy years of atheistic communism. No one would ever think that you could go to a people who knew nothing about God, Jesus, or the Bible and just give them a few trite phrases about God sending Jesus to pay for their sins, then expect them to pray a prayer, and *voilà!*, they want to follow Jesus. Not at all! They needed to learn enough to know *who* it is they're following, *why* they would want to follow him, and *how* to actually follow him.

At Verve, a church we helped start in Las Vegas, Tommy got a job in a tattoo parlor, built friendships, and led three guys to faith, but it took time and learning. When one of the guys, Ben, first started discussing faith with Tommy, Ben asked, "Now I hear about this Jesus guy and the Virgin Mary, but what do they have to do with each other?" People just don't know, and the little they do know gets all convoluted and misunderstood.

Yet many Christians still act like we live in an Acts 2 culture. In Acts 2, Peter simply reminded the Jews listening about all the stories of the Exodus, the words of the prophets, and how Jesus fulfilled what they already knew from the Old Testament. Then he called for repentance, and three thousand people turned to follow Jesus as Messiah.

As James White says, we don't live in an Acts 2 culture like many Western countries did from 1900 to the 1960s. Those were times when people knew and respected the Bible and understood who Jesus claimed to be and basically what he taught. We live in the culture of Acts 14–17. It is a culture more like that of Athens, where Paul had to start with where they lived. Paul began by finding traces of truth hidden in their misconstrued idol worship, he quoted their pagan poets and prophets, he pointed out where God was already at work, and he taught the way of Jesus daily in the marketplace. It takes time, usually six to eighteen months, for people to learn the way of Jesus in order to decide if they want to follow him. The question we must ask is, "Where will they learn?"

"Come As You Are" Venues

Even in a Jewish culture very familiar with the Old Testament Scriptures, Jesus made the effort to create "come as you are" venues. He knew the tax collectors and "sinners" of his day were not about to set foot in the synagogue; that's where they felt condemned by the religious elite. So Jesus taught in the synagogues, but he also created places where anybody could come and learn about the goodness of the Father and the way of God's kingdom.

Consider what Jesus did and how he taught, and then reflect on whether we as his church (Jesus' body on earth) are doing what Jesus did. Matthew says that just before his famous Sermon on the Mount, "When Jesus saw the crowds, he went up on a mountainside and sat down. His disciples came to him, and he began to teach them" (5:1–2). He taught a mixed crowd. On one side stood the pharisaical religious Bible scholars (scoffing because they knew more), on the other side the tax collectors and "sinners" listened in, and in the middle sat the ordinary fishermen who became his disciples. And Jesus taught them all with authority in such a way that everyone could understand: "The crowds were amazed at his teaching" (Matthew 7:28).

Jesus created these open-air venues, safe places, relatable places with relatable teaching, so that even those far from God could come and learn right alongside everyone else. Luke 15 says, "Now the tax collectors and sinners were all gathering around to hear Jesus. But the Pharisees and the teachers of the law muttered, 'This man welcomes sinners'" (vv. 1–2). Jesus responded by teaching all of them about the Father's heart that searches for and runs after his prodigal sons and daughters. He helped all people see the heart of God and what it means practically to trust God and let his kingdom come into a life.

Another time it says, "All the people, even the tax collectors, when they heard Jesus' words, acknowledged that God's way was right" (Luke 7:29). Again and again we see Jesus teaching a mixed audience of "tax-collector-sinners," disciples, and Pharisees: "Jesus said to the crowds and to his disciples . . . '[The Pharisees] tie up heavy, cumbersome loads and put them on other people's shoulders, but they themselves are not willing to lift a finger to move them'" (Matthew 23:1, 4).

Do we Christians inadvertently act like Pharisees when we only think about ourselves: the type of service we want, the worship we want, the teaching we want? Like we want it. When we want it. (If not, we're going somewhere else!) Do we ever even think about those far from God, burdened and without hope? Where can they come and learn about God's grace, "as is," and in ways they can understand? If we are going to be like Jesus in our attitude *and actions*, we must create "come as you are" venues where doubters, skeptics, sinners, and saints can all come and learn the way of Jesus together. That can happen in small ways in any church.

Teach Like Jesus

Jesus never once preached expositionally, verse by verse, through any books of the Hebrew Bible. Instead, he taught about God's character, inspiring people to trust in a God who is good—a God who has good intentions for all people (1 Timothy 2:4). He taught about God's will and ways (his kingdom rule) as they related to everyday life, including worry, prayer, giving, lust, anger, enemies, treasure, people-pleasing, marriage, and divorce. His focus was on getting everyone to trust God fully, whether it was the tax-collector-sinner, disciple, or Pharisee. Take a first step of trust, trust God first, and all these other things will work out (Matthew 6:33).

Personally, I love to listen to and teach the Bible in an in-depth, verse-by-verse, expositional style. I'm not in any way saying this is wrong or bad. I believe Jesus did take his closest disciples aside and instructed them deeper in the nuanced meanings of the Scriptures. (Luke 24:27, 44 and Mark 4:34 indicate this.) But this happened in venues designed to equip Christians to be on mission with him.

If your church service speaks mostly to Christians, then you must find ways to create other venues where all can come "as is" and learn about Jesus. These learning spaces must focus primarily on helping people know God and trust him fully as it relates to living life following God's Spirit. This can still challenge the believer and the nonbeliever.

So let's look at some different ways these "come as you are" learning spaces can be created. Different churches or groups will use different forms, but the function needs to be the same: to create a place that uses language, teaching, and music or art (if that's included) that meets nonbelieving people on their own turf, so they can explore biblical faith without additional barriers being put in their way. This means we simply acknowledge they are there with questions or struggles and that they are welcome. It means we cut out all "Christianese" or define terms so that it doesn't feel like we're speaking a foreign language (see appendix A). It means we are willing to address or at least acknowledge the questions and resistance they might have to these new ideas about God and faith.

It doesn't mean we water down the truths of the Scriptures, but we do need to think harder about their questions: "Why would God say that?" "What's the point?" "Why is God's way better than my way?" "How does that actually work in real life?"

Inspiring Worship Services

One way to create "come as you are" learning space is in a church worship service. Your church might not currently design a service that considers both the believer and nonbeliever (like Jesus' hillside

244

sermons), but sometimes a few minor tweaks is all it takes to create safety for those exploring faith. Some churches will be open to starting alternative services, and we will also explore options other than a church service. But let me explain the values that need to be present in any "come as you are" learning space.

Doubters Welcome

At Gateway, our Sunday service has morphed and changed over the years, but several key values have remained constant that allow believers to be challenged and spiritual explorers to learn. We simply acknowledge and welcome people who are skeptical, doubting, or struggling with faith. We regularly say, "Doubters are welcome here," and "No perfect people allowed," because when people pretend they have no struggles, questions, or sins, they just stay stuck. This is a small tweak that any church can make—acknowledging and welcoming doubting people.

People searching for God come and go through many churches, often feeling like they just don't fit, they wouldn't be welcomed if people knew their junk, or their doubts or cynical thoughts wouldn't be tolerated. Often, all it takes is being welcomed and acknowledged, and they stay and find faith.

Christy said, "I remember my first day at Gateway. A friend invited me, and Ted was giving the message. He talked about how doubters are welcome here, and I thought, 'Wow, this is talking to me.' If ever there was a doubter who needed to be in church it was me, and there I was. So my husband and I kept coming, and we started inviting our friends." Christy soon had twenty nonbelieving friends sitting around her; many of them found faith before she finally did.

Address Resistance

Another value is simply acknowledging people's questions and resistance. No one fully trusts God, so everyone has some resistance, even long-time Christians! If we didn't, then every Christian would tithe, but most don't. Why? Because we don't know or trust God's character, his good intentions, or his will and ways!

The same could be said about most topics: worry, decision making, learning to really love your spouse when it's difficult, patience, integrity at work, debt, . . . I could go on and on. Most people's problems boil down to not really trusting God. So that's where Christians and non-Christians alike actually find common ground! At Gateway, we try to inspire all people to know God's character, to know his will and ways and why his is a better way, and to take next steps of trust in everyday life—whether a first step of trust for a nonbeliever, or a next step of trust for a believer.

Again, this is a tweak most churches could fairly easily make—simply acknowledging the questions and resistance of both believers and skeptics. You would think acknowledging or bringing up questions or doubts would cause lack of faith, but actually it helps people work through those concerns faster.

Teach What Matters Most

Another value we uphold in our services is to teach what matters most. Think about it: The most consistent church attendees these days come two or three times per month. That means the best-case scenario is that a person receives less than twenty hours of teaching from the Scriptures *per year*! (Assuming a thirty-minute message each Sunday). Do we really think we can fully equip and teach the full counsel of God in twenty hours a year? People watch 1,500 hours of TV per year—where are we being spiritually formed?

Consider also that many people move every few years, so we can't even count on long periods of time. So true discipleship and deeper learning of the Scriptures must happen elsewhere—in small groups, in daily reading and study, and in classes.

What we need to ensure in our twenty hours per year of Sunday instruction is that people will be clear about what matters most and be inspired to take next steps to go deeper throughout the week. That's why a service designed for "come as you are" learning for both believers and skeptics must hit on the essentials regularly: emphasizing God's character and heart, how and why Jesus makes a way to be restored to God by grace, how God's Spirit guides us into Life, why the Scriptures should be studied and trusted, the hows and whys of prayer, and the importance of authentic, confessing community.

Use the Arts

When you think about our Western context, what would it mean to contextualize the message of Jesus? Well, the most influential shapers of society without a doubt are movies, music, and video. That's the language of Western civilization. Paul went to Athens and quoted their poets and prophets and debated with the philosophers because that's what people of his day spent their time doing. Just as Paul built bridges from truth he found in the words of pagan poets or prophets, we can build bridges from songs, movies, or videos in our culture to the longing we have for God and his ways.

I'll never forget one soccer team party when David, the soccer dad I talked about in chapter 11, had started attending our services and said, "Man, you guys have ruined more good songs for me. I can hardly ever hear a song without thinking about your message. Like that Lenny Kravitz song, 'Love Revolution.' I was flying somewhere listening to it, and I kept thinking about your message all day." Exactly! The creative expression of truth in music, movie, art, or story not only communicates to the head but also to the heart, propelling people forward toward faith.

An Evil Clown

Verve Church in Las Vegas has a similar service to ours. Warren♦ the Clown came to destroy Verve. You see, Warren was not a nice clown. Warren was a hard-core atheist who worked at a horror show in Vegas. His job as a fire-breathing evil clown was basically to scare and intimidate people for a living. A family member found Verve and asked Warren to try it. Warren decided not only to try it but also to destroy this fledgling church in its infancy.

His plan was to wait until the pastor got up to speak, and then Warren would stand up, curse the pastor out in the foulest imaginable way, throw a chair at him, and force them to kick him out of the church. He planned out exactly what he would say, thinking if he made it bad enough, disgusting and abusive enough, no one would come back. But when he showed up to the service, he was surprised.

The people in the lobby didn't look at him with judgmental looks like he expected; they welcomed him. The band started playing, and it was actually music he could relate to. There was humor, and it was actually funny. He got intrigued by the message about Jesus and understood it. Finally the service ended and Warren realized, "I forgot to do my thing." So Warren came back the following week, and the next.

Vince,♦ Verve's pastor, recalls, "Pretty soon I met Warren and started talking to him. And then I realized that Warren was coming to all three of our identical worship services. I said, 'Warren, you do realize they're all the same?' He said, 'Yeah, ummm, I . . . I just can't get enough of Jesus.'" Between March and September, he listened and learned, got involved in next-step classes to learn more, met a "tribe" of Christians he liked, and about eight months after coming to kill the church, the old Warren was put to death. He got baptized and started following Jesus.[1]

Internet Church

Robert♦ grew up in the Netherlands, came to Austin, and a co-worker invited him to Gateway, where he started following Jesus. He discovered a way to reach out to his friends like his co-worker had for him. Robert invited about fifteen of his unchurched friends in Holland to watch our Inspire worship service over the Internet.

Now they watch, hang out for dinner afterward, and have great conversation with Robert through Skype.

We didn't plan it, but this same scenario started playing out around the globe. As I mentioned in chapter 10, Bryan and Amy started showing our service on a big screen at Denny's for the homeless migrant workers in Branson. Now it's grown to a weekly gathering of close to 100 people. A woman in Austin got her non-Christian friends in New York to watch the service online and then talk about it that afternoon on Skype. Remember Gregg from chapter 10? He's a pig farmer in southern Australia who invited his ranching neighbors to come watch in his living room. Now they have several house churches that network together in Australia to minister to prisoners and their families.

Our Inspire service (Sunday morning service) has been piped into bars, homes, school auditoriums, performing arts centers, and condo clubhouses. Even if your church does not have a service you could invite your non-Christian friends to, you can create your own starting in your home and let it grow, then connect them back into your local church body. Connection into a local church body is critical for growth as followers of Jesus.

As you build relational momentum, serving your neighbors with your neighbors, you can invite them to "come as you are" venues where they can learn the way of Christ at their own pace. Schedule it around a meal so you also have opportunity for laughter and natural conversation. Or take all these principles and create your own venue.

Alpha Courses

A completely different form that achieves the same function of "come as you are" learning space is the Alpha course, or similar seminar-style approaches. Alpha has been successful in many European and North American contexts as a way to expose people to the basic teachings of faith in a way that engages head and heart relationally. Listen to the way Alpha describes their course and you'll hear some of the principles I've been talking about:

> Alpha gives everyone the opportunity to explore the meaning of life in a relaxed, friendly setting. The Alpha course usually meets once a week for 10 weeks, including a one-day or week-end getaway. Sessions begin with a meal, followed by a short talk and time to discuss what's been taught. During the discussion, everyone is welcome to contribute their opinions and no question is considered hostile or too simple. . . . People attend from all backgrounds, religions, and viewpoints. They come to investigate questions about the existence of God, the purpose of life, the afterlife, the claims of Jesus and more. Some people want to get beyond religion and find a relationship with God that really changes life. Others come for the close, long-lasting friendships that are built during the Alpha course. Many guests have never been to church, others may have attended church occasionally but feel they have never really understood the basics of the Christian faith. Everyone is welcome.[2]

Your growing Network could host an Alpha course, or create an ongoing investigative seminar of your own. Our Arts Network is filled with musicians, so they started playing gigs at coffee shops or other venues and then having "Quote Studies," where they bring in quotes from famous people, all based on wisdom that ties back to the book of James. It creates an open dialogue about spiritual meaning in a setting where anyone can come or go freely.

Open Small Groups

Finally, small groups meeting in homes can also provide "come as you are" learning space. It's important that the leader set the tone and ground rules so that the group does not accidentally gang up on a person exploring faith. This can happen if group members quickly correct a theologically errant statement, or if everyone eagerly jumps to answer a doubt, or if they quickly try to fix what's wrong if someone shares a struggle or trial. An open small group must learn to be okay with messy people in process, who may be saying wrong things, still doing wrong things, or struggling to understand some things. The small group must realize that time to learn will sort out a lot of this.

When we first started Gateway Church, I led a small group with three other Christians and nine people at various stages of exploring faith. The first night Ron raised his hand and asked if he and Shannon could take a smoking break. Paul quickly said, "Yeah, I can't concentrate if I don't get a smoke." Things were said in that group that made my theological head spin, and I had to keep praying for discernment, "Lord, do I correct it or let it go?" At times I'd drive away from the group asking, "Lord, is this legal? Is this okay? Because it sure seems messy."

But we also studied the book of Matthew, taking time to talk about what it meant and how to practically live it, and I saw more of the Masterpiece revealed as God did his cleansing work. Within two years, all thirteen people were fully following Christ. They had done things such as overcome addictions to alcohol, cocaine, and cigarettes; found healing from sexual sins of the past; and reconciled a marriage. All were using their gifts to serve others. In time, all but two became leaders in our church or other churches!

If your group can focus on loving community, accepting one another as Christ accepts us, being vulnerable, real human beings, listening and trying to understand the other person's point of view, and sharing your own point of view and understanding of the Scriptures with integrity, this will go a long way. Loving community leads people to faith. Remember what Jesus said we should be known for most? "Everyone will know that you are my disciples, if you love one another" (John 13:35).

Garry Poole has developed some excellent training and material for leading groups with both Christians and non-Christians.[3] I wrote several chapters as well in No Perfect People Allowed to help you understand how to relate to culture, and I give real examples to help you talk to people about tough issues that come up, like questions about other religions, gay people, living together, and sex before marriage.

Whether in a worship service, a seminar, or small group, if you create a "come as you are" learning space, God will use it.

Church Fight

Doug* and Rosey* moved from Arizona feeling no need for God, but their wild party life was not good for their marriage or their kids. Austin gave them a chance to start a new life, get sober, and do a better job raising their children. Doug reflects that their success and wealth from his business disguised all the cracks in the foundation of life.

One night Doug had a vivid dream that someone invited him to church. Doug had run from God for years, but in the dream he accepted the invitation, went to the church, and someone asked, "Instead of just attending, would you like to be a part of this church?" He said yes and found himself up on stage at the center of everything along with a group of people.

A co-worker had invited Doug to play softball with a Gateway team. Doug liked the people he played with, and coincidentally the same week he had the dream, one of the players invited him to attend Gateway's Inspire service. With the dream fresh in his mind, he accepted.

Rosey was an atheist. She grew up in a very chaotic family situation and so concluded there can't be a God. But a mom at her kids' preschool befriended her and invited her to join their moms' group. Dying for friendship with other young moms, Rosey started going and became friends with these moms. Samantha and several other women in the group went to the same church, and they just happened to invite Rosey to go to their church the same day the softball team invited Doug. Rosey agreed to go, only because she didn't want to hurt their feelings.

Doug came home from softball with resolve, but fully anticipating Rosey would put up a fight about going to church. "Rosey, I think we need to go check out church this weekend."

"That's funny you should say that," Rosey replied, "because I just committed us to go check out Samantha's church—it sounds like something I could at least tolerate."

"No, I told Eric and Zack on my softball team that we'd go to their church," Doug responded matter-of-factly.

"We can't," Rosey said, flustered. "I already committed to go with Sam. You can't do this to me. I'm only going because these friendships are important to me."

"What about me?" Doug replied. As soon as he said it, he knew inside this was headed south, but momentum took him down. Doug and Rosey ended up in the toilet bowl of marital conflict, spiraling down the drain into an all-out fight over whose friends mattered more and which church to attend. Sunday came and they were still quarreling, but Doug, the salesman, won.

As they pulled into the parking lot of the church, Rosey burst out laughing, "Gateway? That's where we're going? That's Sam's church!" They had been fighting about going to the same church!

Doug reflects, "We continued going to church for two very different reasons, however. . . . I continued because I had turned my back on God, but I started to see that he was for me, not against me. And Gateway was the only place I'd ever been where people could spill their problems and brokenness, and I could see God actually doing something in their lives."

"I continued to go," Rosey recalls, "because every week, I heard exactly what I needed to hear. Not always what I wanted to hear, but always what I needed. At that point, I could care less about how to get to heaven or some invisible Spirit that lives in people. But as Doug and I started applying practical lessons directly from Scripture in our lives and in our marriage, I started to see that this Jesus guy was on to something."

Four months later, Doug had recommitted his life to Christ, but Rosey still had resistance. "We were headed to the Sunday service,"

Doug recalls, "when we noticed people getting baptized in a pool with lousy water chemistry (sorry, I'm a pool guy)." Doug teasingly said, "Hey, honey, you can get baptized today."

"Not a chance," Rosey mocked. "They can have their fun getting wet without me." But God did something in Rosey's heart that day in the service. She opened her heart to Christ and got baptized.

"I saw regeneration happen right before my eyes," Doug reflects. "I can't think about it without choking up because God has so transformed our family since that day." Doug got in a small group with the men from softball, and Rosey joined a small group with the moms. Doug said their spiritual growth healed their marriage, which was on the brink of divorce. Today Doug leads a men's group and Rosey leads a teen moms' group in our Cedar Park Network.

Having "come as you are" learning space combined with smaller groups for life-on-life discipleship is critical to seeing the Masterpiece restored in individuals and the church raised up out of the culture. A small group is actually where Jesus invested most of his time. Understanding why this was his core strategy is what we'll dive into next.

QUESTIONS AND ACTIONS

1. Reflect on this: Where could you bring people exploring faith where they could learn about the way of Christ? If you can't think of a place, how could you help create one for your church or group?

2. Try this: If you have a place to bring people exploring faith, invite a few people this week. Do not be discouraged if they don't respond right away; it usually takes multiple invites (like 5–7). Even if you're not sure if it's a good place to explore faith, ask for their help: "Would you help me and my friends with a project? We're trying to figure out what would need to change (in our church service) to help people feel comfortable exploring faith if they wanted to. Would you come and just give us feedback about what would help you if you were interested in exploring Christian faith?"

14

Everyone Can Develop Someone

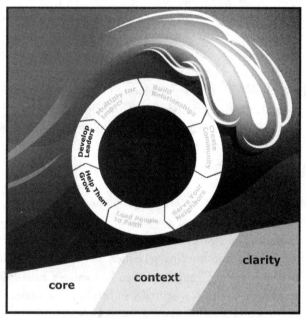

Wave of Impact

J esus had a plan to change the world. It started with serving people at their point of need and helping them learn the way of God's kingdom, but then he focused on very small movements—with twelve—that grew into a powerful wave of influence! As we've seen in this study of Jesus' encounters, for one year Jesus basically said, "Come and see" (John 1:39 NLT).

People would come and go, listening to him teach on the hillsides, deciding if they believed in him. He called people to follow him. How he did this has been the focus of this book, making sure our attitudes and actions match his. But we must also see that Jesus had a plan for helping people to grow deep spiritual roots. He couldn't have a lasting impact on thousands at a time on a hillside or hundreds in a synagogue; it had to be life on life, like one molecule of water transferring God's loving energy to those around them. After a year of people learning to follow Jesus, he did something deliberate that we too must do. He called out and equipped a small group of twelve.

As a Network of people grows up out of the culture around you, it will be critical that you connect people into open small groups where they can begin to develop in faith. This is why we advise that a co-missioned core starts with a Network Leader, Serve Leader, and Small Group/Discipleship Group Leader. As we will see, "everyone can develop someone," but for this to happen, a Christ-follower must be willing to invest spiritually in helping that person grow. That's where Doug and Rosey's story picks back up.

Brandon◆ could not pull himself out of despair. He had always succeeded in everything he had ever done. Coming to Austin for Allie to get her master's degree, plus the GE business opportunity he had been offered seemed so right to Brandon and his new bride. But it became their undoing. *If only I had known. What could I have done differently?* The questions ricocheted like bullets off the walls of his mind, wounding him deeper. *How could she just leave me?*

Doing a Google search, Brandon found our Divorce Recovery ministry. Brandon went, and during those ten weeks, he started to explore faith in Jesus. Brandon met Kirby,♦ who had just started a small group with ten guys, and Kirby invited him to join them. Over the next year, Brandon found faith and the whole group baptized him in a pool.

The group bonded through a weekend retreat where they each told their life story, did a faith-building exercise, and prayed for each other's hopes and dreams. That year, they went through *Morph*, our spiritual formation intensive, did serving projects together, learned to inductively study the Bible through Colossians, discovered how to walk with God's Spirit, and became friends.

The next year, Kirby taught them about Jesus' method of investing in a small group and commissioned them to do the same. He challenged them all to begin praying about who God wanted them to build into spiritually. Brandon didn't feel like he could possibly do that, but Kirby encouraged him, saying, "I'll coach you through the whole thing. You just start to pray about who God's putting in your life." Brandon started a group and Doug (Rosey's husband) joined. In Brandon's group, true transformation began in Doug's life.

Called to Be Equipped

After about a year of exploring faith, many observing Jesus did believe. Now notice what Jesus did: He continued to serve and teach many, but he focused on equipping a few! "'Come, follow me,' Jesus said, 'and I will make you fishers of men'" (Matthew 4:19 NIV 1984). They weren't fishers of men yet; they needed to be equipped, and that's what Jesus focused on for the next year. If you want to make a *huge* difference in the world, focus on investing in a few. This was Jesus' strategy. Why?

Have you ever wondered why Jesus didn't come in the age of technology? He could have blasted everyone's Facebook with his message. He could have started a global TV ministry or his own YouTube channel. Surely that would have been faster. But it says he came "at just the right time" (Romans 5:6). And he had a method for changing the world, one life at a time. Because the message of Jesus is *relational*!

Jesus' message centers on *loving God* by obediently following his Spirit, *so that* he can lead us to *love others* in a new way—that only passes life to life to life. God restores the Masterpiece in us through others, and he calls us to lovingly invest in restoring the Masterpiece in others so that one life at a time, he changes the world. He invested in a few: "He appointed twelve that they might *be with* him and that he might *send them out*" (Mark 3:14, italics mine). Jesus relationally invested time *being with them*, and he made it clear he was equipping them *to send them* to do ministry. Both are critical for spiritual transformation to sink in and pass on.

Jesus called twelve guys who followed him everywhere. For about one year, he intensely equipped them to walk with God. He took them aside and explained things to them, he loved them and built into them, and he prepared them to be able to do the same for others.

Intentional and Transferable

It's important to recognize the developmental nature of spiritual growth. People grow along a path through seasons of faith. (At Gateway, we call these seasons Discover, Develop, and Deepen.) Through each season, they grow deeper in the way of Christ (Loving God, Loving People, Building Character or spiritual fruits, and Being the Body). Though a person needs to grow in loving God during the Discover season, she will have different outcomes than someone in the Deepen season. A person never stops growing deeper in loving God, or any of the areas of the way of Christ.

258

For small groups (8–15) or Spiritual Running Partners (a subgroup of 2–4 people running the race of faith in total transparency), it's important to recognize which season individuals are in and realize that group life will go through phases depending on the season. When a group first forms and includes the Discover season, people are finding faith and the group may be mixed with Christians and those still exploring. The most important thing to establish in this phase of group life is loving community.

If a group of people eats together, laughs together, and learns to be real and vulnerable with each other, then they will be able to go deep spiritually and study the Scriptures for years together. However, if that group tries to go too deep too fast, or gets too studious with no real life or fun or transparency, I can almost guarantee the group won't last more than a year. On the other extreme, if a group stays in loving community but just becomes a book club for years, people stagnate spiritually.

When most members are ready for the Develop season (which should come within six to eighteen months of a group forming, depending on the members of the group) intentionality and transferability are critical. Jesus asked the twelve for a commitment to intentional equipping: "If you will follow me, I will equip you" (see Matthew 4:19). In this phase of group life, a leader needs to challenge people to commit to a season of spiritual development with expectations clearly spelled out for the leader and the group—what are we committing to for this season?

Make sure the people you're going to focus on spiritually developing are F.A.S.T.: Faithful, Available, Spirit-filled, and Teachable.[1]

Faithful—The person is not flaky; you can count on him doing what he says.

Available—Can he commit to be present each week? Sometimes work schedules or season-of-life issues make it impossible to really develop a person. Make sure those you hope to invest in count the cost and commit.

Spirit-filled—Does this person walk with and obey God's Spirit?

Teachable—Is this person eager to learn more about the way of Christ?

Remember, Jesus prayed all night before calling those he would equip (Luke 6:12–13), so take time to pray and challenge them one-on-one and make sure they're F.A.S.T.

There are many ways to equip or disciple a follower of Jesus in the Develop season. There is no one right way or that path would be very clear in Scripture. However, there are principles we see in Jesus that we can pay attention to. Make the curriculum three-dimensional: knowledge, relationships, and practices. Too many "discipleship" curriculums I've used over the years focus solely on head knowledge but neglect equipping people to live in loving, life-giving, conflict-solving relationships, or they don't help people experiment with spiritual practices that develop new habits of spiritual growth.

Whatever curriculum or path you or your church chooses, make sure it's transferable. In other words, you want to equip people to move from the Develop season into the Deepen season, where they can equip others. This happens best if you can say, "Okay, now you do with others what we've just done together as a group." If it is easily transferable, then it can help equip life by life.

Because Brandon had just gone through *Morph* with Kirby and his group, Brandon assembled this new group with Doug, and he did the same. If you're truly seeing the culture become followers of Jesus, new groups should have a diversity of people Discovering or Developing in faith. In Brandon's case, the fifteen guys in his group were mostly new to faith, some more than others.

With Kirby's coaching, Brandon noticed that Doug and three other guys were F.A.S.T.—though fairly new to faith, they couldn't get enough. While Brandon's entire group was not ready for the Develop season, Brandon pulled Doug and three others into a subgroup of Spiritual Running Partners to go through *Morph*— *Love God*, part of a spiritual formation curriculum we developed at Gateway. Within a few years, three of these guys used *Morph* to lead others spiritually. Transferability is key.

Morph

While there are many different discipleship curriculums you could use, there are several outcomes you want to look for in the Develop season. Do they know what it means to truly *love God*? Do they understand God's character and goodness so they trust him? Have they developed habits of reading the Scriptures so they keep learning about God? But even more, do they know what idols usually get in their way of putting God first? Unless we help people understand their deepest desires, they will often give lip service to God, but serve idols in reality. We must help them consider what they think they want—success, fun, money, marriage—versus what they deep down want, and God wants for them—not just success but security, not just fun but joy, not just money but contentment, not just marriage but love.

Do they know what it means to *love people*? Jesus said if we don't love people well, we don't love God. Yet most spiritual formation fails to equip people to actually build others up instead of judging and tearing others down, resolve conflict quickly, listen and care so people feel loved, and understand the essential need for confessing community. "Whoever does not love their brother and sister, whom they have seen, cannot love God, whom they have not seen. And he has given us this command: Anyone who loves God must also love their brother and sister" (1 John 4:20–21). If our discipleship does not produce more loving people, clearly something is wrong.

Do they know how to abide in Christ so that they *build character* (or the fruits of the Spirit)? Jesus said, "I am the vine; you are the branches. If you remain in me and I in you, you will bear much fruit; apart from me you can do nothing" (John 15:5). If Jesus is telling the truth, then teaching people to "abide in Christ" or "walk in the Spirit" is central. Nothing's more important! In fact, if we

261

teach people to study the Bible, pray, fast, tithe, and serve, but fail to teach them to abide in Christ in an ongoing way, what have we accomplished according to Jesus? Nothing! *Soul Revolution* is a book I wrote to lead people through a sixty-day experiment of abiding in Christ, including stories of the amazing ways God shows up when we do what's central.

Do they know how to *Be the Body*? Jesus' church is called his body, but most people don't see themselves as this interdependent, divinely orchestrated movement of uniquely gifted parts working together. We need to help people see their God-given time, gifts, service, and financial resources as opportunities to co-labor with God and his body.

Rick Shurtz and Sherilyn Villareal developed a three-dimensional spiritual formation curriculum called *Morph* (available online at www.gatewayleaders.com). *Morph* is divided into four eight-week modules around *Loving God, Loving People, Building Character*, and *Being the Body*. It's not the only path to spiritual formation, but it's a really good one you may want to assess. Other discipleship curriculum I would recommend considering can be found in the notes.[2]

Even more important than the curriculum or books you choose is clarity on what outcomes you hope the people in your group establish. For a list of the outcomes we shoot for in the different seasons of spiritual growth, refer to lifegroup.gatewaychurch.com/be-transformed.

From Joints to Jesus

Wade got into Rick's Network because his wife had been asking if they could join a small group together. He always resisted the idea because he didn't really care to share his thoughts and feelings in front of a group of strangers, but he decided he would give it a try. When our church did *Soul Revolution*, Wade came to faith during the sixty-day experiment. Afterward, Rick's group started the yearlong *Morph* spiritual formation path. During *Morph—Be the Body*, Rick challenged these newly growing Christ-followers to begin praying about whom God wanted them to minister to. Wade said he could never do that. Rick just asked him to do the exercise and pray, "God, whom do you want to minister to through me?"

Wade came back to the group two weeks later with a crazy idea. For years Wade had gathered with a close circle of friends in one of their garages to watch sporting events, talk about life, and smoke pot! Since coming to faith, Wade quit smoking pot, but still remained close to his friends and continued to gather in the garage to show them that he could still love them for who they are, just as Christ loves everyone. He was committed to living his life by example in hopes that this would eventually influence his buddies in a positive way.

His friends noticed a change in his demeanor and eventually told him that they truly admired him for his commitment to Christ. After Wade prayed for God to show him someone to minister to, one of his friends asked him at the gathering, "Hey, dude, we know you stopped smoking up, but you never told us why." Wade saw it as a sign from God, so, with heart beating fast, he told them about doing *Soul Revolution* and how he really saw God at work in his life.

One of the guys said, "Hey, why don't you take us through that!" So he came back and told Rick's group, "I'm gonna be leading my pot-smoking friends through learning to listen and respond obediently to God! Should be interesting!"

Called to Minister

Churches often wait way too long to get a new Christ-follower involved in real ministry. Don't make the development period too long! If someone can't get involved ministering and developing others after two or three years—that's too long. Once people go from the Discover season through the Develop season of intentional growth, it's time to get them taking others through what they went through—this is the entrance into the ministry phase of group life. We must make sure that Deepen (maturity) does *not* mean constant learning but never changing, never leading, never serving with our gifts, never giving of ourselves. That was not the way of Christ!

After one intense year of equipping, "These twelve Jesus sent out with the following instructions: '. . . As you go, preach this message: "The kingdom of heaven is near." Heal the sick, raise the dead, cleanse those who have leprosy, drive out demons. Freely you have received, freely give'" (Matthew 10:5–8 NIV 1984). Think about this—one year earlier, Matthew was a tax collector sitting at his booth, hanging out with his notorious, immoral partier-friends. One year later, Jesus empowered and sent Matthew out to do the *exact* ministry Jesus had been doing!

"It was not Jesus who baptized, but his disciples" (John 4:2). For the next year and a half, Jesus had his disciples baptizing people, praying for people, healing people, and teaching people. He coached them and supported them. "His disciples asked him privately, 'Why couldn't we drive it out?' He replied, 'This kind can come out only by prayer'" (Mark 9:28–29). The disciples succeeded, but they also failed, and Jesus coached them in ministry.

You can have a powerful ministry, no matter what your past story, if you're willing to follow his Spirit and be equipped. Remember it's not by your power, but by God's power that you can accomplish great things. He says he has empowered you to minister to others, so once you're equipped, that's what you need to do. You *will* feel inadequate, you *will* feel like you don't know enough, you *will* think you're not good enough. Welcome to the club—we all did when we started!

I remember when I got to college, Scott Smith♦ invited me and my friend Ken♦ into a Bible study. I was a two-year-old Christian, and Ken was one of the wildest guys in our dorm, but I prayed for him every night because he was my best friend. That year Ken did turn his life over to Christ, and Scott equipped us spiritually.

He taught us how to study the Bible, walk with the Holy Spirit, pray, serve, and tell our spiritual story so that we could share our faith with others.

After about a year of building into us, he said, "Now you guys can invest in others, just like I've invested in you." We said, "No way, we can't do that!" He said, "Yes, you can because Jesus is with you, and I will help you." I remember how terrified I was to lead my first small group. I felt like I was failing, but Scott kept encouraging me and coaching me.

Here's what's amazing: Scott invested in Ken and me and six other guys for two years, and then he graduated. I started leading a small group of guys and so did Ken, and we helped them grow and start to invest in others, and it started to multiply. Four years later, thinking about all the metaphors Jesus used of how the kingdom of God grows secretly, quietly, like a seed that sprouts into many branches that drop other seeds, I decided to track down how Scott's influence had spread through Ken and me. Do you know that 350 people had been spiritually developed in four years—just from Scott to Ken and me, to the guys we invested in, and then to those they invested in. It started small and gained momentum like a growing wave changing lives—that's what God's Spirit does through willing hearts.

Called to Develop Others 3G

The last thing Jesus said to his disciples was

> All authority in heaven and on earth has been given to me. Therefore go and make disciples of all nations, baptizing them in the name of the Father and of the Son and of the Holy Spirit, and teaching them to obey everything I have commanded you. And surely I am with you always, to the very end of the age.
>
> Matthew 28:18–20

Do you see Jesus' plan to reach the nations? He invested in this one small group of twelve. They couldn't possibly help every nation follow Jesus, so this Great Commission must have been for those they would invest in, and so on, and so on, all the way to you and me.

You can go and lead people to faith, and help them to identify with the Father, Son, and Spirit through baptism. Why? Because all authority was given to Jesus, and he's always with you, and he co-missioned you to do it! And you can teach them to observe all he commanded. You don't have to have a teaching gift or seminary degree because you already have Jesus' authority and his presence to help you do it. Just get into the Scriptures, read them together, and follow his Spirit together in confessing community! Emphasize living it—not just knowing it—and help others live it out.

This seems to be the core of how the early church grew. Paul told his young son in the faith, Timothy, "You have heard me teach things that have been confirmed by many reliable witnesses. Now teach these truths to other trustworthy people who will be able to pass them on to others" (2 Timothy 2:2 NLT). Paul spiritually invested in Timothy (one generation), and then charged him to teach and equip trustworthy people (a second generation of F.A.S.T. people), and to help them pass it on to others also (a third generation).

We encourage small group leaders to think and pray for the same 3G impact (developing three generations of multiplying Christ-followers). Kirby built into Brandon and ten other guys (1G). Brandon built into fifteen men (2G). In the same way that Jesus focused more attention on Peter, James, and John out of his twelve disciples, with Kirby's guidance, Brandon focused on more intensive development of the three "FASTest" guys. Doug was one of the three who, a year later, started his own group with guys he knew. Brandon now coaches Doug and two other guys to help them spiritually invest in the men they lead (3G).

If you invest in twelve, who eventually invest in twelve, who also invest in twelve, those three generations of discipleship (living out the Great Commission of Jesus) become a wave of impact that spiritually develops 1,728 people! Think about that. By making the investment to spiritually equip twelve people to know and follow

Jesus, then coaching them to start groups of their own, your life can impact hundreds of lives. Then as you coach those twelve to become coaches of others, thousands of lives can be spiritually developed.

And don't forget, this is not some money-making pyramid scheme; this is about restoring God's greatest Work of Art! Do you see the exponential power of what Jesus was doing life by life by life? This is how we've seen thousands of people not only come to faith, but lead and equip others to walk with Jesus.

Now, not everyone will be able to develop twelve people at a time. Maybe your gifts are more behind the scenes and you're more of a one-on-one kind of person. Fine, spiritually invest in one to three other people at a time. Think about it this way: Say you loved and served ten people each year, and one of them came to faith in Christ.

Then suppose you built into that one person for a year, and then helped them do the same for one other person the next year, and while you continued to coach them to develop others to do the same, you kept investing in one new person each year. If everyone turned and invested in one new person each year, those tiny ripples would build into a huge wave. That one life built into the first year grows to three lives developed by year two, seven lives by year three, fifteen by year four, thirty-one by year five.

Remember that we're talking about the most important thing in history—partnering with God to restore the loving Masterpiece in life after life! And if that transformation is life-giving and the vision to pass it on to a new person each year sticks, look what happens after year five. The wave builds exponentially, 63, 127, 255, 511, until ten years later, your life has rippled out to develop 1,023 people! You see what Jesus was doing? If this continued, in 33 years, the entire globe would be reached!

Which leads to a serious question. So why hasn't this happened? The answer is self-centered sin. Humans don't see the value of the Masterpiece, so we don't take the time to partner with God in the development of his most precious resource. People lose perspective, get overwhelmed with busyness, and stop developing others. If we paid as much attention helping lives grow and multiply as we do making money and investments grow and multiply, we'd not only have treasure that lasts, we'd also experience the reward of our lives having a huge wave of influence in the world. It can happen through you because it's Jesus' plan. All he needs is your willingness and faithfulness.

A Stripper, a Plumber, and a Mission

"I was headed to hell, and I'm not going back." Paul's[*] intense look and first words shook Lillian as he regained consciousness in the hospital. "I want to find the God who saved me." Paul had overdosed on cocaine that night, and in the ambulance on the way to the hospital, he flatlined. His heart stopped beating.

Paul clinically died and found himself suddenly sober, but in a hellish experience, falling through utter darkness. "I knew what was happening, and in my mind I kept thinking, *I'm a good person. I'm not supposed to be going here*, but no justification stopped it." In desperation, he cried out to a God he didn't even know, "Lord, save me!" Immediately, a loving presence was with him, asking, "Paul, what have you done with the life I gave you?"

Paul recalls, "In an instant, yet in a way I can't explain, I fully relived every moment of my life. I experienced it all for what it was—no excuses, no hiding, the good and bad. I told him, 'I deserve this. But let me go back and tell others—let me live for you and help others.' It wasn't about me anymore. I desired to serve others. Next thing I knew, I came to in the ER."

Paul had grown up in Houston, the grandson of Mexican immigrants. Against her will, Lillian had immigrated to the United States illegally from Brazil at age twenty with her husband and child. Shortly after bringing her to America, her husband had an affair and left her destitute with a child to feed. She got a job at a restaurant, dedicated and determined to provide for her child amidst her own pain. One night, her boss offered her a ride home. Knowing she couldn't go to the police, he raped her.

She quit that job, but then couldn't find work. That's when a friend convinced her to go to the cabaret. Stripping provided lots of easy money to support her daughter, but she hated it. Soon Lillian was snorting coke with the other dancers to take the pain away. Eventually, she started selling it. After ten years, she hit bottom and went to rehab, where she met Paul.

They moved in together, intending to stay clean, but soon spiraled back down into cocaine use. That is, until the ultimate bottom—near death! That night in the ER changed everything. As soon as Paul got out of the hospital, he and Lillian went to a Spanish-speaking church, where they were baptized for faith in Christ. They both got clean and got married in that church. Two years later, after seeing a billboard advertising a play about heaven and hell, they began attending a suburban church that invited them into a small group. Hungry for growth, they went.

Paul recalls, "Here I was a Mexican-American plumber in a white, upper-middle class small group led by an engineer with a bunch of guys just like him. They didn't get me or the world I came from at all! I intended to quit, but my wife convinced me that God brought us here for a reason, so we stayed.

"Even though Tom, the small group leader, couldn't relate to the world I came from, he loved me," Paul reflects. "He saw past my junk and encouraged me in what I could become. He kept telling us how much we encouraged him, because of what God was doing in our lives. Society called me a loser and an addict, yet here was someone successful saying, 'I believe in you, Paul, and you're gonna do something great for the Lord.'"

Because of the way Tom pointed to the Masterpiece in Paul, Paul began to think, *If Tom believes in me, maybe I am worth something to the Lord.* For the next five years, Tom developed Paul, and Paul began to lead others and catch a vision for developing men spiritually. He also grew his business to the point of success like he had never known before.

Paul's aunt lived in Austin and had gotten deep into witchcraft, which had driven her into despair. About to commit suicide, she cried out to Paul for help. Paul led her to faith in Christ that night, and she woke up free and alive the next day. She begged Paul and Lillian to come to Austin to tell her friends about Jesus, and before they knew it, they were making weekly trips to Austin.

Not long after, feeling the Lord calling them to Austin, they sold their home on the golf course in Houston, sold his plumbing business, and moved. Paul started over, building his new business as a master plumber while he and Lillian gathered a few people into their first small group. As they found ways to serve and interact with the second-generation Mexican-American population, that small group grew into a men's group and a women's group.

With a vision for spiritual multiplication, they equipped these new Christ-followers to love and serve their friends, and within a year or so, those they led were leading others. Feeling called to teach and pastor, Paul started a service where people could invite their friends no matter whether they were coming from the strip club or shaking off a hangover. They began to have quarterly weekend retreats to help people understand the basics of turning to God and allowing God's healing, restoring work in their lives.

As Paul and Lillian kept developing leaders who could minister and spiritually develop others, more and more Mexican-Americans found faith and became the church. While Paul was still working full time as a master plumber, life by life about thirty people started following Christ that first year. By the second year, about 150 people were following Christ. By the third year, nearly 350 people were now part of this church that had no paid staff. Developing people in small groups who can then develop others was making a huge wave of impact!

After five years working as a master plumber, and the church growing to over 500 people, Paul sold his business and became the full-time paid pastor of Austin Powerhouse Church. Well over half the people attending came to faith in this church, a vibrant community that has grown out of the unchurched Mexican-American culture in Austin.

Paul and I come from different theological traditions and different cultures, yet what we do share in common—loving people life by life, calling out the Masterpiece in others—that's transcultural, transdenominational, and transferable to any people group. And life by life a growing wave of liberation rolls across the face of humanity. With God's Spirit blowing across the waters of willing, committed hearts, nothing's impossible, as this next story shows. The question is, "Are you willing?"

QUESTIONS AND ACTIONS

1. Reflect on this: Why do you think the art of developing people (taking time to really invest in others) gets neglected so easily? Jesus said loving God and loving people sums up the whole Bible. How does spiritually developing others to develop others fulfill these commands? Pray that your life will multiply Life through others.

2. Try this: If you have never been developed spiritually, ask God to lead someone into your life to help you develop so you can do the same for others. If you have walked with God for a while, you can develop others because his Spirit is with you, so ask God to show you a few people you can build into.

15

Accelerate and Multiply
With Worship and Teaching

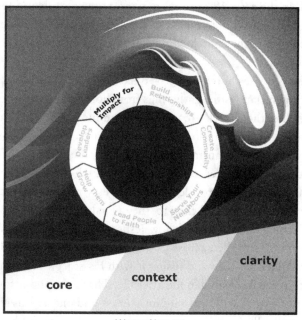

Wave of Impact

In 1966, Mao Zedong made Christianity illegal in China. At that time there were two million Christians in the whole country. Mao expelled all foreign missionaries and leaders from the country, killed all the senior pastors of the churches, and imprisoned all the second- and third-level volunteer leaders in the churches, and for the next decade the Cultural Revolution sought to stamp out the remaining Christians with the worst persecution in recorded history. Many Christ-followers were martyred for their faith.

After Mao's death a decade later, the Cultural Revolution subsided. In the early 1980s, a more tolerant regime allowed foreign missionaries back into China under strict supervision. They expected to find the church completely dead. But what they found was a miracle!

The Chinese church had grown like no other church on earth! Meeting in clandestine gatherings from house to house, investing life by life, the church grew from two million people to an estimated eighty million Christ-followers during a decade of horrible persecution! The mantra of this movement was "Every Christian a house church leader, every church a church-planting church." As they gathered in crowded houses, often with only parts of the Bible to learn from and cling to, they worshiped with lives on the line, risking everything to follow Jesus.[1]

God's Spirit rolled across China like a wave from life to life to life, taking one story and fusing it with his-story—restoring the Masterpiece he created in life after life. That's my prayer for you. That your story will fuse with his-story—and one day his eternal story will tell of a little movement that started in your backyard, that then rippled out and changed your neighborhood, changed your city, changed your world!

Think about it: The Chinese church didn't have worship services with cool bands or angelic choirs; they didn't have great teaching either—in fact, many house churches only had parts of the Bible, if any, to pass around among themselves. No leaders had formal seminary training, and yet these Networks of believers, rising up out of an atheistic, hostile culture accelerated and multiplied.

One Chinese house-church leader writes about how Western Christians who visited China often asked what seminary the leaders attended. He said,

> We reply, jokingly yet with underlying seriousness, that we have been trained in the Holy Spirit Personal Devotion Bible School (prison) for many years.
>
> Sometimes our Western friends don't understand what we mean because they then ask, "What materials do you use in this Bible school?" We reply, "Our only materials are the foot chains that bind us and the leather whips that bruise us."
>
> In this prison seminary, we have learned many valuable lessons about the Lord that we could never have learned from a book. We've come to know God in a deeper way. We understand his goodness and his loving faithfulness to us.[2]

Worship That Accelerates Movement

In the Western church, it is time to rethink what it means to worship and follow Jesus, Lord of the universe, Lord of the harvest. I find too many Christians majoring in the minors: "Where can I worship (i.e. sing songs) where I really feel drawn into the presence of God?" "Where can I be fed with teaching that's new and challenging?" "Where can my kids get the kind of spiritual education that will help them follow God?"

These are good questions in the right context (in the context of being on mission with Jesus). But in the context of just attending church to have your ears tickled with new information, without exercising off the knowledge we've already consumed by engaging a broken world with mercy, it produces a subtle phariseeism.

Worship should not become a weekly "fix" that gives you an emotional high, yet never translates into a heart that breaks over the things that break the heart of God. If that emotion doesn't motivate you to do something, that's just entertainment with a Christian flavor. Thinking one hour on Sunday is going to shape our children into the spiritually grounded, moral, integrity-filled, loving, life-giving adults we want them to become, while we model something less than that the other 167 hours of the week—that's insanity! Unfortunately, what I just described matches much of Western Christianity. That must change if we want to experience God's restoration in us and through us.

Paul said, "I urge you, brothers and sisters, in view of God's mercy, to offer *your bodies* as a living sacrifice, holy and pleasing to God—*this is your true and proper worship*" (Romans 12:1, italics mine). True worship, the kind that pleases God, goes well beyond singing, learning, or an hour of Bible stories for the kids. True worship happens 167 hours a week as we "offer ourselves" moment-by-moment back to the God who has given us every good gift.

In the context of living on mission with Jesus, with his attitude and his actions, the questions of teaching, worship, and molding the next generation are good, important questions because how we answer those questions can accelerate and multiply this surging wave of Life in his Spirit.

Context Matters

Now, before you misunderstand me, I'm not advocating a return to the pure house church model. In some Western contexts, I think that's the most appropriate, effective way to live out what it means to do church where you do life. But I do not believe that all large gatherings for worship and teaching are bad, or all buildings seating more than a hundred are detrimental to a movement of God's Spirit. I've experienced just the opposite! Bringing people together can help to accelerate and multiply movement.

Context does matter, and contextualization is important. Referring back to the Jerusalem council meeting in AD 50, when the church agreed to let Paul strip off all traditional Jewish barriers to contextualize the message of Jesus for a Gentile world, historian Rodney Stark notes:

> By far the most important event in the rise of Christianity was the meeting in Jerusalem . . . the true importance of the Jerusalem council's ruling was not its effects on Paul, but on rank-and-file Christians who now were able to reach out far more effectively to their Gentile friends, relatives, and neighbors—a process that eventually assembled the world's largest religion.[3]

In a media and music driven society, contextualizing services to communicate the gospel in the styles of music, language, and art forms relatable to the culture will be important. And I've seen how large gatherings can create space where people can easily bring friends exploring faith who are not ready for the intimacy of a home.

I've also seen how large gatherings of Christ-followers can be inspired through worship and teaching to take the next steps that accelerate what happens in the neighborhoods and relational gatherings. And worship and teaching in the context of a Network size gathering (20–70) can do so as well. The real issue has less to do with the style of music, style of teaching, or size of gathering and more to do with the hearts of the people involved.

If your Network forms out of an existing church that has not really seen the culture become the church, your church's service can still serve as a rallying point for your Network. Your church service might not be the place you first invite those exploring faith, but it can be the place to gather as a core, sit together, worship together, and learn together in a whole new way, because now you are not just getting spiritually fat, you're exercising the rest of the week on mission with Jesus. You'll have a new appreciation for the service. And hopefully the stories of life change you will be able to tell will inspire others to get out of the seats and into the game.

Of course, if the service is not a "come as you are" learning space for those exploring faith, you will have to create that through some of your Network gatherings. But as people come to faith, it will be important in time to integrate them into the body of the church.

Networks gathering for times of worship and teaching from the Scriptures can be like blowing on the coals of a fire—it just makes it hotter! Find times to gather for worship and encouragement from the Word to stay on mission together. Ministry is not easy. It's a battle against spiritual forces, and it can wear you down without ongoing times of stoking the flames.

We need reminders from God's Word about why this matters. We need to come together to once again yield ourselves to the Lord in true worship, offering surrendered lives, crying out to him to accomplish his work through us. And we need to share stories celebrating what God does among us.

The best worship I've ever experienced and the most fulfilling learning came with ten of us crammed in a small Russian apartment together. Deborah led singing with one guitar, but we poured our hearts out in praise and full surrender of our lives because we were desperate for God. We took turns talking through passages of Scripture, eating it up. Living in a foreign country all year, on mission together, we needed God's Word and his presence, and we needed each other. We had to encourage each other, resolve conflict, and pray for and build up those struggling because we depended on every part of the body. That's church. And God wants his church living on mission together wherever you live.

Birthing New Networks

In the Chinese house church, when they outgrew the number that could gather in a house (sometimes 30 to 50 people shoulder to shoulder), they would send out some to start a new house church. In a similar way here, when volunteer-led Networks grow past the 70 to 100 person size, it's difficult to find community centers or clubhouses large enough to gather, so it's time to prepare to birth a new Network. This is why a Network core group should always be spiritually developing people to apprentice in their roles, those who can one day lead a Network of their own.

Sometimes new Networks form as small groups multiply into six or seven new small groups. Several of the new small groups may be in a part of town where it just makes sense for them to form the core of a new Network that can serve a different population of the city. The beauty of having small-group relationships that can stay together and multiply in the context of a larger Network is that you can maintain your closest relationships in that small group, even as the Network continues to include others and birth new Networks.

One of the greatest challenges Networks will face, especially if most are not connected in close, multiplying small groups, is to become ingrown. It happens to every church, every club, every clique, and every Network! Once we like what we like, we want to protect it from ever changing. Let's face it, new people coming into "our great thing" changes it! But we must remember the parable of the Dead Sea.

The Jordan River flows into two bodies of water: the Sea of Galilee, where Jesus spent most of his time, and the Dead Sea. I've visited both. In fact, we held baptisms in the Sea of Galilee and floated on the Dead Sea. The Sea of Galilee teems with life. The fresh water causes growth in vegetation all around the area, the fishing industry has always thrived because of the abundance of marine life, and it has provided clean water for humans for millennia.

The Dead Sea has the name for a reason—it's dead! The salt content has so built up over the years that nothing can live in the Dead Sea. With a saline content over eight times saltier than the ocean, the Dead Sea is so dense that floating on it feels like lying on a floatie, without a floatie! The land remains barren around the perimeter. No fish or aquatic life can survive the salty environment—it's completely dead! Yet the two bodies of water are only sixty-five miles apart and the same Jordan River flows into both! The difference—water *flows into and out of* the Sea of Galilee. In the Dead Sea, water flows in, but *no water flows out.*

Think People Flow

Networks can become ingrown. People flow in, form community, develop small groups, and make an incredible impact, but in time there is often a tendency to just try to preserve the great thing we've created—and that's death! It may take years for the salinity to build up, but when life does not flow *in and back out*, it will eventually die.

The key to thriving Network life is to think about people flow. We give our Network Leader and core team a diagram of concentric circles as a picture of what Networks are trying to do (see next page). The focus starts with your *Circle of Impact*. Who are the people in your city whom God has uniquely called you to serve? Maybe it starts with your neighbors, or one corporation, or artists, or a marginalized population that your Network will focus on serving until they are following Jesus and restoring others.

Contacts are people you've served, built friendships with, or contacted in your area that you keep inviting to Network parties, serving days, and gatherings. When we started Gateway, this was my email list I used to invite people on the periphery to join us. At times, you may feel like you're bugging them when you invite and they don't show, but I always recall how grateful I am that years ago Randy Worrell kept encouraging me to explore faith. I kept blowing him off, even though deep inside I wanted to figure out this whole God thing. But it's a spiritual battle. Eventually, Randy's persistence paid off as I started attending gatherings, then a small group, and eventually found faith. So remember, it's not about you, and it's good for people to be encouraged to take next steps toward Christ and his community.

The *Crowd* defines those who come and participate each month in some kind of Network event or gathering. The numbers on the diagram refer to minimum and maximum numbers of people for a fully functioning Network. When you have about 25 unique individuals showing up each month to Network gatherings or serving projects, that's when you feel momentum building. Before that,

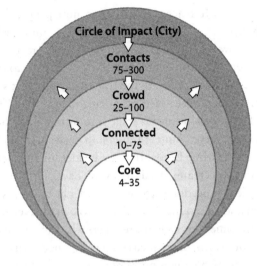

Think People Flow

you're really growing from one or two small groups or a core group into a Network. Usually, in order to see 25 people regularly show up, you have to *Contact* about 75 people you're communicating with regularly about Network functions.

We remind Network leaders to always be thinking about how to help people take next steps (flow), so whenever people show up as part of a *Crowd*, they cast vision for why and how to get *Connected*—either to a small group or serving team. Relational *Connection* is the key turning point for people coming to faith and growing spiritually to become God's Masterpiece. Ultimately, we hope to see the people we serve find faith, grow and serve others, and become part of the *Co-missioned Core*.

The *Co-missioned Core* have grown spiritually in a small group and can now spiritually develop others; they know their gifts and now serve with us in our *City*, and they financially contribute to the church that supports this Network so that it can sustain and multiply. The arrow flows back out from the *Core* to the *City*, and this people-flow movement continues until a new Network is birthed.

When a Network reaches 70 to 100 or more people showing up to something every month, a majority of them connected in small groups and growing, and you have a co-missioned core of 30 or more, then your Network is pregnant with life and it's time to prepare to birth. If the Network falls into the trap of saying, "Let's not serve or invite more people because it's changing what we had," that leads to death. The key to life at this stage is to birth a new Network.

This is why every volunteer leadership position, from Network Leader to Small Group Leader to Serve Leader (or any other volunteer positions you create), needs to always have one or two apprentices. Every leader needs an apprentice leader he or she is spiritually investing in and equipping to fulfill that role in the Network. That way when the time comes, there are others who can step in to lead as a new Network is sent out to focus on serving a new part of the *City*.

The beauty of having a movement of Networks centered on intimate relational multiplying discipleship, connected to larger church-wide or geography-wide gatherings, is that it facilitates growth and multiplication of life without losing relationship. We all have a need for close, intimate, family-like relationships. That happens through Spiritual Running Partners and small groups that stay together but go out to develop others spiritually.

We also need that medium-sized social context of 20 to 100 people (*Cheers* space where "everybody knows your name and they're always glad you came"). Combining the small and medium-sized gatherings with larger weekly or monthly worship services allows Networks to birth while still providing the opportunity to interact with people you got to know in the past. This grows a strong, thriving people flow that can continually flow others in from the culture, send out to the culture, and birth new Networks and groups without losing relational connection.

Finding a Person of Peace

But you don't have to wait for a Network to become full of people to start a new Network. Sometimes new Networks should form because God wants to serve a new people group! Mike Breen has inspired the formation of Networks (which he calls "Clusters" or "Missional Communities") all over Europe. He tells the story of a Network in Sheffield, England, where he started a church of Networks and small groups serving the unchurched populations of Sheffield.

Mike teaches his Networks to look for the "person of peace" Jesus talked about when he sent out the seventy: "When you enter a house, first say, 'Peace to this house.' If someone who promotes peace is there . . . stay there." (Luke 10:5–7). As you serve people, love people, and care about people, look for the person of peace who seems receptive, welcomes you, listens to you, and responds to you—stay there! In other words, focus on building relationship with that receptive person because God's Spirit has probably been working behind the scenes on this person, and he or she could be the link to serve a new Network of people.

There was a large Iranian Muslim population in Sheffield that a few people in one of the Networks felt called to serve. One Iranian man in particular responded very positively to the friendship and service of David, a man in that Network. So David focused on building a deep friendship with Amir. In time, Amir came to follow Jesus. He was that person of peace. As David and others spiritually invested in him, Amir began to introduce David to a new Network of relationships with his Muslim friends. Over several years, these Networks of relationships grew into more than sixty Iranian Muslim people now following Jesus! These sixty Iranians are now a thriving missional community of their own connected to the church in Sheffield.[4]

Restored to Restore Others

God sees a Masterpiece in you. He wants to restore you more and more into that Work of Art he had in mind all along. Don't ever forget that—he saved you by his grace because you are his

Masterpiece, created in Christ Jesus to do the works he prepared for you when you were just an idea in his mind. As you allow him to restore you, that journey will take you into the lives of others who need his restoration work as well. We are restored to restore others. In fact, we can't be restored without allowing the Master Artist to use our lives as tools of restoration in his hands.

People aren't like paintings or marble sculptures that passively cooperate with the Artist; people have wills of their own. They have hurts, wounds, and secret addictions, and people will disappoint you and hurt you and you will disappoint and hurt them. And yet . . . in the mess of our human brokenness, God brings beauty. As we cooperate with him, he restores what's been lost, stained, and broken. As you go with the attitude and actions of Jesus, his Spirit will guide you on the adventure of a lifetime. You will see him do things you never thought possible. You'll realize what Jesus meant when he said, "Nothing is impossible with God" (see Mark 10:27).

All of Jesus' encounters show us this. He entered into the mess with us. He entered into the suffering with us. He entered into deep relationship with us, feeling the disappointment, hurt, and betrayal even to the point of death. Yet in the midst of an imperfect world filled with imperfect people came his greatest work—his Artwork of Grace. And as you learn to worship him with your whole life, living on his mission with Jesus and others, he will restore you and make your life and the lives you encounter into his Masterpiece.

QUESTIONS AND ACTIONS

1. Reflect on this: Have you found yourself thinking about Christian growth as a river flowing into you (to feed you, to encourage you, to have inspiring worship or kids' programs), but never flowing back out to bring life to others? How might giving to others, building into others, restoring others grow you into the Masterpiece God intended?

2. Try this: Start praying and looking for the person of peace. If you've caught a vision for being part of a Network that restores God's Masterpiece in others, make a plan to take next steps to grow that Network. Go to www.mudandthemasterpiece.com for suggested next steps.

Thank You

Solomon said, "There's nothing new under the sun" (Ecclesiastes 1:9). There's also nothing done completely independent of others. I owe many thanks to so many people who helped shape ideas, read manuscripts, gave feedback, and labored for years in the trenches, trying stuff and learning. This book has been a team effort, and I would like to thank those who put time into its coming to fruition, starting with the entire staff at Gateway Church and our awesome volunteer leaders who are the front-line ministers of our church.

I'm extremely grateful to my wife, Kathy, and my kids, Ashley and Justin, for the loving support and encouragement to write. I couldn't, and wouldn't, do any of this without you (God's greatest gift to me). Kathy helped mold and shape ideas, edited, chased down permissions, and cheered me on tirelessly—I love partnering with you in ministry.

Jack Kuhatschek has been an editor and faithful friend for many years now, and I'm so grateful to have your watchful eye and leadership over this project (I'm back!). Michael Warden's editing and insights were superb and flavored every chapter—thanks for your friendship and partnership. Mike Cook has helped get the message out for three books now—thanks for all you do. And Ellen Chalifoux, your editing expertise has been invaluable.

Craig Whitney, who runs our training of church planters, came up with the "Wave of Impact" and much of the process that shaped part 2 of the book. Thanks, Craig, for your partnership and years of proving these concepts out in real life (and for being my global trekie). Lauren Young did the crazy-cool wave graphics for part 2 of the book—thanks Lauren.

Rick Shurtz and Sherilyn Villareal have led the charge forming our Lifegroup and spiritual formation path, and Sherilyn gave great editorial feedback on part 2. Eric Bryant, Jeremy Apel, Gary Foran, Kirby Holmes, TJ Cummins, Karin Harper, and Bruce Gilson have been slugging it out in the trenches alongside our Network and Lifegroup leadership and have contributed to many ideas written in part 2. Thanks for your tireless labor with Jesus and his people.

Tim Hawks and Alan Nagel from my pastors' group encouraged the shaping of part 2 to help churches in Austin and beyond—I love how the Lord is making us One Church in Austin, and I so appreciate your open-handed leadership and encouragement.

Charles Dishinger is the executive pastor leading the charge at Gateway Church, and I can't imagine this book happening without him (thanks for holding up my arms). My assistant Theresa Rozsa keeps me afloat, and I don't accomplish much at all without her constant help. Thanks for your partnership all these years.

Esther Fedorkevich has provided amazing guidance and encouragement, not just as my agent, but as a partner in ministry—thanks for going above and beyond for the greater mission.

Appendix A

Christianese Defined

Christians sometimes use terms that are either foreign to most people or so misconstrued by the culture that we need to redefine them to match their intended meaning in Scripture. I am in no way giving a theologically technical definition here. These are quick explanations for people unfamiliar with Christianese terms. Some of these terms are important and we should not get rid of them; we should simply explain them when we use them. A simple perusal of all the "foreign" terms we use shows you how our insider language can create barriers to those exploring faith.

Baptism—identification with Christ publicly—kind of like a wedding ceremony is the public declaration of a marriage relationship, baptism is a public declaration of relationship with God.

Born again—made spiritually alive by God.

Christian—unfortunately, this term too has been misconstrued, so I find it more helpful to say Christ-follower, as it implies actually following Jesus—which is the real point.

Disciple—a follower of Jesus or a Christ-follower.

Discipleship—spiritual growth in the way of Jesus. Becoming a serious student of Jesus.

Evangelism—I don't use this term anymore because it's been contaminated in our society. Instead, I talk about "serving the spiritual and physical needs of others," or "helping people find faith." It literally means "proclaiming the good news."

Faith, Belief—I like to explain that faith or belief is synonymous with trust. These are relational terms. You enter a marriage by faith or putting your trust in each other to fulfill your vows.

"God told me" or **"I heard a word from the Lord"**—though I fully believe God still leads today, nonbelievers assume that you heard an audible voice, and that's confusing. I will say, "I felt a prompting from God . . ." or "I got this thought in my head that I'm pretty sure was God leading me. . . ."

Gospel—the message about Jesus. God's good news about life with him.

Grace—God's unmerited favor. God is for you, not against you.

Hallelujah—it's a wonderful term, but use it among those who get it and mean it. It's become more of a joke among non-Christians mocking those who seem fake to them. It means "to praise or boast in Yahweh," so tell people about God's great works.

Holy—set apart for God's purposes.

Justified—God paid all our debts for us—past, present, and future.

Lost—If a person doesn't know they're lost, they don't like being labeled "lost." Saying "She doesn't follow Christ" or referring to people who are "not following God" is better.

Mission trips—To many people who have had college-level sociology, this term means imposing your culture on other cultures. We still use this term, but I prefer "serving trips" or "global serving trips."

Praise God—yes, we should and this is also a wonderful term among Christians, but in the company of nonbelievers, something like "Man—God is so good" expresses praise and may even spark curiosity.

Preach—to teach or give a message. "Preach" is rarely used in a positive way in the broader culture. I prefer not being called "the preacher," but rather a teacher or pastor for that reason.

Redeemed—We've been bought back by God at the highest price, and now he's restoring us to our originally intended condition.

Repent—to change your mind from going your will and way to going God's will and way.

Righteous—right-related to God, or in right standing with God.

Sanctified—God walks with us so we can become more and more of the people he intended us to be.

Saved—to be set right with God—forgiven and made right-related to God.

Sin—though this term is still somewhat understood, I often include "wrongdoing" or explain that sin at the core is playing God and trying to make the universe obey my will instead of obeying God's will.

Appendix B

Predestination and Free Will

Throughout the Scriptures we find a tension revealed between the reality of God's sovereign foreknowledge and predestination (P) and the reality that we also truly have free will (F). Failing to embrace this tension (Scripture even presents both P&F together) creates not only poor theology, but destructive practices when it comes to interacting with individuals and a world that is free to choose for or against God's will and ways. God is ultimately sovereign and his will prevails, yet within his perfect will he allows and uses human choices that are against his will. Below you will find a table of all the verses dealing with this tension, which you can study for yourself.

But how do we understand this paradox? Really we can't, because what God reveals to us through the Scriptures is a mystery that only resolves in the mind of God. Hugh Ross points out that our error could come from viewing God's revelation through our finite three dimensions of space and one dimension of time. Time for us must be sequential; it moves in one direction along a "timeline." For instance, if you know with absolute certainty what I will do one hour from now, I cannot have a choice. Either it's been determined

Table of Verses on Predestination (P), Free Will (F), or both (P&F)[2]

Gen. 13:11 (F)	Is. 55:6–11 (P&F)	1 Cor. 4:7 (P)
Ex. 9:16 (P)	Is. 56:4 (F)	1 Cor. 6:19–20 (P&F)
Ex. 33:19 (P)	Is. 61:10–62:2 (P)	2 Cor. 3:4–6 (P)
Ex. 34:24 (P)	Jer. 1:4–10 (P)	2 Cor. 13:9 (P)
Deut. 10:15 (P)	Jer. 8:4–12 (F)	Gal. 1:1 (P)
Deut. 30:19 (F)	Jer. 17:5–10 (P&F)	Eph. 1:4–5 (P)
Josh. 11:20 (P)	Ezek. 18:1–32 (F)	Eph. 1:11 (P)
Josh. 24:14–27 (F)	Dan. 4:4–37 (P)	Eph. 2:10 (P)
Judg. 5:8 (F)	Hos. 4:4–9 (F)	Phil. 2:12–13 (P&F)
Judg. 21:25 (F)	Hos. 5:3–7 (P&F)	2 Thess. 2:7–12 (P&F)
1 Kings 12:15 (P)	Hos. 11:4 (P)	2 Thess. 2:13–15 (P&F)
2 Chr. 6:3–6 (P)	Joel 2:32 (P&F)	2 Thess. 3:3 (P)
Job 1:21–22 (P&F)	Matt. 10:22 (P&F)	1 Tim. 6:19 (F)
Job 7:15 (F)	Matt. 10:28–30 (P)	2 Tim. 1:9 (P)
Job 9:1–35 (P&F)	Matt. 11:25 (P)	2 Tim. 1:12 (P&F)
Job 23:10–16 (P&F)	Matt. 21:21–22 (F)	2 Tim. 2:19–26 (P&F)
Job 34:4 (F)	Matt. 24:24–25 (P)	Titus 1:1–3 (P)
Job 36:21 (F)	Matt. 24:36 (P)	Titus 2:11–14 (P)
Job 38:36 (P&F)	Mark 13:20–22 (P)	Heb. 3:4 (P)
Psalm 14:1–3 (F)	Luke 8:10 (P)	Heb. 3:12–14 (F)
Psalm 25:12 (P&F)	Luke 10:42 (F)	Heb. 4:11 (F)
Psalm 31:15 (P)	Luke 12:4–5 (P)	Heb. 6:4–12 (F)
Psalm 32:5–11 (P&F)	Luke 18:27 (P)	Heb. 6:17–19 (P&F)
Psalm 33:8–22 (P&F)	Luke 22:21–22 (P&F)	Heb. 10:14 (P)
Psalm 58:3 (P)	Luke 22:31–34 (P)	Heb. 10:35 (P&F)
Psalm 110:1–7 (P)	John 6:44–65 (P&F)	Heb. 11:25 (F)
Psalm 115:3 (P)	John 7:17 (F)	Heb. 13:21 (P)
Psalm 119:30 (F)	John 8:31–47 (P&F)	James 1:13–25 (P&F)
Psalm 119:173 (F)	John 10:26–29 (P&F)	James 4:7 (F)
Prov. 1:29–30 (F)	John 15:5 (P)	James 4:13–17 (F)
Prov. 8:10–19 (F)	John 15:16 (P)	1 Pet. 1:4–5 (P)
Prov. 16:4 (P)	John 17:6 (P&F)	1 Pet. 1:15–16 (P&F)
Prov. 16:9 (P&F)	Acts 2:21 (F)	1 Pet. 2:21 (F)
Prov. 21:1 (P)	Acts 4:28 (P)	1 Pet. 5:5–10 (P&F)
Prov. 21:3 (F)	Acts 13:48 (P&F)	2 Pet. 1:10 (P&F)
Eccl. 3:10–17 (P&F)	Acts 17:24–28 (P&F)	1 John 2:5–6 (F)
Eccl. 9:1 (P)	Rom. 4:11 (P)	1 John 3:9 (P)
Is. 1:29 (F)	Rom. 8:19–33 (P)	1 John 4:7–19 (P&F)
Is. 7:15–16 (F)	Rom. 9:10–26 (P)	1 John 5:18–20 (P)
Is. 40:20 (F)	Rom. 10:12–18 (P&F)	Jude 1–4 (P&F)
Is. 40:23 (P)	Rom. 11:7–8 (P)	Rev. 13:8–10 (P)
Is. 41:24 (P)	Rom. 11:25–12:2 (P&F)	Rev. 20:11–15 (F)
Is. 46:10 (P)	1 Cor. 1:2 (P)	Rev. 22:11–17 (F)
Is. 55:3 (F)	1 Cor. 1:26–29 (P)	

and I have no free will, or I can choose, but then you can't know with certainty. That's our one-dimensional experience of time. However, if you existed in two dimensions of time, all that changes! If God exists in two dimensions of time (not along a timeline, as we know it, but in time that extends out from the timeline in an infinite, flat, plane), or if God exists in three dimensions of time, the predestination/free will paradox becomes logically possible: "A three-dimensional time domain or its equivalent would enable God to predetermine every action of every human being while sustaining the operation of human choice [allowing true free will]."[1]

Picture a globe where each moment of our timeline runs from South America to Africa along the equator. God experiences each moment of our latitudinal timeline on a longitudinal timeline extending up to the North Pole (that's how God attends to 2 billion prayers at the same moment—each moment of our "latitudinal" time running along the equator extends his experience of that moment along a "longitudinal" timeline running in a second dimension). In three-dimensional time, God experiences each moment on longitudinal timelines that all come together in a single point of time at the North Pole. "This convergence implies that God can impact events throughout the history of the universe and the course of our lives (and more) in a single instant of his time."[3]

Notes

Chapter 1: A Glutton, Drunk, and Friend of Sinners

1. Chip Heath and Dan Heath, *Switch: How to Change Things When Change Is Hard* (New York: Broadway Books, 2010), 131–34, Kindle location 1927–61.

Chapter 2: Unshockable

1. Chip Heath and Dan Heath, *Switch: How to Change Things When Change Is Hard* (New York: Broadway Books, 2010), 151, Kindle location 2203.

Chapter 3: Restoring Value

1. This study has been disputed over the years and the range of contexts in which effective communication was only 7% verbal as the study indicated questioned, but whatever the exact percentages, the point is roughly the same. See Daniel Druckman, Richard M. Rozelle, and James C. Baxter. *Nonverbal Communication: Survey, Theory, and Research* (Thousand Oaks, CA: Sage Publications, 1982), 84–85.

2. Barry Duncan, Scott Miller, Bruce Wampold, Mark Hubble, eds., *The Heart and Soul of Change: Delivering What Works in Therapy*, 2nd ed. (Washington: American Psychological Association, 2010), chapter 4.

3. The Arbinger Institute, *Leadership and Self-Deception* (San Francisco: Berrett-Koehler Publishers, 2010) makes a great case for this truth.

4. I used this illustration for a message I gave on phariseeism, and I adapted my version of this illustration from an excellent book I recommend: John Fischer, *12 Steps for the Recovering Pharisee (Like Me): Finding Grace to Live Unmasked* (Minneapolis: Bethany House, 2000), 14–15.

5. Associated Press, "White's Rock Quarry Could Net Pitcher Billions," ESPN, February 28, 2007, http://sports.espn.go.com/mlb/spring2007/news/story?id=2783310.

6. John M. Darley, C. Daniel Batson, "From Jerusalem to Jericho," *Journal of Personality and Social Psychology*, Vol 27(1), Jul 1973, 100–108.

Chapter 4: Calling Out the Masterpiece

1. Klyne Snodrass, "Jesus and a Hermeneutics of Identity," *Bibliotheca Sacra* 168, no. 670 (April–June 2011): 136.

2. James March, *A Primer on Decision Making: How Decisions Happen* (New York: Free Press, 1994), chapter 2.

3. Chip Heath and Dan Heath, *Switch: How to Change Things When Change Is Hard* (New York: Broadway Books, 2010), 156–157, Kindle location 2281.

4. C. S. Lewis, "The Weight of Glory," in *The Weight of Glory* (San Francisco: HarperSanFrancisco, 1976), 45.

5. My editor and friend Jack Kuhatschek pointed this out to me.

6. This story, found in Luke 7 and Matthew 8, does not tell us whether the centurion, whom I call Marcus, was a polytheist or not. I took license to paint the background most Roman centurions would have had growing up. Since there's nothing to indicate otherwise, I think it's a good assumption that he had a similar upbringing. We know that he was benevolent to the Jews because he had built them their synagogue, but this does not mean he was a Jew or a worshiper of Yahweh. Perhaps it indicates he respected the "gods" in general, as I implied. All Roman leaders wanted to maintain *Pax Romana*, the Roman peace, and building a synagogue surely would have built bridges to the Jewish elders.

Chapter 5: Speaking Truth in Love

1. Chia Evers, "Laszlo Toth, 'Jesus Christ,' Attacks the Pieta" (May 21, 1972) in *News of the Odd* article 1024: http://web.archive.org/web/20060516211755/http://www.newsoftheodd.com/article1024.html (accessed March 18, 2012).

Chapter 6: Respecting Freedom

1. Akiane Kramarik and Foreli Kramarik, *Akiane: Her Life, Her Art, Her Poetry* (Nashville: W Publishing Group, 2006).

2. Todd Burpo, *Heaven Is for Real: A Little Boy's Astounding Story of His Trip to Heaven and Back* (Nashville: Thomas Nelson Publishers, 2010).

3. Philip Yancey, *Disappointment With God* (Grand Rapids: Zondervan, 1988), 58–61.

4. Dallas Willard, *The Divine Conspiracy* (New York: HarperCollins, 1998), 228–30.

5. An excellent book that delves into this more is John Fischer, *Twelve Steps for the Recovering Pharisee (Like Me): Finding Grace to Live Unmasked* (Minneapolis: Bethany House, 2000).

6. This evolved into an urban legend about Bill Gates and GM, but it actually was just a joke that circulated in the late 1990s.

7. John 8:1–11. The NIV has this note: "The earliest manuscripts and many other ancient witnesses do not have John 7:53–8:11." The IVP New Testament Commentary says, "It appears to have been a well-known story, one of many that circulated orally from the beginning yet that none of the Gospel writers were led to include. But some in the later church thought this one was too good to leave out. . . . Most of Christendom, however, has received this story as authoritative,

and modern scholarship, although concluding firmly that it was not a part of John's Gospel originally, has generally recognized that this story describes an event from the life of Christ." ("Jesus Forgives a Woman Taken in Adultery," *The IVP New Testament Commentary* series, available at www.biblegateway.com.)

8. Dallas Willard, *The Divine Conspiracy*, 133.

9. Don Everts and Doug Schaupp, *I Once Was Lost* (Downers Grove, IL: InterVarsity Press, 2008), 54.

10. *Talmud Menahoth*, 43b–44a.

11. Mark Buchanan, *The Rest of God* (Nashville: Thomas Nelson, 2006), 68.

Chapter 8: Sharing Jesus' Good Message

1. Bill Bright would often say, "Share the gospel, in the power of the Holy Spirit, and leave the results up to God." That's a very freeing way to differentiate our part from God's part.

2. For more reading on how people make decisions, needing communication to the head and heart, see Chip Heath and Dan Heath, *Switch: How to Change Things When Change Is Hard* (New York: Broadway Books, 2010), 8, Kindle location 125.

3. Dan Allender (and Karen Royer) developed this course called Wounded Heart that we have used to help victims of sexual or physical abuse find healing and wholeness based on the book *The Wounded Heart: Hope for Adult Victims of Childhood Sexual Abuse* by Dan B. Allender.

4. Though I could not find the original source of this use of "repent," it has been a commonly held teaching that it was later a Latin military term.

Chapter 9: Hardened Hearts and the Hammer of Truth

1. Ironically, a book I read that tries to clarify the gospel takes Romans chapters 1 through 4 as the outline of the gospel, even though Paul is not sharing the gospel with nonbelievers but explaining theology to Roman believers. The author covers universal condemnation and justification but stops short of Romans 7 and 8—the "so what" of the good news—and the "good" part—God does not condemn in Christ, sets us free from living the law of trying harder, leads us into Life that fulfills the law, adopts us, lets us call him "Daddy," works all things for good, delivers us from fear of condemnation, and nothing can separate us from his love, ever! Stopping with justification without the promise of the Spirit's power to help us live the intent of the law leads to a partial gospel of sin management.

2. The money-changers sold animals for sacrifice and exchanged Roman or Greek currencies for Jewish currency so that worshipers traveling to Jerusalem could buy an animal for sacrifice and pay the temple tax. But greed had distorted the original purpose of this service into using the worship of God as a means of gain, robbing people and charging exorbitant exchange rates. All of this was done under the authority of the Pharisees (John 2).

Chapter 10: Ordinary People Doing Extraordinary Things

1. Spiritual gifts assessments: http://www.churchgrowth.org/cgi-cg/gifts.cgi?intro=1 and http://buildingchurch.net/g2s.htm.

2. Here are the qualifications and description for leaders we use based on 1 Timothy 3:

Qualification	Description
Worthy of Respect	They have exhibited a life that shows they are respected at work, in their family, and at church. Others recognize their lifestyle and show them respect.
Speak With Integrity	Their words are truthful and they don't over-exaggerate the truth. The church would be willing to have this person speak for and represent it.
Free From Addictions	Their lifestyle does not exhibit any patterns of addiction that would harm them or the church spiritually.
Deals Honestly	Have proven trustworthy in their dealings with others, whether personal, business, or church-related interactions.
Obedient to God's Word	Daily seek to know better, understand, and be obedient to God's Word.
Above Reproach	Always seek to take the "high road" in life, leaving no room for question that they are above reproach.
Faithful Service	They have accepted responsibility within the church and have demonstrated a pattern and history of faithful service.
Willing to Perform Duties	They are willing and able to accept responsibility to lead and generally perform the duties required to represent the church by serving in this position.

Chapter 11: Create Relational Momentum

1. Dr. Will Miller, *Refrigerator Rights: Creating Connections and Restoring Relationships* (New York: The Berkley Publishing Group, 2002).

Chapter 12: Serve Your Neighbors With Your Neighbors

1. Jason T. Heriford, *Soul Storming Guidebook* (Austin, TX: Heriford Publishing, 2011).

2. Steve Corbett and Brian Fikkert, *When Helping Hurts: How to Alleviate Poverty Without Hurting the Poor . . . and Yourself* (Chicago: Moody, 2009), 53.

3. Ibid., 61–62.

4. Bryant L. Meyers, *Walking With the Poor: Principles and Practices of Transformational Development* (Maryknoll, NY: Orbis Books, 1999), 86.

5. Corbett and Fikkert, *When Helping Hurts*, 62.

Chapter 13: "Come As You Are" Learning Space

1. For more amazing stories like that of Warren the Clown, and for great ideas on how to serve and love people to faith (and if you like to laugh hard), I highly recommend Vince Antonucci's book, *Guerrilla Lovers*.

2. Check out www.alphausa.org for more information.

3. *Seeker Small Groups* by Garry Poole is a good resource for equipping you to lead a mixed group, and the *Tough Questions* series Poole did can be a great first study to do together.

Soma Communities has *The Story*, which they use in mixed groups to experience the narrative of the whole Bible, and they see many people find faith.

Chapter 14: Everyone Can Develop Someone

1. This acronym, F.A.S.T., was not original to me. I adapted it from F.A.T., which I heard in discipleship circles around Campus Crusade for Christ. Somehow calling people FAT just didn't seem right, and Spirit-filled seemed essential.

2. Greg Ogden, *Transforming Discipleship* (Downers Grove, IL: InterVarsity, 2003) and *Discipleship Essentials* (Downers Grove, IL: InterVarsity, 1998, 2007). Mike Breen with 3DM has a unique, memorable discipleship method: www.weare 3DM.com. Soma Communities have some great discipleship resources (search "soma communities resources"). Willow Creek's *Engage* resource is an excellent individual tool for discipleship: www.willowcreek.com. Neil Cole's LTG Group model is a transferable discipleship path: www.cmaresources.org.

Chapter 15: Accelerate and Multiply With Worship and Teaching

1. Alan Hirsch, *The Forgotten Ways: Reactivating the Missional Church* (Grand Rapids: Brazos, 2006), 19.

2. Brother Yun with Paul Hattaway, *The Heavenly Man: The Remarkable True Story of Chinese Christian Brother Yun* (London: Monarch Books, 2002), 311–312.

3. Rodney Stark, *The Triumph of Christianity: How the Jesus Movement Became the World's Largest Religion* (New York: HarperCollins, 2011), 313–314.

4. Mike Breen and Alex Absalom, *Launching Missional Communities: A Field Guide* (Myrtle Beach, SC: Sheriar Press, 2010), 38–41.

Appendix B: Predestination and Free Will

1. Hugh Ross, *Beyond the Cosmos* (Orlando, FL: Signalman Publishing, 2010), 168.

2. Ibid., Table 13.1, 152–153. Reproduced with permission.

3. Ibid., 169.

John Burke is the author of *No Perfect People Allowed* and *Soul Revolution*, and the lead pastor of Gateway Church in Austin, Texas, which he and his wife founded in 1998. Since then, Gateway has grown to over 4,500 members, made up mostly of unchurched people who began actively following Christ at Gateway. John is also the founder and president of Gateway Leadership Initiative (GLI), a nonprofit organization working to help church planting pastors and ordinary Christians "raise the church out of the culture." John has spoken in fifteen countries to over 200,000 church leaders and Christians about reaching a postmodern, post-Christian culture.

TAKE THE NEXT STEP
WITH **UNSHOCKABLE LOVE**

So what's next? How can I express the truth in this book through my life?

Go to **unshockablelove.com**, where you will find resources that will help you implement the ideas from the book in your life, church, and small group:

- Network Action Guide
- Small Group Discussion Guide
- Church & Leader Resources

unshockable
love

how Jesus changes the world
through imperfect people

John Burke

Go to **JohnBurkeOnline.com** for ongoing thoughts about living on mission with Jesus and each other.

Go to **GatewayLeaders.com** for more leadership training resources from John Burke.